Gloria

Wishing You all
Things Healing
Karma Bae

It's Just an Experience...
Get Over It!

The Spiritual Journey from
Hurting to Healing to Helping

KARMA RAE

BALBOA.
PRESS
A DIVISION OF HAY HOUSE

Balboa Press books may be ordered through booksellers or by contacting:

Balboa Press
A Division of Hay House
1663 Liberty Drive
Bloomington, IN 47403
www.balboapress.com
1-(877) 407-4847

Because of the dynamic nature of the Internet, any web addresses or links contained in this book may have changed since publication and may no longer be valid. The views expressed in this work are solely those of the author and do not necessarily reflect the views of the publisher, and the publisher hereby disclaims any responsibility for them.

The author of this book does not dispense medical advice or prescribe the use of any technique as a form of treatment for physical, emotional, or medical problems without the advice of a physician, either directly or indirectly. The intent of the author is only to offer information of a general nature to help you in your quest for emotional and spiritual well-being. In the event you use any of the information in this book for yourself, which is your constitutional right, the author and the publisher assume no responsibility for your actions.

Any people depicted in stock imagery provided by Thinkstock are models, and such images are being used for illustrative purposes only.
Certain stock imagery © Thinkstock.

ISBN: 978-1-4525-7285-7 (sc)
ISBN: 978-1-4525-7287-1 (hc)
ISBN: 978-1-4525-7286-4 (e)

Library of Congress Control Number: 2013907189

Printed in the United States of America.

Balboa Press rev. date: 7/5/2013

This book is dedicated to all those who have been a part of this amazing journey. To those people who taught me unconditional love and acceptance, and to those who couldn't love me, I send gratitude. To each person who has crossed my path, you have allowed me to grow and heal. Especially to those who were willing to hear the truth and not judge it.

To each person who has empowered me and allowed me to fulfill my soul contracts, I send gratitude and love. To all those who have shown me all that I could be, and to all those who have placed mirrors on the path, because it allowed me to look within and learn the lessons needed to complete my soul's path, I stand in gratitude.

I thank God and my team on the other side for their divine guidance; without you, I would not still be here. And to the doctors who allowed me to see that my connection to spirit was more powerful than any drug.

And most important, to those who have joined me on the path and allowed me to assist them in their healing from trauma and abuse, for you have been the greatest mirror.

I stand in love and respect always.

One could choose to go back toward safety or forward toward growth. Growth must be chosen again and again fear must be overcome again and again.

—Author Unknown

INTRODUCTION

I was lying in my hospital bed contemplating the earlier day's events. I was scheduled for what was supposed to be a routine procedure, to scope my abdominal. However, something went horribly wrong—I died.

I remember sitting up on the operating table and yelling, "Why did you bring me back? I did not want to come back!"

The doctor was at the foot of the table, to the left; he was being consoled by three nurses. Another attendant was cleaning up equipment to the far left. The anesthesiologist to the right was pushing a tray of instruments away from the table. As they heard me yell, they looked, but it was as if they did not believe what was happening. It took them about a minute, and then it registered—I was alive. With their acknowledgment, I hit the table with the full force of my body. I became somewhat conscious and felt my mouth being covered. I started fighting back and took a swing, and then I saw the anesthesiologist's arms in the air as he flew backward into a tray of medical instruments; a loud crash soon followed. Within moments, I heard a gentle voice telling me that they were only giving me oxygen. I knew that they were trying to put me under. All I heard was, "Just take a breath." The oxygen mask went on without further incident, and I slipped into a space of nothingness.

That was where my life ended, and the journey began.

PART 1

HURTING

My Normal

I was the third child born in as many years and was born into a family that was already in crisis. We moved to a small town in Northern Alberta from British Columbia. I started school on my sixth birthday. We lived in a pink-and-white house, and the street we lived on was filled with children.

Most children can say they felt loved and safe growing up. I never experienced that. Most children can look to their parents for guidance. I knew at an early age that I would have to find my own way. I feared my father and would later learn to fear my older brother, because he became his father's son in so many ways. I would learn early that I could not trust my father, and that would never change. Most siblings bond with each other in a positive way, however we were pitted against each other by our father in attempts to control and manipulate us. Separate and divide—that was how he would keep control. As I grew, I would notice how different we were from other families, but I did not understand why.

In grade one I was tall for my age, gangly, and extremely shy. I was left-handed, and in those days that meant I would be reprimanded for using my left hand, in the form of a yardstick being whacked across my fingers. My grade two teacher drew a yardstick across my knuckles as she stated, "If you were meant to use your left hand, it would be called lefting, not writing."

Even beyond that, I was very different from the other kids: I had a secret. That secret would be the driving force in my life and would govern every relationship, every moment, and every decision that I would make from that point onward. The secret was that I was being molested.

This was something that happened from the crib to the age of fifteen. It happened in the mornings before school, in the evenings, and on weekends. My abuser was my dad and later expanded to include my oldest brother. The life that I lived was violent and very scary. I made sure that nothing that I said or did would give the secret away; that would not change for twenty-six years.

I lived in a family where there were numerous secrets. What happened in that house stayed in the house—that was the rule, and we had best not break it. We did not talk about what happened, and life went on. Moments of horror, of sexual abuse, and of violent rages from my father and the delusion of my mother protecting the secret—that was my normal. The days and years would pass with daily assaults and the knowledge that if we spoke of any of it, there would be consequences for our actions.

To the outside world, all was normal. It was a time when people would not speak out, even if they saw something.

My dad coached baseball due to his need to be admired. He would reward the team with root beer after the ball games. He was a good guy, according to them. I would watch how he wanted people to see him. Knowing who he was behind closed doors, I wondered why he would choose to be two different people. Why did the outside world get that other person and we got the angry and violent one?

After a night of my dad being drunk and full of violence, the need for more alcohol beckoned him. He got up and left the house to the bar. His walk would take him past the homes of my friends, and they saw him. We would go to school and our friend share with us that they saw him completely naked, with not a stitch of clothing. They joked with me about it, but I was devastated.

My older brother went home and announced at the dinner table that I had told the neighbors that he had left the house naked, but I had not. My parents were seated at either end of the table, and the four kids sat on the sides, the girls at the back wall and the boys on the open side of the table. My father's rage became evident. He raised his hand up and slammed it down onto the table. He barked, "What happens in this house stays in this house." I felt the table shake as I sat at the other end, and I knew he was not kidding. In a blink, he reached for the cast iron frying pan that held liver and onions, which was to be our dinner. I knew what was going to happen next. I yelled at my youngest brother to duck, and without hesitation he coiled into his seat. The frying pan was thrown from the table over the top of his head, landing against the freezer that sat against the far wall. The contents of the pan splattered everywhere as the pan hit the freezer, leaving an incredible dent. Nothing more was said. We ate what was on our plates and then went to our rooms.

The emotions and trust in the house became more strained. My two older siblings became physically aggressive toward me. They learned that violence got them what they wanted. Banning together, they pointed the finger at me rather than take responsibility for their actions. This would set me up for a lifetime of observing people who didn't take responsibility for their actions, and this would trigger me so deeply that I can't even explain the emotions that it would invoke in me.

Both sides of the family offered their religious teachings, but what happened in our house was anything but religious. The only time I saw my parents in church was for weddings and funerals. However, I did remember my older sister and I leaping out of bed on Sunday mornings to bike off to church. I'm not sure if I was taking refuge, or if I just wanted to make sure God remembered who I was. After all, there were things happening down here of which I was not sure he was aware. I was sitting in church before going down to Sunday school. We were praying, and I had some things that God needed to hear, and as my conversation got heated with him and was at a high point, my Sunday school teacher hushed me. I spoke up, not realizing how loud my voice was: "I'm talking to God!"

The priest said, "Yes, that is why we are here, to talk to God." The congregation then busted out in laughter. Not fully understanding the laughter, I went back to having my conversation silently; after all, this was important, and I felt that it needed expressing.

I questioned God's presence because if he had known what was going on, he would have sent someone to help. Repeatedly my relationship with God would be tested; I stilled prayed, but perhaps there were other people who needed his attention more. I was used to waiting for things—after all, I was from a family of four children by the age of two. I could guarantee you that I was not the first on the list when it came to having my needs met. That would instill my independence at an early age, knowing that if I needed something, I would have to get it myself. Despite the constant fighting, violence, and abuse, I tried to love my family.

Being punished for existing was a good way to describe what was happening in the house. My father's rages would result in spankings, but they were not just a smack on the backside—it was a staged performance on his part. His routine was to take a chair and sit in the middle of the dining room. Then he'd take one of us over his knee. As a final insult, he would rip down the panties of us girls, exposing us to the others. His hand was big enough to cover my entire backside, and he slapped me until he produced welts. If we cried, he barked, "I will give you something to cry about." I learned early to take the punishment without dispute. He needed to be in control, and if he was not, or if he felt we had broken one of his rules, then over his knee we went.

There was also the leather strap, and it could be doubled with a snap at the bottom to anchor the double width. It had no other use than to strap us. That would give way to welts beyond anything one could imagine. Imagine a grown man, over six feet and two hundred pounds, using a leather strap to reprimand his children with force. After the spanking we would be sent to our room. I shared a room and bed with my older sister until the age of eight. Upon returning to our bedroom, we would stand on the footboard of our bed, looking in the mirror to compare the welts, as if to argue who had endured the worst beating. Twisted, I know, but as we seemed to say to ourselves if we could survive this, we could survive anything.

The sexual abuse had started in the crib. First it was oral and touching. By the age of seven, things would change drastically and would continue until I was fifteen, with each assault getting worse as time passed and opportunity presented itself, which was often. Perhaps my consciousness of how wrong this was magnified as I grew up.

During yet another assault when I was under the age of seven, my father molested me. I lay in my bed, confused as to why he would hurt me like this. What had I done wrong? I was a good girl, and I helped in the house with chores. I could not understand, and I needed to know why. I crawled out of bed and went into the kitchen, just outside the bedroom door. As I opened the door, my mother was there ironing clothes, something she did at night. I remember asking her, "Why did Daddy do this to me?" It was in that moment once again that I would make yet another revelation in my crazy life.

She commented, "Daddy was just showing you how much he loves you."

In that moment I proclaimed; "Mommy, if that is what it feels like to be loved, I do not want anyone to ever love me again." I got a glass of water and then returned to bed, somewhat wiser yet more confused by the explanation. Was love supposed to hurt? Was it supposed to make you feel yucky and dirty? That did not make my heart happy. Why would Mommy lie about this? Was she confused about what love was supposed to feel like? My young mind tried to wrap itself around the emotions and the words to make sense of it all. I never came to any resolution. With my proclamation that I did not want anyone to love me ever again, I kept people at a distance.

The abuse would continue. In the mornings my dad would keep me on alternate days to clean house, and the other kids would be sent on to school. After the sexual assault, he would give me a quarter to go get a treat for being a good girl, and then he'd send me to school. My walk to school was done in a blur, trying to understand what had happened, as if I was out of my body looking downward.

As I entered the classroom, late and dazed from the assault, I would take a verbal lashing from the teacher. She asked why I was late again. I could feel the blood drain from my body as I thought of an explanation that would satisfy her. "I had to clean the house." I could hear the words as they hit my ears, and I panicked. Would I be punished for telling? The fear flooded my faint body and I felt as if I would collapse at that moment. I managed to get myself to my seat.

She barked out, "Well, I suggest you do your chores at night, not in the morning."

The morning assaults continued, spanning over three years.

It was my turn to clean house again. I knew what the teacher had expressed to me, and I did not want to get into trouble again. My older sister and I had a plan: she would lower me out the bedroom window and pretend that I was still in my bed. As she lowered me, my feet hit the ground, and I realized that I had no shoes on—and even worse; I had been so intent on getting out of the house that I had not changed out of my pajamas. I panicked, but I would have to go to school dressed as I was. I did manage to slip on a pair of shoes from the back porch. All the way to school, I knew that I would never live this down. I did make it to school on time, but I was picked on all day about my pajamas.

My mind was reeling about what would happen when I got home. Would he be waiting? What would be the punishment this time?

As we all returned home from school, we were standing in the kitchen. My older brother looked around the kitchen and proclaimed, "If you stay home to clean the house, why does it never look clean?" Unaware of my morning descent from the window, he looked directly at me, and the blood drained from my body. I looked at my older sister for help, but all she could do was look back at me. My brother punched me and asked me again. I would not speak, and so he threatened me. I guess he was watching his father and learned that if he wanted something from a female, he should apply force. I still refused to tell, until he beat me up and brought me to tears. He forced me to show him what

9

our dad made me do. I was paralyzed in fear, and he punched me again. I showed him what Father did to me. At only the age of ten, himself that was the day my brother crossed over from being a victim to being an abuser.

The next day was one of terror for me. It was Saturday—no school to keep me safe. I was sent to my room as punishment for yesterday's events. I knew what that meant. My father came into the room and started molesting me, but this time it was different. He laid his adult body on mine, and the weight of his body was crushing my seven-year-old body. I tried to distract myself from what was happening, and I could smell the scent of lilacs coming in my open bedroom window. I liked lilacs, the way they smelled, and how they looked. As he molested me in this way, I could feel that as I tried to breathe, it was getting harder. His weight overwhelmed me, and then everything went black.

The next thing I remembered, I was floating in the corner of the room, looking down on the event. In that moment I proclaimed, "You can take my body, but you will not take my soul." I did not really know what that meant at the time, but I knew it carried weight regarding how the future attacks would affect me—or more important, how they would *not* affect me. I watched the assault from a distance and knew that he would never hurt me deeply again.

As he finished with my body, he looked at me with confusion. I think he realized something had changed. It had, and in a way that he would probably never fully understand.

How could a father do this to his daughter? Why would he impose his adult actions on an innocent child? Did he not know how wrong this was? Most children grow up feeling safe with their parents, being able to go to them when life got tough to handle. I did not have that. When it is your family that creates the unsafe experience, to whom can you go for guidance? Where do you go in order to feel safe, or to have that conversation about all the things a child needs? I lived my life alone. I did not have sibling support, either. Why did this happen? There were more questions than answers, and I did not know whom to go to for what I needed. I made the decision to figure it out myself. Guidance from God would be the place to which I turned.

I had a very important conversation with God that day. I asked him why was he letting this happen, and why was he letting me get hurt this way. It was then I heard something that would again change my life. Very clearly I heard the words, "I did not say that you would not feel pain. I only promised I would be there to walk you through it."

I was taken aback from this—I did not know that God could talk to us that way. In some way, the words brought me solace. I would continue to have conversations with God, and it would bring me comfort and direction. I did not know that most others did not have that ability to hear God this way.

I had emotionally separated from the experience of abuse. I became the record keeper of the family. I watched what my father said and did. All his words were carefully stated to instill fear and obedience. I would challenge his words and threats for the days, weeks, and years that followed because I knew in my heart that what was happening was wrong. This defiance would bring even a greater separation between the others in the house. Divide and conquer. The more the adults could pit the kids against each other, the easier it would be able to live their lie.

There was something happening to me that I could not explain. I noticed as the days passed that I knew when people would be sick or would die. I could also touch things and get information. I would hold a wrapped present and know what was in it. I would use that later and make a game out of it. My siblings would let me hold a Christmas present and get me to tell them what it was. I was not sure what that was about, but it made life a little more exciting, at least. I would not fully understand this for years to come.

I was lying on the living room floor coloring, as I often did. My father would say in a low voice, "You know, if you tell, they would come and take your mom away." I would act as if I did not hear him, and so he would repeat himself. He knew that I was getting confrontational, and he needed to approach this in another way. I got up from my coloring book without a word and went to the kitchen, where my mother was preparing supper. I asked, "If Daddy does something wrong, would the police come and take you away?"

Her answer came fast and firm. "No, they would take *him*."

Armed with the truth, I return to the living room with my newfound information—again he was lying. Our push and shove relationship would continue, but I would always pay in some way or another for my disobedience.

The violence in the house was getting intense. The police showing up at the house became the norm, and the fear grew. Some days, the police would settle the situation and go; at other times my dad would be removed and taken to jail. I would almost hate those days more, because of what happened when he returned; his need to regain his power within the family was stronger. I witnessed the episodes of physical abuse heighten, and the lack of respect for my father would grow with each assault. Weekends were worse: the alcohol was definitely an influence, but there was something more; it was my father's energy that scared me. The fear took me deep, as if I had experienced it for lifetimes. I would learn to read the energy of the house, to determine how the day would play out, some days better than others.

I remembered I was crouched in the bedroom closet with my sister and mom. My father was raging through the house, and I knew that he could kill us that night if he found us, but I didn't understand why. I asked my mother why daddy was doing this. My mother reached across the dark closet and covered my mouth with her hand. In that very second, the bedroom door swung open and crashed into the closet door with incredible force. Frozen in fear, everything became still in that moment. We knew that even the simplest thing, such as exhaling, would result in our immediate demise. As the moment ended, we heard him leave the room and then the house. We sat motionless for some time until we knew that he would not be back at least for a while. My mom put us to bed as if nothing had happened. As I lay in my bed, I heard as she began to clean up the house and returned all that had been tossed in the outburst. The craziness and disassociated existence became the norm. Perhaps if we did not mention it, it would all go away.

The episodes continued. The violence escalated, if that was at all possible. My older sister and I returned home after a night of playing at friend's house down the street. As the backdoor opened, all I could see was blood everywhere—on the cabinets, fridge, and throughout the house. The words came from my mouth: "He killed her!" I looked at my sister in terror. How could someone lose this much blood and not die? We ran from the house back to our friend's home, our speed fueled by our fear. The thought of living with him alone struck fear through my soul. We arrived at our friend's house breathless, and we tried to explain what our eyes had taken in. With the safe presence of our friend's father, we entered our back door again, and my mom was cleaning up the blood. She realized we were not alone and that Mr. S was with us. She quickly started to make excuses to him. He asked if we were going to be okay, and she said yes and dismissed our fear of what took place in the house minutes earlier. Embarrassed, she rushed us to our room to get ready for bed.

The next morning I came from my bedroom. As I entered into the kitchen, my mother was on the phone. I heard her say, "He won't be into work today; he has the flu." She hung up the phone, and I asked her why she was lying; he was hung over, not sick, I proclaimed. She was lying again. God did not like lying—even I knew that.

I wondered what stories my mom had to tell herself in order to allow this to happen and do nothing. Did she not know how this affected us? Perhaps it was a question only she could answer, and she was not talking. What was her buy into this experience? Was there something in it for her that I could not see? I never saw the two of them express affection toward each other. I vowed that day that I would never be so dependent on a man that I would put my children or myself in this kind of danger.

I would go through several incidences where I got hurt and needed medical attention. The first time, my older sister and mom were in the kitchen, and there was a disagreement between us. As usual, there was no resolution to the situation. Mom ordered me to help with laundry. I stood at the top of the basement stairs, which lead into the unfinished basement and laundry area. I was shoved, and I went tumbling down the stairs. I landed on the bottom and knocked out my two front teeth. I was taken for stitches and was ordered to lie and say that I fell. I would go toothless for the better part of two years. Another time I was running from my older brother across the living room to the dining room, and he tripped me. I slid across the floor into the wall vent with so much force that the vent lever cut into my forehead and left me bleeding; more stitches were needed.

I was barely healed from that when I was out sledding. I had been pushing the sled up the hill, and a friend was pulling it. As one of the other sleds headed down the hill, the people grabbed the string from my friend's hands. My mittens had frozen to the sled, and I was whipped around and flung down the hill. The culprits released the sled, and it slid to the bottom, heading directly toward the ravine. I was screaming, and I couldn't get my frozen mittens off to let go. Within seconds the sled hit the one and only tree separating me from the ravine and a twenty-foot drop. With the speed and impact to the tree, the corner of the wooden sled cut into my forehead. People came rushing to me, and I could feel the warmth of the blood as it ran over my forehead and into my eyes. Someone grabbed me and flipped me on my side; the once white snow was soaked in the deepest red I had ever seen. I heard a man asked whether I was all right! I blurted out, "Do I look like I am all right!" I always wondered why adults asked question when the answer was so obvious. I had a stream of blood pouring from my head, and I was hauled up the hill by my arms to a friend's house; his mom was a nurse. More stitches, and the doctor made a comment, "You're making a habit of this, I see." Was I putting myself in harm's way in the hopes of dying?

The next incident was a little more intense. I was sitting in the front seat of the car with my older sister, waiting for our dad to come out of the tire shop. My sister had taken his cigarette and was pretending to smoke, and so I wanted to smoke too. I reached into the glove compartment to find something that would make do, because there were no more cigarettes. I found a bullet to a hunting rifle, I stuck the bullet into the cigarette lighter, and in what seemed like seconds, there was an explosion, and people were running from all the buildings along the block. I looked down, and the bullet had exploded and shot through the front seat, directly between the two of us. I was scared that my dad was going to punish me for this. The car door flung open, and we were pulled out of the vehicle. Unsure at the time of what could have happened, my dad examined the car. The bullet pellets had shot not only through the front seat but also through the back seat and into the trunk, and pellets sprayed the trunk from the inside. I realized then I came close to dying that day ... and in some way I wished I had.

I was in a constant emotional battle with what I felt and what I saw and heard. I would continue going to church, and as I sat, I could heard the priest say, "Honor thy mother and father." Every part of my body shuddered, and my thoughts spun in my head. *Even if they are hurting me,* I wondered. I wanted to ask the priest, but I sat there with my thoughts, so I did what I knew, and that was to ask God. I was having my conversation with God as I sat beside my Sunday school teacher, and she hushed me again, embarrassed. But I continue with my questions to God. I wanted to know why God had not made him stop hurting me. I would conclude that because my dad did not go to church, perhaps God could not speak to him. I would continue trying to figure out this life that I had stepped into, and I tried to make sense of what for the most part was senseless. Why did what was happening only seem to affect me?

Summer brought with it pleasure and pain. We did not have school, but that meant more time at the house and more opportunity to be abused. The relationships within my family based on fear and control grew more hostile. The only information I did trust was when I talked to God. I learned to trust my feelings. It was as if I could walk into a room and read everything that people were feeling and thinking; perhaps that was my survival instinct kicking in. This ability would put me in a state of alertness, as if it would keep me out of harm's way, or at least I'd be warned about what to expect from the experience.

The summer weekends would include baseball tournaments for the team that my dad coached. I remember a tournament that was in Peace Country, and some of the team was loaded in the homemade camper. En route, the boys find dirty magazines under the mattress in the camper. I was shocked at what I saw. The boys were hovered over the magazines, and my fear of being trapped in there with them was overwhelming. I sat with my back pressed into the corner of the trailer, not knowing if I would be safe. I knew what the males in my family were capable of—what would other males do, if given the chance? Some of the boys noticed my fear and tried to joke with me, but I would have none of it. When the doors to the camper opened upon our arrival, I bolted for safety, wherever that was. The tournament ended without incident this time.

Later that summer the family went camping at the lake, and the drinking did not stop; neither did the violence. One night the booze ran out, and my father's urge for more sent him seeking the next bottle. He headed out walking, but the only problem was what he craved was miles away. Hell bent on getting what he wanted, he set off. Shortly after, my mother loaded me into the truck. I was reluctant—why was she taking me? Was I being used as bait? We caught up to him, and he was staggering in and out of the ditch. She pulled the truck beside him and yelled at him through my open window. He was reluctant and continued on his mission. She pulled the truck just ahead of him and cranked the wheel, and she hit him. As he tumbled head first into the ditch, my instant thought was to hit her foot on the gas and end all this craziness, but I did not. He managed to make his way into the truck, and within minutes, he had his hands on me. Perhaps that was how my mother survived: hand over her children, and she would not get hurt. I fought my thoughts, and he would live to see another day. I was unsure he deserved to live, but I guessed God had a plan even for people like him. The weekend ended, we make it back to town, and life continued.

Kick the can was the game of choice for the neighborhood kids. We would gather in a yard down the street and pair off. One night two of the boys were fighting to be my partner. I hated this fighting because I just want to play. They continued, and I had had enough. I left, went home, crawled into bed, and fell fast asleep.

Hours later, I was jolted out of bed. Apparently the other kids thought they had lost me and had spent several hours looking for me. I explained my dilemma: I was not going to put up with fighting. In later years that decision would have me walking away from conflict. I knew early that if I was going to fight, it would be for my life. Nothing else was worth the emotions that fighting stirred in me.

One day while playing kick the can, we were paired off, and this time I was with one of the girls. The can was kicked, and we ran down the back alley and ducked down behind the fence. The next yard didn't have a fence. We heard a man's voice from behind us. We had never gone this far down the back alley before. The tall, gangly young man came closer, and as he did I noticed his eyes were weird: one was straight and the other shifted to the outside. He scared me. He explained that if we wanted to play in his yard, then we had to come and give him a kiss. My body became rigid, and I told him kissing his was not allowed. My friend went with him. In terror, I ran home, and I never went there again.

THE SUMMER I DIE

We got to spend the summer with our cousins in southern Alberta. The cousins melded into our family as far as ages went. The situation at home carried into the summer at my cousin's home. My dad was out drinking, and he phoned the house looking for a ride. Like a dutiful wife, off my mother went with my aunt to get him. They were barely out the door, and my father came into the house, as if he were waiting for them to leave. All those remaining in the house felt his presence. The kids were up in the attic bedrooms, and we heard his voice commanding my sister and me to come to him. I froze in fear. *He cannot be doing this now!* Would they find out? He had never done this in front of others before. Had he let his guard down? Was he that far gone that even he could not see what he was doing? Our cousins commanded us to go—they did not want him to come upstairs. I lay in my bed and prayed for God to make my mom come back right now. Fear grew in the attic bedroom; the others insisted that we go downstairs. As my feet hit the top of the stairs, I heard one final command: "Bring some panties with you!" I could not understand this and was embarrassed—after all, we did not talk about this. I gathered my panties and prepared to go downstairs, still praying for my mom and aunt to return.

As my older sister and I entered the kitchen, he stood there angry that it has taken so long. He grabbed the bag of panties from my hand and reached for the door. As he did so, the door opened from the outside; my aunt and mother were home. I was relieved, but I still knew it was not over. My mom grabbed the bag from him, saw what was in the bag, and looked at me in disgust. She yelled at us to go back to bed, as if this was our fault. Just as I turned, I saw her slap him across the face. I quickly rushed back up the stairs and prayed again, thanking God for bringing them home. I slipped off to sleep knowing God had not forgotten me.

The next day arrived, and life went on. My auntie and mom went shopping, and they left me in the supervision of my older brother and male cousin. As they drove away, the boys soon tried to ditch me. I followed them upstairs, but they continued to insist that I was not allowed to go with them. They headed to the bathroom in the top floor attic area, and they crawled out the window. I started to follow, and my cousin informed me I couldn't come out onto the roof. I waited until they were around the window and then peeked out to see that they were not in sight.

I did what I was told not to: I crawled out and stood up. Having never been on a roof before, I would soon learn the lesson of gravity. I fell down, hitting the back walkway. In the seconds prior to impact, there was a blank bit of time; I did not feel the impact of the ground. In the next second, I felt my right hand extended above my head. I looked up and saw my grandfather from my dad's side escorting me from my body. I was unsure of how I knew who he was, because he'd died when I was only three months old. I looked back and saw my physical body lying lifeless on the ground. It was my energy body that went with

Grandpa. I asked if we could wait to see if anyone found my body; I was unsure even at that age, just shy of my eighth birthday, that anyone would care enough to look for me. He agreed, and we sat on a branch of a tree that was parallel with the window from which I had just crawled.

This experience intrigued me. I liked this energy body. We chatted about many things. I was having feelings and thoughts, and I noticed it was nice not to be in my physical body. I felt free; it was as if I remembered something about that freedom that I had forgotten, and I was unsure as to why. I asked him that if I had all these thoughts, feelings, and understanding, and the ability to communicate in the energy body, why I needed the physical body.

My grandfather explained. "The soul wanted to matter, so it formed matter; we call that the hue-of-man (human) experience." We talked about allot of things, and he told me things that were possible to experience in the human body could not be experienced in the energy body. He told me that being in the physical body allowed the ability to create things physically. I listened intently and loved the time that I spent with him. I realized something else: he was telling me the truth. I never questioned his honesty. His words touched me deeply, not like when I talked to my dad. The time passed as he showed things to me; much of what I saw was beyond my years, and I would not grasp the wholeness of what was being explained to me until much later in life—especially the impact of knowing these things long before I should, knowing things that would come to be long before others would know, and seeing things that many would never witness in their lifetime. While witnessing these things, there was a different appreciation for what was to come, and perhaps a calmness of knowing that with all the changes to life, it all had a purpose. For the first time,

I had a feeling of trust of things that I knew. I understood then that there were things that I could not control, and that things would happen that had a purpose; even if I did not approve or fully accept them, they were a part of a bigger experience. We were here to experience things and learn and grow in each experience, and more important not to get stuck in the experience, in hopes of leaving this world knowing more and being better than when we came. He explained these seven main things to me.

1. Everything we endure is of choice.
2. We are accountable for who we are in this experience.
3. Our happiness is separate from our experience.
4. We are responsible for our feelings.
5. We are a part of a consciousness.
6. We are here to experience this journey at four levels to be complete· physically, emotionally, mentally, and spiritually.
7. Our journey needs to be lived within our truth and knowing.

I took in all that was shared and knew it to be true. I was shown all that I could experience had I stayed in the physical body.

Time passed, and then something caught my attention: my auntie's car had pulled up to the curb. They started up the front walk and then stopped and turned to come through the back gate. My lifeless body lay on the ground. My mother grabbed my physical body and started slapping my face. I was confused as to what she was doing. I could not feel the slaps, but nevertheless I was yelling at her to stop. She did not respond to my screams. I turned to Grandfather and asked why she would not stop hitting me. He stated she couldn't hear me. "Was she deaf?" I asked. After all, I was screaming at the top of my lungs. He explained to me that I needed to be in the physical body for her to hear me. I asked if I could go back in. He said yes, and in a blink of an eye, I was in and yelling at her to stop hitting me. When she stopped, I turned to get back out of my body and to go back to Grandpa. I couldn't get out. I screamed to him, "I can't get out, I can't get out." My body filled with panic and then terror.

My mom grabbed my face, turned it toward her, and yelled at me, "Who are you talking to?"

I told her I was talking to Grandpa. "I don't want to be here anymore! I want to be with Grandpa!"

She grabbed my face and said I was not going anywhere. She held me tightly and would not let me go. I turned to Grandpa, hoping he would help me out. I saw as he held out his hand, he shrugged his shoulders as if to say, "Sorry, kiddo," and then he floated away. I was furious with him. How dare he not get me out of my body! Once back in my body my mother dismissed the experience and told me to go play. She did not realize that I had just fallen from the window, and she did not seem to care what all of this was about.

The day continued as if nothing had happened. I wrestled for days with the abandonment I felt from my grandfather leaving me here with them! I vowed that he and I would have a chat about this.

All I really knew about what I had been through was that I was here to do my best, and anything short of that was cheating the world and myself. I would take the gift of being human very seriously from that point on. Being here was a privilege, not a right; I knew that in the physical body we worked toward creating greatness, if we allowed it. I made a promise to God and my soul that day that I would never be less than my best.

We have a choice of who we are in each experience. The best way to explain that is if someone casts anger at you, you have a choice to throw anger back or love. You do not have to become the experience, you only learn from it. The difference shows itself whether or not you get stuck in the drama of the experience.

This was big stuff for an eight-year-old—even the choice to come back in to my body would prove to be an incredible experience, because I would later find out not to many people did that. I knew that I was going to choose happiness over what was happening around me and to me, and no one could take that from me.

It was an eventful summer, and then it was back to life as I knew it. Somehow things had changed, and I was unsure of how. After all, I was only eight years old; all that had come to me this summer would take years to integrate into my knowing.

Something else happened: Grandpa would come and visit. I would tell my mother, "Grandpa is here!" She would tell me to stop saying that because it was crazy. He was there—I saw him, and he would talk to me. I learned that telling anyone that I saw him was a bad thing. I would continue to have visits from him, and we would chat. He liked it when I would color, and he would play with the crayons as they scattered on the floor beside me. It was our little game. This would be our time, no one else could share it, and that was okay with me. This knowledge allowed me to be happy despite what was happening; I knew that there was an end to this harshness. I would survive, things would be different, and that brought me joy. Perhaps the others did not understand my happiness.

Even a simple thing as coloring was dictated by my not wanting to break the rules. I would outline each image and color within the lines; going outside the lines was like breaking the rules. My fear of what would happen to me if I did not follow rules would govern my life for years. I knew that if I broke the rules, someone got hurt. That fear resonated in my bones.

Now that I was going into grade three, I had started Brownies. There was a uniform that we were supposed to wear, and my older sister went, too. The only problem was that we only had one full uniform, and a part of another. We were inspected for our uniform. Snowy Owl, the group leader, was telling me that I would have to pay ten cents each time that I did not have my full uniform. For the first time I was embarrassed that we did not have money. I did not tell her that we only had one uniform for the two of us. Each week that came and I could not wear the full uniform, my anger that my father would rather buy alcohol than buy what was needed for the family would surface.

False Freedom

t was my eighth birthday, and I got my first bike. I was excited: it was blue and white and just the right size. I was learning how to ride without training wheels. It became my new favorite thing to do. However, things would change. I would find more often than not that when I wanted to ride, the spokes would be missing, making it unsafe. My dad came to the rescue, or at least that was what I thought. He loaded my bike in the back of the vehicle, and off we went to get it fixed. But we were not going to the tire shop—we were heading east, out of town. I knew what that meant: he would take me to assault me in the vehicle and then get my bike fixed on the way home, if I was a good girl. I hated him.

This game of his continued, until one day as he parked on the dirt road, I jumped from the truck and ran down the road. A car was coming but slowed; the driver and I locked eyes, and I knew he could see the terror on my face. He pulled up to the truck and said something to my dad; we were in a small town, and everyone knew everyone. Then I heard my father's voice: "Get in this truck right now!" I could feel the blood drain from my body and knew that I had better do as commanded. As I walked back to the vehicle in defeat, he grabbed me by the back of my hair, lifted me into the truck, and threw me across the seat. Fixing the bike did not happen that day. The bike was supposed to symbolize freedom, and instead it was just one more way of being controlled.

THE KNOWING

⚯

s time passed, I realized that I would just know
things, as if I tapped into the incredible knowing.
I could feel emotions in others. I could sit beside
someone and know his or her tummy was angry. I would
know how to fix things that were broken. The ability to sense
information from people and things got stronger. I still did not
know that others could not do this. This knowing would get me
into more trouble. I would challenge what was happening around
me, and to me this became very matter-of-fact when faced with
adults lying. Some days this would get a chuckle, and other times
it got a reprimand, because the adults knew that they had been
caught in a lie.

I did not like the feelings I had inside when I was around
others who were angry, sick, or in pain. I tried to comfort people
to make them feel better so that I would feel better. It was as if
I was a sponge for others' emotions, and I took on the task of
healing the emotions of others through my body.

When I would pray and talk to God, I would hear the response.
In my childhood innocence I assumed everyone heard guidance,
so I never questioned this. I would be twenty-six before I found
out differently.

There were rules to be followed within this family, and we
knew that if we did not follow them, there would be consequences.

I remember one Christmas we were threatened not to get out of bed early, or all the gifts would be sent back by my father. Our belief in this was so strong that the next morning when we did in fact wake up early, the four of us snuck out to the living room. We quickly sorted the presents accordingly, hauled them back to our rooms, and hid them. Later, our mother woke us and asked if we were going get up and open presents. We knew we would have to confess what we had done. We were able to put the presents back under the tree before Dad got up.

The school year passed, and life continued as it had for years: fear, hurt, lies, and abuse. Things again would change in my life: a new baby was coming, and we would move to the country at the end of July of that summer. I would be nine in September.

This one day was different. I woke one morning in mid-July. I was extremely excited and yet unsure as to why. As I entered the dining room, I couldn't find my mom. I asked my dad where she was. He laughed and said in his disturbing voice, "They came and took her away." I started screaming and running through the house, and he stood there laughing. His used words as weapons any chance he got. My grandmother appeared, unsure of why she was there or when she got there. She grabbed me and lifted me into midair, looked me eye to eye, and explained my mom was in the hospital having the baby. I demanded that she take me to the hospital, now—I wanted proof that they had not taken her away as my father had said. I managed to hold things together until we left, but I still did not trust him. His threats over the years had tainted everything that came from his mouth.

I was in the hospital, and there was my little sister. I proclaimed to my mom that she was mine. I felt the baby's skin; she was soft and tiny, and I loved her instantly. My world changed that day. For the first time in nine years, I felt what real love was like. Perhaps with the first three children born so close in age, celebrating each other's existence was not there. It seemed that the fighting was ingrained in us. The struggled to have basic needs met created a constant battle, and that was being acting out. This new baby was different; I could feel it.

We had to move from the rented house. We were moving out to the country; the property belonged to someone that my parents knew. There was a house and a shed, and that was about it. I remembered an argument between my mom and dad about the farmhouse. She vowed she was not moving if the house was not finished and there was running water. As the days got closer, she would resolve to move anyhow, uncertain of what that meant. I was excited that my new sister was here. I think perhaps this was a point of contention with my older sister, because I did not love her this way; she was just there, and I had to put up with her.

How Would God Know

The house was cleaned, and the vehicles were loaded with stuff and kids. I was in the empty house with my mom and asked how I was going to get to church. She said I wouldn't be going to church because it was too far. I freaked out—I ran through the house screaming, "I did not tell God we were moving! How will he know where I am? How will he keep me safe?" She stood there laughing. I was scooped up and placed in the truck with the others. I cried most of the way to the farm. If I did not have God, then what would happen to me?

I liked the country: there were many trees and lots of room to run around, and we would get animals, but I soon realized the there was no one to protect us. At least in the city, we could play at friend's house to escape the violence at home. I was stuck. There were many chores to do that to would be used as weapons in the battle of the house. I also realized what a house that was not finished meant. There was no running water, and the only doors in the house were the porch, the main door, and the folding bathroom door. There were promises made that all this would be fixed and everything would be fine. Well, that was not true—my dad did manage to get water running to the house, but I guess you could say it was seasonal. The water line would freeze in the winter, which would prove to be a huge strain; laundry would be done in town. We would have to haul water from the well for bathing and doing dishes, and we would rely on the neighbors to get drinking water. For heat, there was a diesel-burning stove, and the boys' room was the only room completed. They had all their walls and carpet. The other bedrooms had framing and the roof. The exterior wall had insulation with plastic and no doors on any of the bedrooms. Nothing much would change in the six and half years that we lived there.

While growing up, I would pray that one day I would have a house with walls, doors, and plumbing that worked all year long. That seemed simple, right?

One thing that did change was that we had to ride the school bus, so there were no morning assaults. That did not mean the abuse stopped. Now the assaults came from the two of them, and I was in a constant mode of self-preservation. What could I do that would keep myself out of harm's way? The answer to that was not much. Any separation from who was in the house meant risk of assault. With the setup at the house, there was no privacy, so people knew about anything that happened. No doors to protect privacy, so then why did nothing change? How could a grown man over six feet tall and over two hundred pound manage to get out of a bed that rested against a wall on one side, with his wife sleeping on the outside? Why would this woman not protect her children? There are no barriers to hide the obvious. By surrendering her children, would she avoid abuse? Was it not a mother's instinct to protect her children? I learned quickly that what I needed was not the concern of anyone's in the house. If I wanted something, there was a price to pay. I decided that the price was too high and I keep my needs to myself.

My ability to sense energy heightened, and the sense of knowing what would happen in the house became stronger. I would be able to sense the energy for the night and who was going to abuse me. I would hide under my bed, crawling into and wrapping my body into the framing of the wall, in hopes of avoiding another assault. I was anchored in this position. My father was the abuser of the night. As he realized that I was not in my bed, he reached under my bed. My body pressed as tight as I could get into the framing. I felt his hand go across my hair, which stretched across the floor. I quickly grabbed my hair and looped it over my shoulder. He tried again, but he now only touched the floor. He gave up and moved to another room to get what he needed. I continue to hide in different areas of the upstairs, but I knew that this would not last. At my next haircut appointment, I got my hair chopped off to my shoulders. The hairdresser was stressing over this, but I instructed her to cut off the hair, which then reached down to my waist. My hair was once my pride, but now it was something that put me at risk. I would continue to cut my hair shorter with each appointment.

I would start a new school on my ninth birthday, and it was horrible because I felt out of place. I had started going through puberty over the summer. I was the only girl with a bra, and I was again the tallest in the class. I was an easy object of ridicule for the kids. I would take my jabs and pray for the days to end. There were two other girls who were being picked on, and I could feel how sad they were and how much pain they were in. I stood up for them, and that also made me a target; I became their friends anyhow. I continued to hold my secret inside.

SIBLING RIVALRY

*I*t was my older sister's and my birthday, and for our birthday that year we got dolls. My doll had blonde hair to match my then blonde-brown hair. My older sister got a dark-haired doll. I loved this doll, and I thought it was prettier than my sister's doll. In a rage one day, she took my doll and cut all of its hair off, and she wrote all over the doll's face with a pen. I was sure she was just expressing what she would like to do to me. I kept the doll and would remind her that my doll was still prettier than hers. I would keep the doll until I was fourteen, and I displayed it proudly. Our hatred for one another would grow. She would constantly pick on me and go out of her way manipulate me. I would grow to despise her. There was definitely no love there. I was unsure why she hated me; I did everything I could to be a good sister, but she was not as gracious. As time passed, if I had something, she would go out of her way to destroy it, even going as far as going after the boys that I liked and having sex with them. Her jealousy superseded her anger toward me. I'm not sure what she was jealous of—after all, I worked hard to fit into this family and was never accepted. It was as if I had done something that made me unworthy of the love and acceptance that the others received without trying.

I would focus on my younger sister. I would play with her, babysit her, and even make clothes for her when I began to sew.

She was my little doll, but better. I became very protective of her and did what I could to protect her, even though I knew that I could not win that battle. However, I would love her and comfort her in the hopes that would be enough. It was at least more than I got.

Our friends from town came for a visit, and I was excited to show them our farm animals. They were not so happy about these animals or the farm. I heard their father tell my dad that he could not let us live here like this. That would be the last time that they would visit.

The anger and fighting in the house was at an all-time high. My youngest male sibling, now seven, yelled at our mom that if she didn't stop doing something he was calling Zenith 12345—that was the abuse line years ago. Our mother barked, "If you think this is abuse, I will *show* you what abuse is!" My jaw hit the ground. Was she kidding? If she did not see this was abuse, she must have been crazy. I knew at that point she was in so much denial that we would never be safe with her as a parent. I tried to console my brother. I wondered what God would say to my mom when they had their talk.

I thought of the many things that I was shown when I was with my grandfather. I would continually wonder why my family members were not being accountable for the actions.

DREAMS

started to dream a lot. My dreams were full color and full audio, and I saw things in them that would later come true. If someone lost something, I could find it in my dreams. I could also fly in my dreams. There were dreams that were from the past as well, as if I had stepped back in time. The images made sense to me, but I knew I had not lived the experiences in this life. I did not know anything about reincarnation or past lives at that time. I would ask my mom what it was about, and she would just tell me I must have seen it in a movie. At that time, we had two television channels, and I had not seen a lot of movies at the theater. The words and the details were as if I had come from another time and space. I would later come to know that this type of dreaming was called astral travel.

I would have one dream that would reoccur I was female and wore clothes from another time. I was tied to a large wheel and set on fire, in the dream. This dream was terrifying to me. Between the dreams and the abuse, I did not sleep much.

GOING INTO SURVIVAL

꧁꩜꧂

The homemade camper was in the yard, and I would go out and try to get sleep after school or whenever I could. This would help somewhat. I was running on adrenaline and was always tired. I was sleeping in the camper in what I think was my safe place. My older brother had broken into the locked camper, and I woke to him raping me. He was his father son in every way, taking what he thought he was entitled to. My disdain for him grew daily.

There are many distractions on the farm: the animals, gardening, and fieldwork. I learned early that being active took me to a place of safety. While growing up, the boys did not do housework; according to my dad, housework was women's work. More important, women were here to serve men.

Life on the farm was definitely different from living in town. I got up early to do chores real chores, and then I got on the bus for our hour-long ride to school. The only thing that I liked about riding the bus to school was that I was out of the house early.

It would be in grade four that I had my first male teacher; he taught physical education. He was good looking, and the girls were smitten with him. During class after running laps, I would get incredibly red in the face. This glow would continue for hours after class. The gym teacher was concerned and suggested I go to the doctor. My mom took me get a check-up.

The doctor examined me; he had me lift my shirt from my back to check out my breathing. He stepped back and then asked my mother to leave the room. I could see a look on her face, as if to tell me not to say anything. After she left the room, the doctor turned his attention back to me and asked, "How did you get all those bruises on your back?" I explained to him that my brother and sister beat me up, which was what happened that time. He looked at me knowingly that there was something more going on but said nothing. He suggested that I stay away from my siblings if wanted to stay alive. If only he knew the truth of his statement.

With the examination complete, my mom re-entered the room. I could see in her face the look of fear and the warning look that I had better not have told. When we got to the vehicle, she asked what that was about, and I explained what the doctor had said. It was a very quiet ride home. That was what happened with her: if she was mad or couldn't control something, she did not speak. I think even then, she knew that I would be the one to tell—perhaps not now, but one day.

As the abuse at home got worse, I vowed that when I got bigger, this was never going to happen to me again. I found out how powerful my words would become. I began to gain weight, and a lot of it. I was getting bigger, but not in a way that was positive. By this time, my older brother had started abusing me more often. He took his lead from Father about what it meant to be male. Perhaps he craved the power, demanding that he be served like some king. I went deeper and deeper into my world of walls. Not wanting to get hurt anymore meant not letting anyone else in. The layers of fat on my body were like protection against the assaults. My world was small: school, chores, the animals, and my younger siblings. The separation from my older siblings grew; their constant physical assaults would increase if they wanted something for me, and they would beat me into submission. My father would attack me verbally about my weight, telling me no one liked fat girls, and no one would ever marry me. "You are fat and anger. No one could love that." Well, perhaps I had fulfilled my need for protection from men: stay fat and angry, and they would not want to be with me.

Finding My Voice

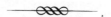

*O*n grade four I started writing reports. Putting my words on paper brought me joy: I was able to investigate things and find out the truth about stuff, no longer relying on others for information. For the first time I felt smart. For my first report we had to write a letter to a company, get information from them, and then tell a story about the product the company made. I wrote about a salt company. The next report was about bears. I remembered getting very good marks, and for the first time I was being acknowledged for it. I also learned how powerful words could be; they made me feel good when I could express them. I came from a family that did not communicate, and this acknowledgement was huge. I loved school from that point on. Learning was a passion for me, and no one could take words from me.

There was a new topic: we were to write something about our family. My body screamed in fear. Unsure of what the teacher expected from this report, I talked to the other kids in my class; they were writing about when their parents got married and how they met. I went home and start asking questions. My mom shared that they were married in the summer of 1961, and she showed me a picture of her: she was in a short white dress, she had a small waist, and she had simple shoes as she stood there by herself. I thought that was weird but did not say anything. As usual my mind went into overdrive with details—something was not right, but I couldn't put my finger on it. I realized that she could not be telling the truth. My oldest brother was born in the fall of 1961, which would mean that she would be seven and a half months pregnant in the picture. *Nope, one more lie,* I concluded. I asked who I was named after, and my dad told me it was one of his old girlfriends. My skin crawled with disgust. I made up a story for school because the truth was ugly, and I did not want anyone to know the truth.

My Body

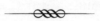

*M*y body would continue to change, and in many
ways I hated everything about being in this physical
body. The emotions that I felt from others were
getting stronger, and I did not know what to do with them.
Dealing with my own emotions was hard enough. I would try
to make people feel good around me so that I would not have to
feel their pain or discomfort, as if it was my job. I did not know
what this experience meant for many years. This brought to me
an awareness that if I could make people happy, then I would not
have to feel their pain. This would set me into a cycle of pleasing,
and putting others emotions before mine. It was as if I was an
open vessel for the emotions of the world around me, and I did not
know how to manage them. My body continued to gain weight,
as if that would protect me from the emotions.

The year continued, and I became aware of how protective I
was with what I shared with my classmates. I learned to navigate
through their emotions, and as I got bigger, I would try to fit in
with my classmates.

It was the summer before my tenth birthday. We had been
weeding the garden. We had a huge garden with every sort of
vegetable, and gardening gave me a sense of purpose and joy. I
liked the process of planting seeds and something good coming
from it. I went inside to use the bathroom, and I came out and

shared with my mother that I was bleeding. My mom was angry; she took me to the house and gave me the supplies needed and then told me to hurry up and get back out to do the weeding. Somehow I thought there should be more to this than what was expressed.

I was unsure of what this was, despite what was happening to me sexually. There was a separation of the magnitude of what this was. I didn't know what bearing that would have on the sexual abuse that happened so often. As my body changed, I realized that despite all that had happened to me, I was naive about the body. The body was an object to be controlled by men; the feminine part was made to feel dirty and shameful. I hated everything about my body. My dad would constantly tell me that women were put on earth to serve man. Those words would make me shudder to the bone each time I heard them. In his eyes women were objects to be owned and controlled. I wondered why he thought this way. Where did he learn that being angry was his only choice? Did he not see how this hurt his family? Did he not know that this only made us hate him? My mind spun with questions about his adult choices.

THE ATTEMPT TO ESCAPE

———— ✺ ————

The summer continued, and we have a visitor: my uncle from the west coast, I would get so excited when he came. He always brought fish to eat, and being from a farm, I thought fish was a treat. He would never let us know what we were eating until after we decided it we liked it or not. He brought things like abalone, octopus, salmon, black cod, and ling. He brought his outside world into ours. I wished he was my dad, and I think my dad knew it. The time while he was there seemed to fly by. His morning wake-ups would consist of him yelling upstairs, "Okay, you hippies, out of bed!" When it was time for him to leave, I struggled with it. I had a plan this time: I would hide out in his camper, and he would not find me until it was too late; he would have to keep me. I snuck into the camper and sat quietly. Everyone was gathering to say good-bye to him, and he was yelling for me so that he could say good-bye. I remained in the camper. He was relentless, and for some reason he opened the camper door and looked in. He saw me and was confused as to why I was in there. He scooped me out and gave me a big hug good-bye. My dad was furious with me—he knew exactly why I was there. I was not getting out of this family quite so easily.

The Day He Broke Me

The assaults would become more difficult, with all the people in the house and no doors to protect the secret. Being taken in the vehicle down the road to be molested was a second choice. I was struggling with my dad, and he was grabbing me, trying to take me and put me in the truck. I fought him. I was not getting in that truck, even if I had to die trying. He finally got frustrated with me and said, "You think you are going to win this, really?" He went into the house and came out with my two younger siblings. I started screaming for him to stop, and I was throwing rocks at the vehicle, trying to get him to let them go. He put his hand out the window and waved. He broke me that day. I was overwhelmed with emotions. I did not go into the house but rather into the trees just beyond the pasture. I cried from my soul that day; it was as if every part of my being had died. I sat on a fallen tree and sobbed uncontrollably. I couldn't stop the pain that was leaving my body; as I cried, it was almost a purge of all that I had held in over the years.

I realized I was not alone. All of a sudden, there was energy around me like I had never felt before. I was scared and thought that perhaps it was a wild animal. I slowly lifted my head and saw that I was surrounded by our horses. I was in the center of a perfect circle; it was as if they were trying to heal my pain. I realized I was safe in their energy. My head went back down, and

I allowed the energy to fill my emotionally empty body. I fell into a very deep state of safety in their presence.

Unsure of how much time had passed, I raised my head again, and the horses were gone. I got up to go back into the house. He had returned. With nothing said, I went upstairs and held my little sister. I held the guilt that I could not protect her deep in my soul.

THE VOW TO ESCAPE FOREVER

I knew that I did not want to be in this family anymore, and I made a plan to get out. I would work, save money, and move away, never to return. I started to babysit and helped people by doing odd jobs. Later I would get a job months before my thirteenth birthday, so that I would have things of my own. I believed that abuse happened to people who did not have money, so my plan was to make money, and then I could get away from this experience.

I tried not to let people in. I was afraid that I would not be able to keep the secret for much longer. I could see where I would be overt with my responses to my abusers. I would get a look, and almost in defiance I was saying, "Yeah, what are you going to do about it? I dare you to push me."

The county school that I went to had great people, but I could see how my decision to keep people from my secrets affected me socially. I also noticed how my older siblings kept me from the groups. When I would get close to being a part of the circle, my older siblings would make comments and insult me, and I would retreat. I craved friendship, and I did not know how to balance that. I did not want to have to lie to someone I cared about. Truthfully, I knew my life was nothing but lies: one more lie to protect the last, trying to remember who I had told what lie to. It took a lot of energy that I did not have.

I Don't Want to Die

We went camping on the weekend with a family that we knew when we lived in town. I would turn thirteen at the end of that summer. We headed to a popular camping site, and I was excited to see our friends, but I wasn't happy about being there with my dad. The weekend consisted of fishing and playing. My dad decided he needed to play father. He was drunk and wanted to take the three oldest out in the boat, perhaps to create that false sense of family. I think even he knew that we did not want to be around him, especially when he was drunk. I didn't want to go and I made my opinion known. He forced me to get in the boat, and we head out on the lake, but I continued to protest. My dad reached over to me and threw me out of the boat. I started to splash about; I was not a good swimmer. I could not keep my head above water and started yelling. I went under the water, my survivor instincts kicked in, and I managed to surface. I was yelling, "I don't want to die, I don't want to die!" As I went under and came back up, I saw my two older siblings sitting motionless, not trying to save me. I went under for the third time, and I felt my body sink to the bottom of the lake. I could feel my body coil onto the bottom, and everything went dark.

I was unsure of the time that I was under water, but the next thing I recall was my right arm was extended over my head, and

I was being pulled from the lake, with water splashing against my face from the force and speed that I was being pulled. I could feel my knees hitting the bottom of lake, now in shallow water. I heard, "Stand up, you can stand up." I gathered my strength and stood up. I looked on the shore of the small piece of land in the middle of the lake; no one was there. I was confused. I looked into the lake and saw the boat was about fifty feet from where I stood on the shore. I couldn't explain this experience. All I knew was that some force pulled me from that lake. From that point on, I had a very deep hatred for my siblings. Despite all the abuse and neglect from my family, I knew that I would have tried to save them. Their actions let me know I was not wanted in their family—that was very clear. I couldn't wait until I was older, so that I could leave and never go back.

SELF-DISCOVERY

I would start to learn who I was. I loved being around the dogs, cats, and farm animals. I liked cooking and baking, and most of all I like photography and sports. These things allowed me to focus on something other than the abuse. When I was not doing those things, I loved to read. It was as if I was able to create a life beyond abuse. I learned that I was not the abuse; abuse was what happened to me. That was what my grandfather shared with me when I left my body at age eight. Slowly I was beginning to understand what that meant. Time passed, the abuse continued, and no one talked, so nothing changed.

After yet another assault by my dad, he asked me, "When are you going to make me a grandpa?" My stomach turned, and I shuddered to my core. I vowed in that moment that he would be six feet under before I would have children. He was looking for his next victim, and he sickened me. Who would be next for him? I vowed that I would never let him have access to any of my children. If he ever touched my kids, I would kill him with my bare hands. I would not become my mother. Just when I thought I couldn't hate him any more than I did, his words spun through my head for days and weeks to follow. The thought of that haunted me.

I wanted to fit in at school, but my weight had become an issue; I was just another target for people to treat me poorly. In grade eight there was a boy I liked, but I was too shy to do anything; more important, I did not know what to do. The ex-girlfriend of my brother invited me to a party, and the boy that I liked was there. I found out he that liked me. He made his moves, but I kept him in line. People noticed that we liked each other, and that got back to my brother.

At home the next day, my father was yelling at me to come downstairs. As I stepped onto the second to last step, I looked my father directly in the eye as he waited for me. The family congregated in the area at the base of the stairs. I was being asked if I had had sex with this boy. I said no. My older siblings were taunting the situation, and the younger two siblings stood there waiting for the outcome. My father called me a slut, and I was shocked! The rage in me boiled over. I looked him in the eye and I say, "Yeah, well, if I am a slut, then I guess you made me one now, didn't you?" The jaws began to drop from the others standing there. My father said nothing. I turned and went back to my bedroom, and nothing more was said about the situation. I pulled back my emotions that I had for that boy and any other boy after that, for some time.

I went to my bed and asked God if he could kill me. I did not want to be a part of this family. *Just let me die,* I prayed. I was done. I fell asleep hoping God would take me in my sleep. Unfortunately, he did not.

The days continued and my anger with God started to grow daily. Just let me die!

JUST LET ME DIE

———— ∞∞∞ ————

*M*y father was not satisfied with just the after-school
assault. He would start coming to the school and
telling the teachers that I had an appointment. He
would drive from the school and across the highway onto a dirt
road minutes from the school, and he would assault me. His
assaults became more often, and I was sick of it. I would have
nightmares about him coming and taking me. The next time he
showed up at the school, I was in my homeroom, just feet away
from the principal's office. I was called out of my classroom,
and as I entered the hallway the principal and my dad were
standing there. I froze. The principal commented that my dad
was there to take me to my appointment. I yelled, "I don't have
an appointment," and I turned to go back to my class.

My dad yelled at me, "Yes, you do!"

I firmly said, "No, actually, I don't."

The principal was confused as I made my way back to the
class. I knew that I would pay for that. But just maybe he would
be mad enough that his anger would escalate and he would
physically assault me and I would die. I did not care anymore; I
was emotionally overloaded, and if dying was the only way out,
then I was ready for God to take me from this pain. I thought
about death more and I remembered when I was with Grandpa in

my energy-body. I wanted to feel that way again. If only I could leave my physical body and all the pain it held.

I would attempt to take knives to my bedroom. My older sister would rat me out to our mom, and she would ask, "Why do you need a knife in your room?"

I looked at her and yelled, "What the hell do you think I need a knife for? You sure as hell are not protecting me." She took the knives from me again and again over the next few months.

The relationship between my mother and I continued to become strained. I could not understand why she could not love me. I was a good daughter, I helped in the house with the younger kids, and I did well in school. What had I done for her to hate me so much? She did not love me; if she did, then she would have done something to keep us safe, but she did nothing.

The siblings were fighting and yelling, and my mom yelled, "Why can't you kids just love each other?"

"Are you kidding me? You are going to open that door?" I barked at her. "And where would we have learned that? Oh yes, all that love we have seen from our parents, that's right!"

She looked at me as if she has no idea what I was saying. The others stood there with their mouths open, waiting to see what happened next. I shook my head and pushed past my mom in the kitchen. *Is she seriously that stupid?* I wondered? What would it take to get her to step up, be the adult, and protect her children? What world did she live in? What was her reality, to allow this to happen?

THINGS ESCALATE

The weekend came, and the old man was drunk again. He called from town and wanted someone to pick him up. My mom recruited one of the older kids to go with her to drive the other vehicle home. I actually refused to get my driver's license for that reason; I did not want to be a part of the rescue program. My mom returned from rescuing him from town. The kids were upstairs in bed but not asleep; we knew what was coming. He demanded cigarettes, but there were none. I knew my older sister stole them from the freezer. The rage was building in him—it was palatable, and we could hear him beating on her. I shared a room now with my youngest sister, and she crawled into my bed for safety. The boys were now out of their room and standing at the top of the stairs, outside my room.

The intensity of violence escalated and my older brother ran down the stairs; we could hear him physically charge our dad. The battle began in the next minute. My oldest brother was running up the stairs, and as he was starting up the second tier of steps, our father was right behind him. My dad grabbed his legs, and his body slammed into the top of the stairs. My dad continued up the stairs and overtook my brother; he flipped him over, put both hands around his neck, and began to choke him. The color of my brother's face changed. All I could think was that this was it—he was finally going to kill one of us. We were all yelling at him to stop, but all that did was fuel his rage. He would do what he wanted; that was obvious. Finally, my mom came up the stairs with a broom and whacked my dad over the back of his head. It did not knock him out, but it brought him back into a state of reality. He looked at my brother, turned to my mom, went downstairs, and headed to bed. *What just happened here?* I said to myself. I was sitting on my bed and was crying.

My mom appeared upstairs, looked at me, and said, "What are you crying about? This has nothing to do with you!"

Really, I was supposed to witness all this, and it should not affect me? Was that how she dealt with the abuse? It was not happening to her, so it was none of her business?

One day shortly after, my dad was not living in the house I was unsure of how long, but it was not long enough. I was just starting to feel safe from his nightly assaults. It was daytime, and I heard a vehicle pull in the driveway. I went outside, and my mom was standing in the doorway to the porch. My dad was outside with a bouquet of flowers. Mom was standing there with a sense she had made him change by making him move out, but I knew differently. She said, "He has brought flowers."

I felt the betrayal boil in my blood. "Oh, so that's what we are worth, a bouquet of cheap flowers?" She yelled at me to be nice. "Thanks, Mom." I pushed past her in disgust. All I could see was a weak woman when I looked at her. I knew she would never be strong enough to make me safe. The abuse would start shortly after his return.

The anger between my father and I got worse. He would look for any reason to physically assault me; he knew that he had lost control of me, so the physical assaults were his last-ditch effort to gain some level of control. My older sister, being the master manipulator, would give him all the reasons she could to direct his anger at me. After all, she was a victim here. I never understood why she was angry with me; I had done nothing to her. I was being abused just like her. Perhaps because she knew I had a plan to get out, and with that I had hope. I refused to be a victim of what was happening to me any longer. He may have won the battle, but I would win the war. I vowed that he would never win!

My sister was having one of her moods again and was out to prove her power when it came to our father. We were to alternate doing dishes, and she started an argument with me about whose turn it was, My mom just wanted quiet and told me to do them. I told her that I did them the night before. Again my sister started to contest that it was not her turn; she claimed she had done the dishes the night before. I was the one who cooked dinner, and I knew what dishes I had done.

My father was getting enraged with the bickering. I was standing in the kitchen in protest, and he came to the kitchen, grabbed me by the hair, and slammed my body into the cabinet. The force that he used makes me black out, and I could feel my body start to slide down the cabinets as I fell to the floor. He grabbed me again and slammed my face into the sink of dishes, and he commanded me to do them. I turned, and my sister stood there smugly, one more success in her world. She played him like a fiddle and got what she wanted from him, perhaps for services rendered. I hated her more and more each day. As I did the dishes, my anger came out, and I was braking glasses and slamming pots. My father barked, "If you break one more thing, I will come out there."

I thought to myself, *just go ahead*. I placed the biggest knife by the sink and knew that if he came near me, I would stab him to death. Unfortunately, he did not come to the kitchen again that night.

I started working that summer. If I was not going to die, then I needed a plan to get away from this. I would work at a hotel cleaning rooms, and I would do odd jobs to get money. My job at the hotel started with being a chambermaid, and then I went to laundry and then to the office over the eight years that I worked there. I liked the group of people I worked with, and despite what was going on in my life; I was naive about what I would experience here. The hotel filled with the same people for years. There was an oil boom going on with no houses to be rented, so the hotel rooms were rented for years on end by the same people. It created a community of sorts, with a lot of laughs and a sense of belonging. I experienced a healthy side of relationships for the first time. Not all men were scum, I would conclude. That was huge for me to acknowledge. I finally had men in my life that had my back, ones whom I could trust and who made me feel good about being me. I would create bonds with them as friends, and again my naivety would prove to protect me, thinking that they were just friends. I would later learn that some of them wanted more in our relationship. We would laugh about it later, but I realized that being so focused on getting out of this town meant that I was not open to relationships. I guess you could say I missed being with a few good men.

Money and Betrayal

he money had started to build. This made my mom mad, and she made a point of letting me know.

We would sell eggs, milk, cream, and butter. The money we generated from selling these was for movie nights or to buy tack for the horses. It was Friday night, and we loaded up and headed to town for the movie. I was at the back of the group, and when I went in the movie theater, the lady at the ticket booth yelled I had not paid. I told her I was with them, pointing to my family. She stated that they did not pay for me. I looked at my mom and said, "What is going on?"

She said, "Didn't you bring your own money?" Back in the day there use to be family rates at the theater. The message was clear: I was not part of this family. I hated her.

I did have five dollars in my pocket; the movie, pop, and popcorn cost $1.25. I paid for myself. I was so hurt that I got my treats and sat by myself in the theater. It was not the money; it was about how she treated me differently. If I had not taken money, would she have made me sit in the truck? I saw them looking for me, and they were laughing. I got it—I did not belong. I regularly questioned being born into this family. Perhaps that was the day I quit trying to be a part of the family. My independence grew more each day.

If I wanted clothes, my mom would tell me to buy them myself, and I did. That created a rift between my siblings. "Why does she get that?" they'd complain.

I would say, "I paid for it." They would question where I got the money. "I worked for it—that is where I got it." Unlike them, I saved my money; I did not spend it on booze and smokes. That also made my mom angry, because she saw I could do it without her help. I was independent because I had learned early she would not protect me or provide for me.

When it came to birthdays, I would be asked what I wanted. When I stated what I wanted, I was told, "You don't want that." *Actually, I do!* I would not get what I wanted, and usually I did not get anything. One Christmas, I asked for a clock radio, and my sister got it instead. From that point on, I would keep fifty dollars from my check and buy what I needed. I started buying things for when I moved out. I no longer asked for anything.

Christmas became a payout program. The tree was lined with gifts. Perhaps they thought that the presents made up for the abuse. I would get resentful to those in my life whose actions were less then honorable, and then they would show up with gifts. I would state my disappointment in those who would act in that way. My first question to someone bearing gifts was, "What did you do wrong?" I would struggle this for years. I learned later that gift giving was supposed to be an act of love. For me, it was a "buy back love" experience.

EATING DISORDER

⸺⊗⊗⊗⸺

*W*e had been visiting my grandparents and uncles, who still lived in a small mountain town. We all went out for Chinese food, and my dad tried to be the big man at the table, he said he would pick up the check. This was before debit card or credit cards. He quickly realized that he couldn't pay the bill. He turned to me and said in front of everyone, "You eat so much now that I can't afford to pay." I was not only shocked but incredibly embarrassed. I knew I had barely eaten anything. Shame filled my body, and my uncle was quick to help pay for the meal. This experience would trigger my eating disorder.

I had heard there was a singer that had starved to death by not eating, and this intrigued me. I had seen enough violence that I could not kill myself in a gory way. Therefore in the summer between junior high and high school, the process started. I would not eat for days, making excuses that I had eaten before or would eat later. I got thinner and thinner, sometimes not eating up to four days. If I had to eat, I learned that by exercising, I could burn all the calories that I had consumed. I started running and doing five hundred sit-ups a day. When I had to eat, I would then go out to the field and throw up. A girl I worked with was ninety-eight pounds soaking wet, and she went to a doctor who gave her diet pills. I was much larger, so surely it would not be a problem to get pills myself. The pills were so strong that just taking one meant I would not be hungry for days. The weight continued to drop away. No one knew any different, and neither did any of my family. As long as I made their dinner, nothing else mattered.

As my body changed, I began to notice it. I was walking down the street on Saturday, and I caught a glimpse of someone I knew in the window, so I stopped to look. I saw my reflection for the first time. I was thin—really thin. Later that week I was in the bathtub, and I realized the amount of space that was in the tub. I no longer filled the tub with my overweight body. How much weight had I lost? In that moment of self-awareness, the bathroom door was yanked open, and it was my brother. I started screaming for him to get out. He was taunting me, and so I continued to scream for him to get out. My mother yelled at me to shut up. She defended his actions again. He turned to me in the tub and started urinating on me, and he would not stop. I was screaming again and told Mom what he was doing, but again she defended him. I was humiliated and disturbed. The worst insult in my mind was to urinate on another person. He stood there laughing. That small moment of self-awareness was shattered, and I became aware again that I had no power.

When school started, again, I had dropped sixty-five pounds. I continued with the binging and purging, or just not eating when I could get away with it. This would continue for the next ten years that followed. I didn't realize the long-term effect that it would have on my life. Binge eating became my way of life, and it was one thing that I could control. When my emotions would get the best of me, I would stuff them with food to the point of needing to throw up. I liked the way it felt when I threw up. From that point on, when I felt sick,

I would make myself throw up, and it brought me a sense of relief. This gave me some sense of control in a world where felt like I had none. The purging would become something that I did daily.

POWER AND CONTROL

My plan to get out of this family would create more tension between my mother and me. My mom resented me for my ability to save money, and she could see that by having money, I had choices. Back before ATM machines, I would give her my paychecks, which would be on average $525, for her to deposit into my bank and update my bankbook. Twice I noticed that the bankbook had not been updated. I asked her to explain, and she stated that she did not have time to update it. My next paycheck came, and she updated my bankbook, but the last deposit was still missing I confronted her—she was stealing from me! She got aggressive with me. The next check I signed but write "for deposit only" with my bank account number and she freaked out. I would not allow her to take my money anymore. If she needed money, she needed to ask, not steal from me. I wondered how many times she had taken my money and I simply did not notice.

I was now in grade ten. I was excited to be in high school; my body was slim, and perhaps there would be a new level of acceptance. I quickly realized that the kids from elementary were here, and I panicked. What would they say about me? Would they remember what happened in the pink and white house? I found myself trying to hide from them, in fear of my past coming forward.

In high school there were option classes, and I signed up to take auto-mechanics and carpentry. I was excited more about carpentry because then I would know how to build things, and I could have a bedroom with walls and perhaps even a door. The boys in the class made sure I knew they thought this class was for boys, not girls, and I needed to get out. They quickly squashed my dreams of being able to fix my room. I withdrew from the class.

I was in English class, and there was an announcement over the class speaker calling me to the principal's office. I was not sure what it was about; was my dad coming to take me again? Was I in trouble for something? I entered the office, and the principal explained me about my outstanding school fees of thirty-four dollars. I was confused. I asked the principal if my older siblings' fees were paid, and he said yes, I asked to call my mom. Her response was, "You have money—you can pay them." My eyes filled with tears with the realization of the situation. So because I did not let her steal from me, I was fully on my own financially. I turned to the principal and promised him I would have to go to the bank and get the money to pay the fees. He looked confused but accepted my promise to pay. I paid the fees as soon as I could get to the bank.

The Unthinkable Happens

had taken control of my body. My weight disappeared, and I was now thin, but there was something else going on: I could feel something moving in my stomach. My period had stopped a few months earlier. I was pregnant from the abuse. I kept the secret for a few more months, but then I got scared. I shared with my friend in the hopes she would know what to do. Instead of helping me, she did the unthinkable: she disclosed my secret. I had gotten on the school bus at the end of the day to go to the farm, and the girl I sat with said that there was something written on the bathroom wall, and I needed to go and remove it. I bolted off the bus, knowing what she had seen. With eraser in hand I went back into the school, and sure enough there it was for everyone to see. She wrote that I had told her I was pregnant. My friend had done this. After everything that I had helped her with over the years, this was my thanks. It was obvious that asking for anyone's help would get me nowhere.

My thoughts flooded my mind. How could I be pregnant? I saw the words scrawled on the bathroom wall, I was mortified, my heart sank, and I was alone again. Who had seen it? I was always afraid of someone letting my secret out. I realized that there was no one that I could trust, and that made me sad. Then I thought to myself, *why did the girl that I sat with on the bus not erase it when she saw it?* Shame ran through me the whole way home. I retreated to me room and tried to figure this out in my head.

At that point, I had decided that I would keep the baby; at least that way I would not be alone, and I would have someone to love. Perhaps I would run away, maybe to my grandparents' house, and raise it. Perhaps I would live in the tree fort that my younger brother had made. I could use the money I had saved, I could do this. This was the mind of a naïve, sheltered girl not even realizing the ramifications of what was she was about to embark on.

My older sister caught wind of the situation and informed my mom that I was pregnant. Later, I was in the bathroom, and my mom and older sister confronted me. My mom asked me when the last time was that I used the monthly supplies. I lied and said three or four months; I knew it was getting closer to five months. My sister would do anything to get me into trouble, and she did not care that I was pregnant and what that meant. Her only goal was to get me into trouble. I looked my sister in the eye and wished her dead for the first time in my life. I pushed past them and went to my room, dazed by all that was happening to me. I was trying to wrap my head around this. After all, I did not go out and have sex with some boy—I was being molested. Now would be the time for my mom to step up and realize what was going on, but she was judging me instead. I went to my room ashamed of this experience.

My mom came up to my room and instructed me to take off my pants and to lie on the floor. I did as I was ordered, thinking that she was going to check my stomach. Within moments I could feel pain in my abdominal. She had inserted a coat hanger into me and was trying to take the baby. I could feel the coat hanger scrape my insides, and I begged her to stop and not take my baby.

The fear and pain hit me all at once, and I blacked out. That was the last that I remembered about the situation. This event was something that I would block out for many years to come.

There was a void in the weeks that followed. I then realized the baby was no longer there and was unsure of what happened. The details were completely blanked out of my memory. My mind reeled trying to make sense of it all. How could one make sense of a senseless situation? My mind did not grasp what my body had gone through. As my body tried to rebalance, there were huge emotions; crying was my main state of being. I sought answers from my mom, because I thought I was going crazy. Her only comment was we were all a little crazy. Why was she so uncompassionate? What had I done to deserve such neglect?

After the abortion, I started to think of death more. The wave of self-loathing would send me into a cycle of self-abuse, alcohol, smoking, and more purging over the next several years. With each action I hated myself more, and I was unsure of how to get out of this rhythm of self-destruction. My hatred for my family and myself grew daily.

I had what would be my last conversation with God for a very long time. I expressed to him that I wanted to die if this was how my life was going to be. Trying to be a part of this family was killing me emotionally. I even went as far as having my little sister hold a pillow over my face until I passed out. However, I realized how that would affect her when she got older. I was glad in that moment of desperation, I was able to see past my own pain and see how that event would change her life. If I died, who would protect her? The truth was I knew that I couldn't protect myself, let alone her, but I hoped that my presents would at least lessen the impact on her.

I began binge eating more. Binging and purging became a way of life for me. I did not want to feel—I just wanted to be empty. I went to school and continued to have emotional breakdowns. One day my older sister realized I was not well. She called me out of class and took me to the bathroom across the hall. I was unsure if she realized what our mother had done that night she shared my secret and the role she played in it. I felt myself sink to the floor in tears and sobbed, not even sure of why myself. All I knew was that I was done. It was that day that I knew I was broken and did not know how to fix myself.

We would soon move from the farm and back into the city. I was unsure of what sparked this, but I did not care—moving back was a good thing. It was winter and the middle of grade ten all I wanted was to be back in town.

Moving Back to Town

As we prepared for the move back to town, again my mom confronted me with a money issue. She informed me that she needed two thousand dollars, or she couldn't pay the mortgage. Had she asked the others for money? Why was it my job to give her this? I did give her the money, but I emphasized it was a loan, and she had to pay it back. That was my money for college. I had ten thousand dollars saved by then, and I was proud of that. She would bitterly mention my savings any chance she got. I could not wrap my head around why she was doing this. Most parents would be proud.

As we planned the move to the new house, my parents were ordering furniture. I wanted a new bedroom suite, and they told me that I would have to buy it myself if I wanted it. I did, and I thought to myself that was fine, because I would take it when I moved out. All the other kids got new bedroom suites and did not have to pay for them. We moved in, and I settled into my room; it was in the basement, beside the stairs and under the kitchen on the main floor. My new furniture fit perfectly. I finally had a room with walls and a door. It was a good start.

I went upstairs, and my mom summoned me to her bedroom. She was standing in front of a large steamer trunk open on the bed. I looked into the trunk; it was filled old pictures. She was holding a piece of paper and acting weird as she handed me the paper. I looked and realized that was it a marriage certificate from Sacred Heart Church, Alberta. The certificate was dated on the bottom: June, 1965. I said, "I see you were married in 1965." She grabbed the certificate from my hands and would not let me have it back. No worries, just another lie to the pile, she had said they were married in 1961 for years. I left the room. Nothing more was said about the exposed truth.

It would not be long before the abuse started again. I was asleep and woke to someone coming down the stairs; it was my dad. I knew he was coming to molest me. I quickly moved a chair that I had been using to block the door so that he couldn't get in. I slipped back onto my bed, curled into the corner. The door handle rattled, and I could feel the terror in my body. He realized what I had done. He managed to get his hand into the small crack that he was able to create. The chair slipped, and I realized that if he got in, I would pay for trying to lock him out. The door opened just slightly, and the legs of the chair hit the footboard of the bed. The door did not budge any further. He gave up and returned upstairs.

I realized that my door was what would keep me from nightly attacks. My older sister was out most every night, so she had also realized that not being in the house during the night was her survival. I surrendered myself to the belief it had stopped, not realizing that he had already chosen his next victim.

It was now summer and I requested more hours at the hotel. I volunteered at the hospital and played sports. My time at the house lessened, and I created a false sense of peace for myself. The family was almost tolerable at this point.

I realized something else as I volunteered. I noticed how grateful people were. Complete strangers were willing to express their appreciation for the things I did for them. Why was it so hard for my family to express gratitude for the things I did for them? Volunteering was a way of feeling appreciated—something I did not get from my family. I would continue to volunteer any chance I got, and it became a way of life for me.

FAMILY

*L*ater that year my uncle in the same town hosted a family reunion. There had not been any family gatherings other than weddings and funerals, so this was a first. Each parent would go up and introduce his or her kids and grandchildren. It was my father's turn. "These are my kids, and they are all sterile." My jaw dropped as I stood there. Was he serious? He did not understand how inappropriate he was being. Derogatory and sexual comments were his norm; perhaps he thought he was being funny, but it was so far from the truth. I pushed down my urge to say, "And that is my father. He is a rapist." I avoided him for the rest of the day and focused on my cousins and relatives.

TIME TO REFOCUS

committed myself to school. I managed to stay on the honor roll, holding an average of 75-80 percent. Perhaps for some it was not that impressive, but considering what I was going through, I felt proud of my marks. I graduated, and again it was no big deal. My father showed up to the ceremony drunk. I wished he would just leave, but he grabbed at me. His touch sickened me. I managed to make it through the ceremony and dinner. Time spent with them and the false sense of family disturbed me, putting on a show that somehow this family was strong.

My goal was to leave and go to college in the city, hours away. My mother explained to me I was only seventeen and was not allowed. I knew there was more behind her resistance. I reluctantly registered at the local college for business, and I studied accounting and management. I wanted to understand the money part of the world. I would pay my own way and would continue to work a forty-hour week to ensure that I would have money. I saved money, buying only what I needed, and with each paycheck I was closer to my goal of leaving and never coming back. I honored the vow that I would never be so dependent on a man that I would put myself or my children in harm's way, and making money was the only way I knew how to do this. I would also conclude that being poor and having no education was what allowed for the abuse to occur, so I created a belief that if I had money and an education, I would eliminate abuse.

It was my birthday again. I told my mom that I wanted a spice cake. She replied, "Well, I guess you had better make it then." I was shocked. I baked and decorated cakes for everyone, yet she couldn't honor a simple request to have someone do the same for me. I was unsure why that bothered me so much, because celebrating my birthday was not important and never was. I did not get a birthday cake that year, or any other year for that matter. As I reflected, I never got one unless my sister was home, and then it was a dual-purpose cake.

RELATIONSHIPS

ollege was interesting, with new people and a new way of doing things. I submerged myself into my new daily routine. It was as if I had stepped through a veil, and everything was different: not being home to be abused, no longer living on the farm, and realizing I had choices. There would be a new sense of confidence. I was aware that men were showing interest in me. I was so focused on getting out of town and moving to the city that dating was really not my focus, but I realized having male friends was something I wanted in my life.

I acknowledged my fear when it came to relationships. I did not want the sexual escalation that was a part of this interaction, and I always kept men just out of arm's reach, if you will. Those men presented an interesting part of a relationship I had not before explored. I would see their frustration with me as I did not allow the sexual part of the experience to develop. I did not want to feel that shame and fear in my body again.

There would be someone who would catch my eye, and I could feel he was different. He would not push me sexually I became good friends with him, even his best friend. It would be years before I would let anyone into my space sexually, and even then it was a horrible experience. I'd have flashbacks and would shoot out of my body energetically. I would sense the frustration as I lay there, letting the sexual act occur. I did not know that as an adult, I had a right to enjoy this experience. For the most part, the sexual experience was horrific, and I would avoid it as much as I could.

Later that year my older sister moved back home. She had a sense of entitlement—what she wanted, she got. I got up to go to college, and the vehicle I had been driving was not in the driveway. I called my mother at work and asked her who took it. She told me my sister had. I asked how I was supposed to get to college, and of course the answer was to take the bus. That made sense: get on the bus and take an hour to get to the college, instead a fifteen-minute drive. I jumped on my bike instead and got to school.

I get home, and that was the discussion of the night. End of story, I would not get the vehicle. After all, it was more important that she have a vehicle so that she could go for coffee and go to the bar. I went out that weekend to buy my first car. I would buy a silver Dodge Aspen and paid in cash.

This situation was not going to control me, and I let them know it. The vehicle gave me a new freedom, and I made sure they were aware that they no longer had control. I did not have to rely on them any longer. My siblings questioned how I could afford a vehicle. I surrendered to the fact that no matter what, when I wanted something and they knew, it would give them control. I did what I needed to did to take care of me. My sister came and went from the house, and her life continued to twist through her own issues.

BIRTHDAYS

The year passed, and it was July. For my mom's birthday, I did not make her a cake that year, and neither did I get her a present. She was pissed and proclaimed, "What, I don't get a cake?" The situation was perfect. I said, "Well, if you want one, you should make one. I have to bake my own." She did not talk to me for the week that followed.

Two months later, it was my older sister's and my birthday. She had moved away, and I was going to see her. Time and distance had given us a new prospective; we could at least be civil to each other. My car was loaded, and I was in the foyer of the house. My foot was up on the stairs as I tied my shoes. There was a thud on the landing above me. I looked up, and there was present there. I said, "Oh, a present for me?"

My mom barked, "No, it's for your sister."

I asked, "Where's mine?"

She commented, "You don't need anything."

I gave up. There was no hope for her; she truly could not see how her actions wounded me. I wondered how many people got things that they did not need, and how many people got presents in celebration of their birth? I guessed in her mind, my birth was nothing to celebrate. My thoughts reeled over this as I drove to see my sister in the next province. I got there and gave her present to her. She thanked me; I did not tell her it was from "her mother." I officially disengaged from the person that I used to call Mother; she was obviously incapable of being a parent.

Spiritual Awakening

The summer ended, and college would start soon. I realized that the choices that I made were changing my life. I would no longer allow my family's decisions to affect me. College presented its own challenges, and I did not engage in the traditional activities; it was class and then work and I would also play volleyball and curl. Other than that, I would focus on getting through this until I was old enough to leave my hometown.

One of my college friends asked me if I would be interested in coming to a workshop that she was teaching. I had never gone to a workshop, and so I did not know what to expect. I agreed to go to support her, because that was what friends did.

The course was about energy. We practiced different techniques of feeling energy over the weekend. It all felt natural, but it was the last part to the workshop that made me feel connected and scared all at once. There was a point where the instructor, my friend, wanted us to put what we learnt into action. She asked me to go first because she knew me, and I agreed. I did a grounding technique that we learned, similar to a meditation. She gave me a name and address of someone that I worked with to prove that what we had learnt was real. I focused on the address that she had given to me, and I went there energetically. As I did this, it was just like when I left my body at night and floated. She asked me many questions about what I saw and felt. I described the building that I stood in front of, and she asked me to knock on the door and ask if I could come in. I described the inside the home of the woman that greeted me. I felt many emotions from connecting to this person I had never met. I could see the inside of her house and knew what she was thinking. I was asked to scan her body and tell what was wrong with her health. As I did so, I saw a red spot in her chest. I continued giving answers to the questions that I was being asked by my friend. The depth of information that I getting was powerful, and I saw what has caused her illness and what she needed to heal.

After what seemed like forever, she instructed me to return to the classroom and my physical body. As I did, I realized I had cried, and my shirt was soaked in tears. I was embarrassed by my response. As I become fully aware, I saw that everyone in the group was holding a paper. They provided me with a copy of the sheet, and I looked at it. It had information about the person I had just visited in my energy body. The information on the sheet were the answers to the questions asked during the session. There were about twenty significant things.

One of the other students asked; how would they know if all the other stuff was true; it was not on the list. My friend and teacher said, "I know that it is true, because that was my grandmother." I was taken aback by this experience and was unsure if I wanted to know all that information or feel the emotions of someone else this way. I was trying to shut that part of me off, not utilize it. I stepped away from this process. However, after doing this I was more open than I would like to be. I would experience a connection to the people around me and did not know how to shut it off. I certainly did not want to tell people what I knew about them. It was 1982—not a time that disclosing this ability to others was safe, at least not for me.

The truth about who my college mates and teachers were became very clear. As I sat in class, I was picking up information about my instructors, and not all of it was good. I couldn't shut it off, and I did not know what to do with the information. If you could see people's truth, what would you do with that information? What if you knew they were hurting people, or if you knew when people were lying? This experience put me into turmoil. How did you tell people what you were getting without physical proof? I kept my thoughts and information to myself.

The energy class that I had taken was surfacing more in my life. I was aware of when people would be sick or when they died. I also know if they were going to have accidents. The first person was my grandmother. She was sick, and she did not live near us, so I called her to talk when I could. I had not done this before, but I knew that I needed to tell her I loved her—not something our family members said to each other. Our conversations were different from those we had before. I guess when you know someone is passing, you say what is important.

I started having dreams again that would come true more often. I would dream about my college mates, some of whom I knew through sports. For one of the people I played volleyball with, I dreamed that he drove a red soft-top Jeep, and his brakes would fail and he'd have to ditch his vehicle. I found him and asked if he drove a Jeep. He said yes; I even got the color right. I explained to him I knew that what I was about to tell him was weird, but it was important that he listen. I explain to him what I saw in the dream and told him to get his brakes checked; his brake line was cracked and would fail if he drove home at Christmas.

He found me a few days later and confirmed what I had shared with him, and then he asked, "How did you know?" I explained I did not know how, but I got information. He was grateful, and that was all I needed.

I got another dream around Christmas. One of the girls from our class was heading back home. I felt extremely sick and knew she would be in an accident and would be killed. I tried to convince her not to go and wait a few days. She was insistent and headed home with a group of friends rather than taking the bus. I was unable to persuade her differently. I went to her funeral that month. I did not tell people what I saw in my dream.

I enjoyed college. The time passed quickly, and we went through a graduation ceremony. I got my diploma in business administration. I did not invite my family for this. Why would I? They had not wanted to celebrate anything in the past, so why would they want to be a part of this? My younger sister questioned why she did not get to go. I heard my mother bark, "She's embarrassed." No, I was not embarrassed—I just didn't see why they would celebrate anything I did. They certainly did not celebrate my life in the past. I saw how my mother was using my sisters' emotions to play the victim. It was the first to go to college, and perhaps with her shortcomings, she needed to live through me, but we were so different. Her false offering of support came too late and was certainly not trustworthy. *What is in it for her?* I wondered.

I was sitting at the kitchen table having breakfast before work, and my mom proclaimed, "Well, your dad and I decided that we would start putting money away for your brother to go to college."

I thought to myself, *He doesn't want to go to college, he hated school. Yes, save money for him, but don't help me out—that would be ludicrous.* I guessed my wish to be invisible had come true. At least my mom could not see me. Now if only my abusers would follow suit.

My Failing Body

℘ returned to college to certify in accounting. I was constantly doing things and slept even less. My relationship with food was strained. Again, my time at the house was limited. I created a false sense of safety from sexual assaults, however the abuse turned physical and verbal.

It was a complete delusion, I know, but it worked for right now. The busier I stayed, the less I thought of the years of abuse. If only I could manage to push it deep enough, I might survive after all. I could feel my body getting sick. Going all the time, not eating, and not sleeping enough was taking its toll. I knew my body was starting to process the emotions of the years for the abuse, and my thoughts reeled into the old events. I continued to try to convince myself that if I just kept busy enough, the thoughts would get pushed back into that dark place of my mind.

When that did not work, I began drinking. However, that created a whole other set of problems. The loss of control put me in danger, with plenty of men standing in the wings to take advantage of the situation. It became very clear to me that I did not want to become an alcoholic like my father. The drinking would stop, and it would take everything I had to push the emotions down. I was losing the battle. I would try to keep the smile on my face despite it all. I told myself that I would not let my life slip away, and I struggled to keep up. The nightly flashbacks were still coming, so not sleeping solved one problem but created another.

I was not winning this battle. I was so sick and could barely get out of bed most mornings. My mom came to my room and yelled for me to get out of bed and get to class. She was not paying for this; it had nothing to do with her. I laid my head back on to my pillow and asked God to please let me die. With the battle of shutting off the emotions of the abuse, and the strain of working and college, my body was shutting down. Adding to the stress was the fact that my grandmother passed away. I was devastated by the loss of her and was emotionally maxed out. My physical body failed me.

I could feel my body was not well. I felt the poison in my body, almost tasting it. Everything that I had eaten seemed to make me sicker. I sought out medical help, but they couldn't seem to pinpoint it.

At a friend's wedding, I decided I would have a drink—something that I had not done in a while. I ordered a salted Caesar. I had a few sips, and then I could feel my lips start to tingle. I realized that I was given a spiced Caesar. I thought it was too spicy, but I did not think anything of it until my date for the wedding persisted in getting me to go to out to the vehicle. As I slid into the truck, I felt a sharp stab in my leg, and I turned as I let out a squeal. As I looked at my leg, I saw I was being stabbed with an epi pen, an injection used for someone who was having an allergic reaction. Still unsure what was going on, I asked why he had stabbed me, and he told me to look in the mirror. I looked into the rearview mirror and saw my lips swollen, and we raced off to the hospital. By then my body was sporting walnut-size welts and my tongue swollen and had peeled five layers deep. I was not given drugs and was sent home; they told me to go see my doctor. *Excuse me, are you not a doctor?* I shook my head at the experience. They did nothing about my peeling tongue, and they told me the epi pen was enough; perhaps I could get some antihistamine from the pharmacy.

I did go to my doctor and was tested for allergies. My arms were covered with over a hundred skin pricks that ran up and down them. The results said I was allergic to fifty-two things, mostly food, and I had asthma. Food was life for the body, and I did not want to live—was my body giving me what I wanted? Was I dying? The doctor offered me allergy shots so that I could eat the foods to which I was allergic. I said to him, "If my body says it does not want it, why should I continue to eat what was poisoning me?" He was angry at my decision not to get the shots. I managed to get a grip on what I could and could not eat. The list of cans was small, but I did not eat for days in the past and knew that I could do this.

The tests showed that I was allergic to foods that touch every food group, leaving me with very few food choices to select. No dairy, chocolate, celery, tomatoes, apple juice, oranges, wine, peas, carrots.... Most restaurants sauces contained tomato, cheese, or cream, and most soups or stews would contain celery and many of the vegetables to which I was allergic. It was easier to tell someone what I *could* eat rather than what I could not. I would read every label and have to question any food prepared at restaurants. It was easier not to go out for supper because the inconvenience and the judgment of others were huge. Allergies were not yet understood by the masses; most did not even know what ingredients were in their products. Staying at home and eating was safer. I would be on a path of discovery of how the body utilized food. It would take me hours to get my grocery shopping done, reading labels and watching how things where processed. I studied everything

I could about nutrition. I remembered when I volunteered as a candy striper, when we handed out food trays, there were special dietary dinners, and we needed to make sure that people did not get the wrong trays. I now knew how important that was.

JUDGMENT

———— ⊗⊗⊗ ————

While my arms were covered in marks from the allergy testing, I was unable to wear long sleeve shirts; I had to keep my arms exposed as they healed. One of my college professors made a comment, implying that perhaps I should get off drugs. I was shocked. I thought to myself, *I must be an accurate druggie because the needle marks are evenly placed up and down both arms.* He would continue to verbally make snide remarks for the remainder of the year. I would later find out *he* was the one with the drug habit. *Interesting,* I thought to myself. He was a tall, gangly man with one eye that would turn outwardly while the other was straight. He gave me the creeps.

My diet consisted of very limited choices. I would eat clean long before it was the thing to do. No packaged foods, only real foods. I became a great cook if nothing else, learning 101 ways to make chicken and hamburger.

While still living at home, I sat down to supper. My mom cooked that night, and each dish of food circled the table without me taking any. My mom barked, "What, nothing good enough for you?" I could feel my eyes filled with tears, and I commented there was nothing I could eat with my allergies. She shot back, "Well, if you think I am going to make special meals for you, you are mistaken!" I got up from the table and said, "Of course not—that would be compassionate." I left without anything to eat. I separated more from the family and took care of myself. Where was the button that made me invisible? I could not wait to finish college and complete my plan to leave.

That summer I focused on working. My weight that I had gained while being sick was melting away effortlessly. I realized that when my body was healthy, it did not carry weight; that meant emotionally or physically.

MONEY AND FAMILY

*C*ontinued with the plan to leave home. I had left my family emotionally; all I needed was to leave physically. I worked several jobs to save money, so that I could get away. Every Friday, I was paid, the stream of money continued, and my bank account grew. Money for me was not about status; it was what would ensure my safety and freedom.

Time passed, and the energy changed in the house, at least somewhat. Perhaps it was the fact that my time in the house was less. Not that I felt safe; it was just different.

My older brother was selling his stereo equipment, and I said I would buy it. At the time it was about seven hundred dollars, and he asked where I would get that kind of money. My mom barked, "She has ten thousand dollars in her savings account!" He jumped in and asked where the hell I got all that money. My response was, "I have a job, you know!" I bought his stereo. I did not understand my mom's anger about my money; perhaps she was jealous of what it gave me: a way out. All she could focus on was the money that I had. My mother forgot that I had bought everything myself since I was thirteen—clothes, car, and my education. She was not there for me. She would use my ability to save money—and more important, spend what I had wisely—against me like a knife. She would pit my siblings against me, using my money as a weapon, triggering their lack issues. This would set me up with huge money issues. My fear of people taking my money would make me very protective of what I owned. Over the years, judgment would come for what I could afford from boyfriends, friends, roommates, and coworkers. They commented that I could pick up the tab at the restaurants, and if they needed something, they would make guilty comments like, "Well, if I had your kind of money, I could get that." Interesting enough, I never let people know how much money I had. I did not do flashy things and was unsure of what that was. For most people, I would play poor as a safety measure.

It was the summer I was working five different jobs. My dad came to me and demanded my social insurance number. I knew that this was private, and I yelled no. He demanded it again, and I asked him why he needed it. His rage increased, and he demanded I give it to him. I again protested. He got physical with me, and I surrendered the information. He did not tell me why he was taking it. Time passed, and I forgot about the situation.

I was at one of my jobs, and he showed up and demanded to talk to me. I was hesitant as to why he needed to see me. There was no relationship with him other than disdain. I went out to the vehicle, and he slapped a paper on the hood of the truck and then handed me a pen. He ordered me to sign the paper, and I refused. I went to grab the paper and saw that it was actually a paycheck. I saw my name was on the check and began to question him. He grabbed my arm and slammed it on the hood of the vehicle. My eyes filled with tears as he commanded me to sign it in the voice I had come to know too well. I signed it and walked back into work. My anger for him grew. I forget about the situation until it happened again. I refuse to sign it. I found out later he was having it signed by someone else.

Executing the Plan

*L*ater that summer, I ruptured my eardrum in a swimming mishap, and I needed surgery. I would have to travel to south of the city to see a specialist. I got on the Greyhound bus and embarked on the seven-hour bus ride. I met with the doctor and would have the surgery the following day. I went shopping and exploring. I realized the college that I wanted to go to for commercial baking was in the city, just blocks from where I was. I went to the tech school and applied, not really thinking anything about it. I got my surgery, and my parents came to pick me up so that I did not have to get on the bus—probably the first act of support they had shown. On the ride home, they complained about the hotel room that I had booked and paid for the night before. They used the room for the day of my surgery. My dad began to smoke, filling the car to the point of being airless and triggering my asthma. The radio was blaring, and my ear was sensitive to sound. I asked him to open the window to get air, and if he could turn the radio down or turn the speakers up to the front of the vehicle. Again I was reprimanded by my mother. "You are so selfish. You never consider anyone else." I couldn't believe what I was hearing, so I tried to fall asleep so that the trip was tolerable. All I could think was, *Thank God for the drugs that I have for the pain.*

My ear would heal as the days passed, and after the drugs wore off, I remembered that I had applied to the college. I shared the fact with my mom, and she rebutted, "Well, you have to be accepted first." I responded that I would be. She did not speak to me for the following week. I reminded her she needed to pay me the money she borrowed, because I would need it for college. She said, "What money? I don't owe you any money." I reminded her of the money she got for the mortgage, and she went into denial about owing me the money. She threw the emotional wall up and did not speak to me again about the money. Aren't parents the ones that are supposed to support the children, not the other way around? Or perhaps they should get a little excited for their children's successes? I would never understand the lack of support from my parents. Perhaps I was delusional with that expectation of them. I would make the decision to take care of myself, and no longer worry about being part of a family who so blatantly expressed that I did not belong with them.

I made a trip to the city to find an apartment, and as I drove around, I realized how big the city was; the traffic was crazy. I was at my limit and needed to get off the main road and refocus. I heard intuitively to turn right at the next turn, and I parked, caught my breath, and got out of the car to stretch my legs. I turned slightly and right in front of me there was a huge sign: "Apartment for rent." I chuckled at the situation. I rang the manger's buzzer, and the apartment was perfect. I signed papers for mid-August.

INTUITIVE BODY

9 was getting sick again; I could feel it. My intuition told me it was my appendix. In May 1985, I went to my doctor and expressed that it was my appendix. He asked how long I was sick, and I stated two weeks. He said it would not be my appendix. I continued to be sick, but I did what I learned when I was sick before: certain foods helped cleanse my body. I would use what I learned, eating only fresh foods and no processed food. My body would get better and then sick again. I could not control this. However, I would manage it. I left shortly after to go visit my uncle from the coast. I looked forward to the time away, hoping the rest would help.

As I spent time with my uncle, I knew I was getting sicker. There were no hospitals on the island. My usual routine of getting up with him before work did not happen. He checked on me, and I commented I would see him when he got home from work. I put my head back down. After what seemed like minutes, I heard his voice again, calling me, and I yelled back, "I will see you later." The bedroom door opened, and he told me he was home from work. I had slept the day away. I knew then I was very sick. We make plans to get me on the next flight out to see a doctor.

I got back to my doctor, and he was reluctant to do anything, saying again it was probably just the flu. I knew he was wrong, though I took the antibiotic he offered. They pacified me for a while. I went back to my jobs. I continued to get dizzy and lost more weight, but not in a healthy way, and then I started blacking out. I continued to try to get him to check my appendix, but he refused with the qualifier, "It can't be your appendix—it has been too long." He checked my blood, and there was no infection, so he was certain it could not be my appendix.

It was now summer and I did get accepted to college. I got ready to move to the city, hours away from my family. I took my furniture and all the things I had purchased over the years as part of my plan to get out. I left my friends, my family, and my world. I would create a new existence. My parents reluctantly moved me, but my mother made a point of letting me know what an inconvenience it was for them. I pointed out that it would be a non-issue if it was any of my siblings. I thought of how they had moved my older sister more than once, and they even handed her money at every turn. Soon their presence in my life would be less, and that would be okay with me. I was tired of having to justify my existence. My furniture was moved in, and my younger sister helped with the unpacking. She was having fun, but with the realization that I would not be near her starting to sink in, she started to get moody. She stayed with me that night, and we have fun, but both of us realized that tomorrow would prove to be hard.

When it was time for them to leave, I hugged my sister and said she should call me whenever she wanted. My parents got in the car and yelled at her to get in. I yelled good-bye to them; it went with no response.

PART 2

HEALING

Reclaiming My Life

I was safe for the first time. I was living by myself, and no one could abuse me. My attention shifted to my new experience. I was within walking distance of the college and all the amenities—let the fun begin. I loved baking, and the program came easy to me. I had my business courses behind me, so now I could learn the business I wanted to open. Baking brought me peace and joy.

I would play sports and explore this new city, but I would continue to feel sick. I reconnected with a girl from Business College who had moved to the city, and with her help I located a new doctor. It was mid-August.

I was sitting in the exam room in the little paper dress. I was almost twenty-two and was in excellent physical shape with six pack abs. I simply felt sick. The door opened and a man's head poked into the room. We connected eyes, and in a blink the man slipped out of the room and closed the door. I thought to myself, *what the hell!* Soon there was a knock on the door, and the man returned to the room and introduced himself to me as the doctor. He went on to explain he had left the room because he was expecting someone older. I was quick to reply, "So was I." He explained the nurse had written the year I was born instead of my age. He took offense to what I said, and I explained that where I came from, most of the doctors were old. We have a chuckle, and then I explained what was happening to my body.

I told him I thought it was my appendix. Like the others, he stated that it would not be my appendix because it had been too long. In desperation I said, "Please find out what is wrong—it is scaring me."

He got to work with a battery of tests that would take us from August to mid-December, and nothing was coming up in the testing but I was getting worse. He was as frustrated as I was. He proclaimed he did not know what else to check. I asked him if he checked for my appendix. It was now eight and half months from the time I went to the first doctor. He said it would not be my appendix; he had checked my blood for infection, and nothing was showing up. I said, "Humor me. Check for my appendix. If it is not my appendix, you can put me in a padded room and keep the key."

If he knew my past, perhaps that would not have been such a bad idea. He explained that it was not a very nice test. *Really!* What I had been going through was not every nice. I just wanted to be well. He scheduled the test for my appendix.

I arrived for the test. It was a barium enema: they injected a fluid into the colon and, with a magnetic imaging machine, took pictures of the colon. I was laying on a cold slab for the exam as a large imaging device hovered over me. The size of this machine created a sense of fear: surely if it fell, I would be crushed. The radiologist took one picture and then came in and made another adjustment to take the second one. As I heard the click of the machine, I heard a soft voice in my right ear: "They found it." My body became instantly calm and serene. The voice was that of a spirit, not of a human source.

I left, and the doctor was right: the test was not much fun. My body wanted to purge this substance. I took the rest of the day to rest. I had plans later to meet up with my college group for dinner and dancing before we broke for Christmas. Just before I left the apartment, the phone rang. The man from the lab urgently stated that I had an abscessed appendix. I told him I already knew that, and then I hung up and left for my evening out.

Dinner and dancing was great; we had a good outing and shared some laughs. One of our friends was in the hospital, so we head over to spend some time with her.

I returned to the apartment, and as I entered the main door to the building, I could hear the phone ring, and ring, and ring. I thought to myself, *I don't think anyone is home.* As I continued up the four flights of stairs, I realized it was my phone ringing. I rushed into the apartment and grabbed the phone. "Hello?"

There was a male voice on the other end. "Where the hell have you been?"

"Wow, I don`t remember having to be accountable to anyone to warrant that. Who is this?"

"Your doctor," he proclaimed. "You have an abscessed appendix."

I casually said, "I knew it!"

PUSHING THE LIMITS

*H*is urgency in this matter was evident. He had arranged a meeting between the surgeon and me. I explained to him that it was not going to work. I was in college and had things scheduled that next day. He was trying to get through to me how serious this was. I joked with him. "Do you not think if God wanted me dead I would be dead by now? One more day will not make a difference." He adjusted my appointment.

I met with the surgeon, and he made this a priority. He wanted to do the surgery right away. I told him, "Look it is Christmas. You do not want to be here, and neither do I want to be in the hospital over Christmas. How about we meet up on December 27?" He looked at me and expressed that he couldn't believe we were negotiating this, but he agreed with the caveat that if I so much as felt a twinge, I had to get back into the hospital. I agreed.

I head home for Christmas in the hope that the time away would prove to have made a difference. It did not, except for the fact that I missed my baby sister. We headed out to our farm friends because they always hosted a party on Boxing Day. Food, people, and snowmobiling were the events of the day. I went out on the snowmobile as a passenger. I got bucked off the machine without the driver realizing. As I sat with my butt anchored in a snow bank in the middle of a farmer's field, I looked up to the night sky and a full moon, and I realized I had pushed this too far. My friend returned, and he realized I was not well. He asked if I needed to go back, and I nodded with no words spoken. I asked God to keep me safe. I now understood that my life was at risk, and I had pushed this as far as I could. I returned to the house and then went back to town.

My mom was vocal about her disappointment that I made her leave. I replied, "Don't worry about me—I am just dying." I arranged for my trip back to the city and my meeting with the surgeon.

I endured the eight-hour bus ride with the winter roads and the milk run route that stopped at every spot along the way. I could feel how sick I was and knew that I may not get to the hospital on time. I talked to my body, asking it to let me get to the hospital safely. I got to the bus depot toting my stuff. The taxi driver did not help me in or out of the vehicle, and certainly not up the stairs of my fourth-floor walk-up apartment. I managed to get everything in to the apartment by stopping on each flight. I acknowledged now how sick I was; this should be an effortless event, but it was taking everything I had to do it. I checked the time: it was five in the morning. I was supposed to be at the hospital at seven. I put things away and packed a small bag with things for my hospital stay. I then crawled into bed because I did not want to bother anyone by showing up too early at the hospital.

I fell asleep but was jolted out of bed by the sound of a male voice yelling, "Wake up, you're dying. Wake up, you're dying." I looked around my bedroom in terror. *What the hell was that?* I became aware of my space and then quickly my body. Yes, I felt like I needed to throw up. I ran to the bathroom and did so. I felt a little better. I decided to walk to the hospital with my bag.

The man who lived across from me was coming in the front door of the apartment from his night shift, and he asked where I was going so early. When I said the hospital, he offered to drive me, and I accepted.

Upon my arrival at the hospital, I checked at admittance and told them I was there to have my appendix out. They give me a funny look and told me to take a seat. I sat for about half an hour and then was taken into a curtained-off area for an exam. I was thinking this was routine. The doctor, quite young and probably a resident in emergency came and asked what brought me in. I explained to him I had an abscessed appendix and I needed to have it taken out. He dismissed me and stated, "You probably just ate too many sweets over Christmas."

I explain again to him. "No, I have an abscessed appendix." He left with a little attitude. In came another doctor of the same age; he too gave a few pokes and jabs, and then he left. The stream of doctors continued. Was this a test to see my tolerance, because if it was, things were running a little thin!

In walked the sixth doctor and I told him that if he touched me, I would break his arm. He stopped and looked at me, and I told him, "Please call Dr. J and tell him that I am here to have my appendix out, any questions?" He gave a meek no and exited. Moments passed with no more visits from any other doctors.

Then the curtains pulled back as my tall doctor appeared. He smiled and asked if he could bring some people in. I knew that I would be seeing the six doctors that had been in prior, and I chuckled and agreed. The curtain slid back, and the doctors entered the small area. Dr. J said, "Gentlemen I will be removing her appendix today, any questions?" A no came from down the line of now embarrassed faces. He dismissed his group, and off we went to get me ready for what would happen next.

Intuition Meets Medicine

I was placed on the surgery floor. The first process was to cleanse my digestive system and elimination track. I was placed into the bathroom with tubes that went up my nose and into my stomach, to push the bags for solution through to clear the internal systems. It was thick, and I could feel it enter my stomach. This was done bag after bag, and they checked for the outcome, to measure results. The process was taking its toll. I was cold and shaking and requested a blanket. The nurse was angry and barked, "You cannot be that cold." I was shaking and my teeth were chattering. Whether it was nerves or actual decline in body temperature, I did not care—I wanted a blanket. They draped a heated blanket around me as the process continued.

There was not a lot of waste leaving my body as the process continued. The nurse was yelling at me for flushing the toilet, but I had not. "Great, now we have to do another bag," she snapped. Then she hooked the next bag and cranked it open. The solution was filling my stomach, and I told her it was going in too fast and was going to throw up. "No, you're not," she insisted as she stormed out of the room. I jumped from the toilet and started puking in the sink. She heard me and came back in mad, but she realized that she had in fact put it on too fast. She adjusted the flow of the solution without much speaking, and then she was gone.

I was more scared than I had ever been. This was all new to me. Perhaps it was her normal day, but it was not mine. She scared me with her unfounded aggression. I told the next nurse what happened, and that I did not want the first nurse anywhere near me. The nurse that was aggressive no longer attended to me.

I was scheduled for surgery later that next day. I got up in the morning and showered; the tubes remained in my nose and throat, in order to pump my stomach. No more food until the surgery was complete. As I returned from the shower, there was an orderly there to take me to surgery. "No, I am not supposed to be until this afternoon," I said.

He laughed and then he told me I was bumped to first class, so off we went. I was scared and alone, but I trusted my doctor and knew it was time to deal with this.

The surgery was complete, and I was in the recovery room. The nurses there were very attentive, and I was in and out of consciousness. They gave me lemon sponges on a stick to suck on, to get the drug taste from my mouth. They were joking with me and telling me what a commotion I had caused in surgery. I was unsure of what that was about, and I drifted in and out as they moved me back to my room.

I slept most of that day. I woke the next morning to a room full of nurses and the surgeon. The doctor was tall, and his hands were probably one and half times the size of mine. He was at the bedside, and his hand was palm up as he kept asking, "What do you do?" I was still heavily sedated and not fully able to figure out what he wanted from me. I told him I was a student, and again his large hand was there, as if he was holding something. He then said, "Your stomach muscles—what do you do?" I realized now that my six-pack abdominal muscles were in question. I told him all the sports that I did, and I weight trained, not to mention the hundreds of sit-ups that I did daily.

"Your stomach muscles are bigger than most men's. I could not cut through them—it would have taken you six years to heal." He went on to tell me that he had to peel back my muscles to get to the appendix. The surgery should have taken a few hours, but it turned out to be three times that. They found that not only was the appendix taken, but also a foot of my ascending colon. The eight and half months of this being in my body had taken its toll. There would be no food for me until my colon healed. What that meant was that I would have tubes up my nose into my stomach to pump the bile out of my stomach, so as not to contaminate the surgery point.

I was a little overwhelmed by all the attention and information. I drifted in and out, trying to process it all. The buzz of medical staff lessoned, and the energy of the room was gentle. I heard people talking; the voices were my roommates. This was back in the day when four-bed wards where the norm in the hospital and where there was care still left in the health care system.

I had visitors that day: my mom, dad, and youngest sister come in. I was in pain and heavily drugged. They are there for about fifteen minutes, and I asked if they wanted my keys so that they could stay at the apartment. My mom proclaimed, "Well, we are not staying; we are going to see your brother." My younger brother lived an hour south of the city in which I lived. Why would I expect anything more from them? They left and did not return for the remainder of my stay. I felt my resentment toward them grow within me. I let myself fall asleep in order to shut off the emotions that ran through me. Yet one more chance for them to show compassion, but obviously that was too much to ask of them.

It was a new day, and I heard the patient to my left was saying how cute I was, even with all the tubes attached to my face. I realized then that no one had ever called me cute. I feel myself smile and drifted off again.

I was attended by a resident doctor who was there to check my progress and start the process of removing my drainage tubing. It was a clover leaf tube, and he struggled to move it. He gave it a yank, and the tubing came out completely. He knew that this needed to be in, so he reinserted it. I said, "Did you think that was going to work?" He said nothing and left. That was the last time I saw him.

My increasing need to go to the bathroom took main stage in my thoughts. No one was letting me out of my bed, and the side rails were up so that I couldn't get them down. Three days went by, and I finally asked a nurse if I could get out of bed to go to the bathroom. She explained to me that I had a catheter. I asked what that was. She explained, and I was disgusted that they did this to me. A sense of violation flooded my body, but then more pressing issue came to play. I had to go to the bathroom. The nurse taught me how to utilize the catheter, and even she was shocked at how full I was. I remembered my time as a candy striper and saw the bags, but I never put much thought into the process.

It was late at night, and I was jolted from my sleep. There was a nurse standing at my bedside. She was new, short in stature, and native. She told me, "We need to look at the incision. Something is wrong." She assisted in removing the bandage, packing, and then the sterile strips. One by one they were removed, exposing the incision. As the last sterile strip was removed, the room went dark, and the nurse was gone. I tossed the blanket over my exposed stomach and called out to the nurse. "Hello?" No one responded. I buzzed the nurses' station. A few minutes passed, and one of the regular night nurses appeared and asked if I was okay. Confused, I asked where the other nurse was. She says that it was just her and Mary-Anne on duty tonight—there was no new nurse. I was a little freaked out, and I told her I thought I was in trouble. She asked why. I flipped the blankets back and she saw that all my dressings and packing were removed from my abdominal. She asked me to tell her what happened. I told her about the native nurse, and she was more than shocked. She repacked my abdominal and tucked me back in.

Again I was the talk of the department. My doctor came in, and we talk about the night's events. He was trying to take off the packing to check things out, and he was having some difficulty removing things. I joked with him and said, "I could do that in my sleep." He chuckled. We tried to make light of what we cannot explain. All I knew was that I wanted off the drugs. It was now about ten days into what would be a twenty-one-day stay in the hospital. They were concerned about taking me off the drugs and made a point of saying, "You do realize you have just had major surgery." Just in case I missed that part. I insisted, and they agreed with the condition that I could have pain killers any time I needed them.

I was getting restless. I could not remember when I had been motionless for so long, and it was stressing me out. I asked if I could start walking, and they agreed. They did not realize just how much walking I intended on doing. My morning walks would be about ten laps of the surgery unit and would soon include the surrounding units. It would become my routine before the doctor's rounds, and it would continue throughout the day. My body was already lean when I went into surgery, and I would manage to drop another seventeen pounds by the end of my stay.

On one of my walks, I ended up in the maternity and surgery department. I was resting in their sitting room, and a young mother came in. She had her one-day-old baby and asked if I would like to hold him. I said, "Are you sure?" She nodded, and I took her up on her offer, honored that she would allow me this privilege. As I took in the magnificence of this experience, I thought to myself that if this little baby were mine, I would do anything to protect him. No sooner did that thought entered my mind there was a crabby old nurse that came in and barked, "Oh what, having second thoughts?"

I was confused with her aggression. "What?" I challenged her outburst.

She barked, "Well, are you regretting having your hysterectomy?"

Astounded by her outburst and her judgment, I snapped back, "Actually, I just had my appendix and a foot of my colon out, but thanks for being such a bitch!" The new mother was shocked at what had happened in front of her. I excused myself and went back to my room in tears.

The nurses from my department came in to see if I was all right. I told them what had happened, and they were hot over this and stormed out of my room. I knew they were out to fight this battle for me. As I lay in my bed, I questioned why people needed to attack me.

I still was not able to eat anything other than ten ice chips a day. I was becoming emotional and overwhelmed—no food for what would be twenty-one days. My body was going through all this and feeling alone. After years of stuffing my emotions with food, all the emotions were raw and came up easily. I knew that even if I ate, I would throw it up, but I yearned for that feeling of release, and the only way I knew was to binge and purge.

My throat was getting swollen from the tubing and dry from the hospital air. My roommate had company: her grandchild was there and had a popsicle. I thought, *Now there is something I would like.* The day nurse was in the room, and I asked if I could have a popsicle. She said it was okay. I headed out shortly to the patient fridge to get half of a popsicle. As the cool, wet ice melted and ran down my throat, I was in heaven. I could feel it soothe the inflammation from the tubing. I lay there reveling in the satisfaction of how something so simple could bring a sense of relief. I slipped off to sleep in my sense of glory.

It did not seem long before I was jolted from my sleep by a swarm of nurses. They buzzed around me, and I could feel their panic. I was awake instantly. One nurse asked in a hurried and scared voice, "Have you had anything to eat?

I said no but then remembered the popsicle. As I disclosed the information, it was like a switch was flipped, and the energy settled. The nurses now stood around my bed, and the next question comes. "What kind was it?" I told them grape. They began to laugh, and I was still confused. They explained the tubing was pumping my stomach of any fluid. The bile was green normally, but by adding a grape popsicle, it came out red. They thought I had ruptured my stomach wall when they saw the red fluid in the reserve. We agreed that if I got another popsicle, it needed to be on my chart. I was sure by this time they were counting the days to my release.

I was now able to walk each day, and I looped the unit again and again. I was restless and was not used to being bedridden. I needed to move. I was up early and began my walking. Not much was happening this early on the unit, so I cruised about. I came across the nurses' station and heard a doctor say: "Well, if they think I was going to operate on him again without insurance,.

they are crazy." I was shocked to know that someone may need surgery and could not get it. Did I have insurance? Could they refuse me surgery? I was unfamiliar with the medical system and was shocked by this doctor's outburst. Was it not his job to help people? This brought a lot of awareness and fear about my situation.

After what seem like forever, I still remained in the hospital and college had come back into session ... I expressed my urgency for getting out of the hospital. Day twenty-one came, and I got to go home, but not before they removed the tubes from my stomach and throat. Other patients explained how horrible it was, and I was scared. I was willing to leave with them still in—that was how scared I was. The nurse was obviously mad that I was resisting, and she told me she would do it on the count of three. "One, two ..." Then with a quick yank, the tubing came out of me with a shocked gag, and it was done. The disappointment that she'd lied; was quickly followed by relief that I could now go home.

Life resumed. My body began processing out the drugs; even with not taking any drugs for days, they were slow to leave my body. I became fully aware of the harshness of the drugs and couldn't image someone willingly putting them into their body. My body healed, and again I was aware of every movement my body made and the signals that it gave me when I pushed it. Even the simple things such as making the eight-block walk to college took its toll. I was not supposed to lift anything for several weeks. I knew that it was a big part of the training. I managed to do my part, and others helped when I couldn't, for which I was grateful.

MORE BETRAYAL

I was back at college, and it was tax time. I received all the tax forms in the mail from up north. As I started to go through my papers, I saw a T4 from a company that I did not recognize for thousands of dollars. I knew that I had not worked for this company, and then I remembered the check that my father had made me sign. I was furious and called my mom and ask her what the hell was going on. She tells to process it and be quiet. It was for thousands of dollars, and it would affect the taxes that I had to pay. I told her that I would have to pay instead of getting money back, but she did not seem concerned. I knew this was wrong and illegal, and I was furious with them both. My dad was collecting unemployment insurance and working for this company, and they used my social insurance number to record the income. I did not know what to do other than process it. The following month, I got a letter from the government bursary department telling me that I would lose my loan from them because I did not claim the money from that company when I did my budget. I did not know how to tell them what the truth was. I called my mom and told her she had to pay me the money she owed me, and she had to make up for the money I was losing because of what my dad did. I make sure she knew that if I did not get the money, I would tell the government what he did. I got the money, or at least some of it. Miles separated us, yet they still found a way to manipulate me.

Listening to My Body

Three months passed, and things were getting back to normal. My lean body had shed seventeen pounds while in the hospital, and my clothes were still loose on me. I decided to go back up north for Easter because I missed my friends. As I drove, I felt a need to undo my pants—all of the sudden they felt incredible tight. As I drove and shifted in my seat, I felt as if the muscles were rolling over something; it seemed like I had a golf ball in me. I managed to get to my destination but was physically exhausted. I thought that perhaps the six-hour drive was too much. I decided to sleep, and it was not long before I was in a deep sleep. That was what I did most of the weekend. I decided that something was wrong, so I phoned my doctor to see if he was working Easter Monday. He was, and so I headed back the following day. My mother was quick to complain that all I did was spend time with my friends and sleep; she showed no concern that I was sick again. I know I would never be enough for her as a daughter, no matter what I did.

I went to the doctor's office and told him there was a golf ball-size lump in my abdomen. He laughed at me and said, "I doubt it." I get onto the examining table, and he placed one hand on my abdominal wall and tapped with the other hand. He turned to me and said, "I will meet you at the hospital in half an hour." I thought he was joking, but his face told me something else. It was as if the blood had drained from his face and fear had replaced it. I did not want to go back in, but I knew at a deeper level that I had to. There was no messing around this time—that day I was in the hospital!

I had a secondary abscess where my drainage tube was from the last surgery. My doctor was quick to say to me, "You're not normal!" *Well, thanks for clearing that up for me. My life was not normal, so why should I be?* I thought to myself. I remembered the native nurse had said that something was not right; perhaps this was what she meant.

I was back in the ward that I had stayed at before. The nurses were shocked to see me back. Apparently if you were to get infection from surgery, it would be instant, not three months later.

They suggested a new procedure to me. They did not want to do surgery, but rather irrigate the area. I agreed to the new procedure. I was in a room with one bed, and there was a doctor there, but I did not know him, and there was my surgeon as well. The procedure involved the use of ultrasound to scan my abdomen, and then they inserted a tube into the area of the abscess. There was a monitor there to see the tubing as it entered my abdomen. I was fully awake; only a local anesthetic was given. My doctor asked if I wanted to watch the procedure. Of course I said yes. As the radiologist was attempting to insert the tubing, he was struggling. I couldn't quite see what was happening, so I turned the monitor to see what going on. Less than pleased, he said, "I need that to see!" Oops!

He couldn't make it work. My surgeon started to chuckle. Both the doctors were trying to make the insertion, and I looked at him, feeling a little lost as to the inside joke. My surgeon asked me, "Can I tell him?" It was as if I could read his mind.

I was instantly embarrassed. Now the radiologist was the only one left out of the conversation. I nodded to the surgeon to let the radiologist know. The surgeon told the radiologist about my six-pack abs. Each time he tried to poke the tubing, I tightened my abs—not intentionally, but I did so nevertheless, and it was prolonging the procedure. The surgeon left, and I knew he was up to something. He returned with another doctor who was very tall and extremely handsome. The new doctor asked if he could hold my hand. "Hell yeah, you can hold my hand." He put his hand on mine, and I melted. I said, "So was he your secret weapon?" We all laughed. I was embarrassed, but it worked. The tubing was inserted and the irrigation began. Unfortunately, the procedure of irrigating the abscess would take days, not hours like I thought. The irrigation was slow—and even slower that it should've been, because no one was trained to do it. My frustration rose because I was in a lot of pain and felt like it was going to rupture.

The doctor instructed me on how to do the irrigation so that I could show the nurses as they rotated in and out of their shifts. The irrigation needed to be done hourly. The nurses were not comfortable with doing it, and the pressure was building in the abscess. I told the head nurse that it was not being done regularly enough, and I was feeling increased pain. She had not done it, so I told her I would show her, and she was insulted. I told her the doctor had showed me so that I could show them. I wasn't trying to step on any toes—I just wanted this done so I could get out of there. Days passed, and the procedure was not being done enough. I was getting frustrated. I asked to see the surgeon, and I complained. I told him to get me the supplies, and I could do it at home. It was a new process and they wanted to monitor it. As a result, there was a training process set up with the nurses, and then things began to happen. I returned to college, finally. My time absent from college was getting close to the allowed limit, without being kicked out of the program. I managed to return to college in time with the abscess drained, and I was feeling healthier.

RETURNING HOME

───── ⌾ ─────

The year away from my family had given me a new perspective on what options I had. Eight months of no abuse or violence was the longest I had gone, and there was a sense of safety that came with that. The revelation that perhaps this was the way it was supposed to be was refreshing. Unfortunately, it would not last.

College would end, and I would move back up north. I would have to work in northern Alberta for two years, and then I could move south again. As I slipped into the old way, I knew that I did not want to be here. I would keep the focus on being there for only two years, and that kept me going. I had applied for a job at one of the bakeries and started shortly after I returned north.

CLARITY COMES FAST AND HARD

I had racked up many miles on my vehicle and decided to buy a new one. I got up to go to the dealership, and my dad wanted to come. I reluctantly let him. I test drove a few, found one that was smaller, and thought it was the one. My dad suggested I take it on the highway before I decided. Off we went with the car, trying to make this a fun experience. The radio was playing, but he said to shut it off. The next instruction was to go down a back road to see how it handled. I drove for a bit, and then he told me to stop the car. I was confused but did so. All of the sudden the energy shifted in the car, and then I looked out the window and got my bearings as to where I was. I got a sick feeling in my stomach. I reached to start the car as I told him what a jerk he was. My mind was reeling, and I was still trying to grasp what had just happened. Was he kidding? The clarity of who my father was came that day: everything he had ever done was cold and calculated. That place on the dirt road was the spot he would take me to molest me in junior high school. Yes, everything he did was conscious; there was no longer any question about that for me. If possible, I hated him more than ever.

As I got back to the dealership, I jumped from the car and went into the building, to safety. I was rattled by what had just happened. As I stood there, the salesman noticed I was in distress and approached me. I announce to him I would take the car, and we started the paperwork to take my mind off what had happened. I told my dad to leave; I did not need him there, and neither did I want him there. I got into my old car with what I needed to transfer everything to my new car.

My older sister was home again for some reason. I was on the stairs when I heard my dad offer her a hundred dollars. As I entered the kitchen I said, "I need a hundred dollars. What do I have to do? Shovel gravel?" My dad had a construction company at the time. My sister spun her head and gave me the look of death, and I got a sick to my stomach feeling. The hundred-dollar offer was an offer for a sexual favor. What the hell was wrong with him? His blatant attempt to get sex was shocking, to say the least. If he ever made that kind of offer, I would have killed him on the spot. He was fully conscious of his actions—that was no longer in question.

I think that with the realization he would not be getting what he wanted from his daughters, he went out on a drinking binge. The next day there was another night of fighting, and he was beating on my mother. I intervened, and as I did he grabbed me by the throat and threw me against the portable dishwasher. The pain shot through my body as I sank to the floor, and I blacked out. I felt him grab me by the back of my hair, as he had done so many times before. He spun my body around and slammed me into the fridge, where I dropped to the floor, and he walked away babbling something. I felt myself fade in and out of consciousness until I finally passed out completely. I was not sure when or how I make it back to my bedroom, but I did.

The next morning came, and I was so disgusted with him. I was at the top of the stairs, and my mom called me into her bedroom. She showed me the bruises on her arms and legs, as if she was showing me her badge of honor. Emotions of disdain with her filled my body. I asked her if she was proud of the bruises with as much sarcasm as I could muster. I hated how weak she was. What was her reward for her silence? I tried to make sense of their relationship but quickly realized it was a waste of my time.

I could no longer tolerate this—he had pushed me as far as I could go emotionally. I went into the kitchen, and he was sitting at the table. I started making myself something to eat, and I said nothing to him. He knew I was shutting him out. He couldn't take it and barked, "What, too good to talk to your old man?"

I was quick to respond, "Yes, actually, I am. You think you can pull that shit you did last night, and all is forgiven?"

"I never did anything to you!" he proclaimed.

"Really?" I showed him my bruised neck and arm. "Just like you never did anything to your wife last night? Why don't you go down the hall and see how you didn't do anything last night, you asshole!"

He got up without another word and headed down the hall to his bedroom. Shortly after I heard a large thud, and I went down the hall. He was on his knees. Had reality finally set in? I left and finished breakfast. I never heard an apology from him, but I never expected one. Was he ever going to accept accountability for what he had done to his family? I believe one has to admit one has a problem before one can heal from it. Would he admit his problem now?

I hated the fact that I needed to be up north to work off my bursary. No matter how screwed up or dysfunctional one's family is, one tried to hold hope. My hope died that day.

I was at the house for barely a week, and my mom told me that if I thought I was living there for free, it was not going to happen—she wanted rent. Funny, how things never change for some people. I recalled that as many times as my sister had moved in and out. She had never paid rent—in fact, they were quick to rescue her financially at every turn, while she stole money from me any chance she got. I made the decision to move out. It would solve so many problems. She could live in this craziness, but if she thought that I would pay to stay there, she was wrong.

I soon found an apartment and moved out. I moved my stuff in and tried to hold some level of relationship with my parents. I wasn't truly sure why, but I did. I invited them for dinner at the apartment. The table was set, and I had prepared a home-cooked meal. As we sat at the table, my mom was quick to address the fact that I had a tablecloth on the table and fancy dishes. If the five-dollar table cover and the twenty-dollar dish set were going to be an issue for her, then there was no sense her being there. I was almost reluctant to serve her. Of course she was also quick to judge what I had made to eat. My years of anger with her started to surface. Had I outdone her again? I could never truly understand her resentment toward me; none of the other kids were treated this way. Perhaps I had learned to survive without her. Was that it? Was I was a better cook than she was or better with money? Was it that I was determined, or was it that her husband would rather have sex with me than her? I knew that no matter how long I processed this, I would never come up with a reasonable answer for the years of abuse and neglect. That was the last time that I would invite them to my home.

LET THE BAKING BEGIN

———— ∞ ————

During one of my breaks at my new job, I was greeted by a few of my old schoolmates, who said, "You're the one that they were talking about." I was confused as to what they were talking about, and I asked for an explanation. They had been discussing the new girl and asked about her training. Perhaps my schoolmates were surprised with what I had done since our last encounter. I was excited to bake; it was my passion. I loved the creativity and the physical aspect of the job. What I did not expect was the jealousy of one of my coworkers; she was apparently fearful that I was after her job, and she did everything in her power to sabotage my products and relationships with the other bakery staff.

I worked in the bakery, did sports, and enjoyed life. I started playing soccer and biking, two of my other favorite things to do. I would remain active; it seemed to keep me in a good headspace and supported a healthy body. I tried to resume my circle of friends, but I did notice that a lot of them had gotten into drugs, and there was resentment from some of them that I had left. I wanted so much more for myself, not in judgment, but I did not want to get sucked into what I had come from; none of my friends knew what happened in our house. I would continue to work and picked up a few different jobs, anticipating the move that would come. The two years that I needed to work in northern Alberta would pass quickly, and then I could move away again.

I would continue to work at the bakery and at a hotel doing accounting. I also served at banquets at nights. I did product implementation in a small, independent bakery. I realized I did not know how to be still.

Reclaiming My
Feminine Energy

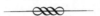

I had reconnected with a former boyfriend. The connection that we had was powerful and beyond words; the intensity put me into fear. I was still working on my body issue and the whole sex thing. I again kept him at arm's length as I tried to figure everything out.

Our group of friends did a lot of activities together, so the date outings were more group events rather than one on one, which made things easier for me. The sex part of the relationship was hard for me. I knew what it was to surrender my body, but I would black out during the sexual act. I knew there had to be more about sexually intimacy that I needed to learn. It was still hard to talk about the sexual part of relationships. I wanted my body back; I wanted to feel good when I was touched. Each time I was touched sexually, I would have flashbacks to the abuse. I would disappear in the experience, blacking out or floating above my body—the two things I had learned from my childhood attacks. No one knew about the abuse that I had been through. Learning about who I was at this level was a huge part of self-discovery. Fortunately, I attracted a good man that allowed the needed time to shift the old experience into something healthy, but the process would take many years to resolve. I learned that everyone brought their sexual garbage into the relationship, and each needed to be handled independently in order to heal fully.

Interesting enough, I realized that I did not trust anyone enough to tell what I had experienced. This would continue for years, and when I was ready, I realized certain men did not want to hear what I had to say. One response was, "If this is going where I think it is, I do not want to hear it." We'd break up shortly after. I did not want to make this the theme, but I needed to know that the person in my life would support me in figuring this out, not just take from me.

It's funny how things happened. A friend invited me to a lingerie home party. I did not wear things like that! I sat there quietly and watched the others as they went through the items. Then I heard the salesperson say that this was not about selling sex—it was about connecting with one's feminine energy. Every cell in my body heard the words; it was as if I was getting a tingling sensation in my whole body, feminine energy, what was that? I was not sure what that meant. Was I allowed to be connected at the level? I got up and started to look through the items. I found a nice red one-piece in which to sleep. I thought if nothing else, at least I could start tapping into this feminine energy in my own space. Realizing that this was not about a man, that it was about me, I purchased the sleeper and was surprised with how embarrassed I was that I had done so. The others gave me a hard time about my shyness. The item arrived, and I stuck it in my dresser drawer and left it there for months.

One day I got home and felt less than pretty, and certainly not feminine. I showered, hoping to wash away my day. I remembered the sleeper, and as I pulled it from the drawer, I thought, *let's try this*. As I slipped into it, my body felt the softness of the sleeper's satin and lace. It did make me feel soft and gentle. Was that the feminine energy that the lady had talked about at the party? I would continue to put this on when I was not feeling gentle. I found that I wore it more and more. I went to another party and got another piece. I liked this feminine energy thing, and it was not about sex. In my revolution of being in my feminine body, I felt my body image shift. I had a sense of pride, an internal knowing that feeling good in my body was allowed.

People treated me differently. I reclaimed that part of me that was lost—or should I say, what my abusers took from me. Who would have thought that this small piece of red lingerie could melt those walls that were built over the years? I liked how this made me feel, and I wanted others to get what I had learned. I started selling the lingerie. I did well because I shared with my clients what I had learned. I also wanted them to reclaim their feminine energy.

I worked and played sports with several men, and I noticed their attention toward me was changing, or perhaps I had become more receptive. For the first time in my life, I felt worthy of love. I would date more over the next few years. I was learning what I should have known years before.

INTUITION HEIGHTENS

$\mathcal{S}$omething else had happened: I was sensing energy again, now feeling the energy of plants and animals. I was leaving the grocery store that I worked, and as I got close to the door, I heard, "Take me home" in a high-pitched voice. I stopped and looked around; no one was there. I chuckled to myself and thought I needed sleep. I was leaving the store the next day, and the same thing happened; the same high-pitched voice stopped me in my tracks. I looked around, and there was a three-tier plant stand with hundreds of plants. I walked over and intuitively said, "Whoever said that, let me know where you are." Within seconds a beam of light came from between two large plants. I walked over, and there was a twenty-five-cent pot; the plant was about three inches high and had four leaves on the top of it. It was the worst plant I had ever seen. I felt bad for it and went to purchase it. The girl on the checkout laughed and asked if I could find a sadder looking plant.

I took the plant home. One of my allergies was to mold on plant soil, so I repotted the plant in hydroponics. I had the plant for three months, and it grew straight up. It became a foot high, with the original four leaves. A friend was over and told me how ugly it was. I picked up the plant and in a stern voice told it to grow leaves, or it would be in the garbage. I returned it to its place on the plant stand and did not think anything more about it.

Two weeks later, my friend was back. I was in the kitchen getting drinks, and she said, "Oh, you got a new plant." I tell her no. She kept insisting that I had a new plant. I was getting frustrated with her insistence and walked over to the plant stand. The four-leaf plant was sporting about thirty leaves. I was shocked, and then I remembered what I had said to it. I felt bad for what I had said. I jokingly told it I was sorry, and I commented on how beautiful it was with all its leaves. That plant continued to flourish and needed to be repotted more often than any other plant that I had. I would continue to read the energy of plants, knowing where each wanted to be placed in a room and when it needed nutrients. My friends joked with me about this but did notice when they moved their plants to where I told them, they did much better. I became the plant whisper for my friends.

TAKING RELATIONSHIPS
TO THE NEXT LEVEL

$\mathcal{I}$ had asked one of my male friends to accompany me to a wedding out of town. I cared about him and even thought one day that there could be more. We had a unique connection, but both of us were unsure of what that would look like if we took it to a different level. I had sex with him for the first time on that trip. I was trying not to disappear during the experience. His touch was gentle, and we connected at a level I had never felt before. I heard my internal voice said, "That is what it is like to be made love to." I was at peace for the first time after a sexual encounter. He then rolled away from me, and with that came an incredible surge of emptiness that filled my body, as well as emotional abandonment. I lay there until he fell asleep, and then I went to have a shower. I needed to wash away the dirtiness that had flooded my body as I laid there in my aloneness. As the water hit my body, my thoughts reeled in my head; my body was confused from feeling loved to being empty in a matter of seconds. I went into a zone of emptiness, and the next thing I remember, the shower curtain was being slid back. I was sitting in the tub with the water now cold flowing over me as I looked up, and he was standing there. Without words, he wrapped me in a towel and took me back to bed, where I fell asleep in his arms.

That night changed me. I had let someone into a place that no one had been before; it was as if he touched my soul. I did not know how to express what that meant to me verbally. It scared me and made me feel safe at the same time. I knew that he felt protective of me from that point onward. We would not talk about this but rather kept it sacred. In the past, when I admitted that I cared about someone, my sister or friends would make it their mission to sleep with them. I did not want anyone to take him from me and kept it close to my heart. I did not think he could process the level of connection that happened. I knew the connection was deep, but he was not a good communicator, and I needed him to talk me through this, to take charge in some way. This was all new to me, and perhaps it was to him; I did not know.

Time passed, and his job took him all over, so our time together would fluctuate. It was out of sight, out of mind. I would pull back my emotions and closed the door to what I was feeling. I needed more than what I was getting, and that hurt left me confused. The cycle of turning my emotions on and off was getting exhausting. I would start getting resentful and would start pulling back, becoming unavailable with my time. Instead of healing the relationship, he made the decision to seek out what he needed from others. His rebuttal was that I was not the type of girl a guy dated! I was crushed by his words. He then added, "You're the type a girl a guy marries." Thanks for clearing that up. I guess he was not in the market for a wife, just someone to use for sex! I retreated emotionally. *Yes,* I thought, *he was just another man taking what he wanted.* Time would pass, and we would see each other through our friends, but things would never be the same, at least not for me. I did not know how to separate the resentment from my past and the resentment I felt for him for allowing the separation to occur. After all, men where the ones that decided whether a relationship would move forward, not women—at least, that was what I thought.

A few months would pass and I find out I am pregnant not realizing all the antibiotics that I had been on had neutralized my birth control. I would lose the baby shortly after. I did not tell what I went through. I didn't want him in my life out of sympathy.

EMOTIONAL IMPACT TO THE BODY

My focus shifted from relationships to my body. I knew that years of burying my emotions were taking its toll on my body. I was not feeling well and went to my local doctor. I told him what I was going through, and despite all my physical activity, I was in a lot of pain. He was quick to pull out his prescription pad and jot down three things. I asked him what it was all for. He explained one was an anti-inflammatory, one was an antibiotic, and the other was a painkiller. I sat there dumbfounded and told him I was not there for drugs; I wanted him to find out what was wrong. Again I went over my past surgeries, thinking he would understand that this was something more. I knew that intuitively.

He barked, "If you are not going to take what I give you, how are you going to get better?" Better? What was that in the medical field? Numbed out, pacified, and drugged?

I knew there was more to this, and I trusted my inner knowing. I was not stepping down on this. I would not settle for a pat on the head and being dismissed by this doctor. I rebutted, "You do not even know what you are treating!"

"It's probably just women problems!"

Well, considering the pain was in my abdomen and I was female, he was at least in the right ballpark. Our voices were getting louder, and we bantered back and forth. I was exhausted.

My final assault was, "You know what? Don't worry about it. I will go back to the city where there are *real* doctors!"

"I *am* a real doctor!" he spouted.

"Then start acting like one, and find out what is wrong before you throw pills at me!"

I got up and left the exam room. As I left the office, the receptionist acknowledged me and gave me a small smile for standing up to him.

I went back to my surgeon in the city, who ran more tests and sent me home with requisitions to get more testing done over a period of a few weeks. I was to send the results to him.

When I got back home, I took the requests to my local doctor, and he was willing to dance circles for me once he found out who my city doctor was. He was quick to tell me they went to the same school, and he was now willing to do whatever I needed. It was funny how all of the sudden I was actually getting tested and we were running off of results, not off of someone's opinion. I resisted my urge to do a smack down with him. I knew the surgeon had explained my ability to know what was wrong with my body. I was suddenly treated with a little more dignity than the last appointment, and he did what a doctor should do: run tests. We managed to work together without further incident. However, it was also without any resolution to the pain I was feeling.

A year and half had passed, and I was getting restless. I knew that I needed to be back in city; my guidance was pushing me to leave. It was now December 1987. I was having problems with my relationships; one of the women that I worked with had pulled a knife on me, ranting about me taking her job. Well, there was no difference between what we did, so I was unsure of what her issue was; most likely it was jealously and fear. I wanted to disappear again, and what better place than a city of a million people?

REFLECTING ON MY CHOICES

⸻

As I contemplated leaving, I sought out transparency from my friend. I wanted clarity to what, if anything was between us. It seemed that he was putting more energy into dancing around than simply talking about it. All I wanted was cards to be put on the table. I called him, needing to find out where we stood, and a woman answered. I asked for him, and she asked, "Who are you?" I explained the situation to her, and there was silence on the other end of the phone for a few minutes. Then he got on the phone. I tried to talk to him, but he was evasive. I asked if he wanted me to call him back later. He hesitated again, and I asked if this was an overnight guest; still no answer. I guess I got my answer on where I stood in his life. I become very aware of my separation in relationships, coming from abuse where men took and demanded what they wanted. I did not know how to be in a relationship with one who sat back and had a hard time expressing what he wanted this was unchartered territory for me.

I hung up the phone and headed over to where I worked to get boxes; then I went back home to pack up my stuff. As I was taking things off the walls, it was as if I snapped out of a trance. My body was numb, and I had shut down emotionally. One more person who needed to lie, I was done. *Thank you for showing me what I did not want in a relationship.*

I become aware of what it was I needed in a relationship, and betrayal was not on the list. I wondered *if love is not enough in a relationship, then what was needed. Why do people not do their work when it comes to loving one another?* I would never understand why people sabotaged relationships; was it a test to see if the other would get jealous or beg for attention? Was stepping into and supporting the values in a relationship too much to ask? I was not going to fight to be a part of my family, and I certainly was not going to beg someone to be in a relationship with me.

I had started applying for jobs in the city. I had packed the majority of my apartment and gave my notice at the places I worked. My life was filled with people who needed to attack me and hurt me. What was the lesson in this? Did I need to reinforce the feeling of not being worthy of a healthy relationship? Why was being my best such a problem for others? More important, why did others choose to be less than they could be? Perhaps my ability to see others' potential was not an ability that others had. The ability to see the greatness in someone and then see them hide from their own greatness made my heart sad. Never had I done things to intentionally hurt anyone. Perhaps what I was shown when I left my body at eight was the driving force to be the best me I could be. Perhaps I'd never be enough for my family to accept me, and it set me in a process of doing more to be accepted. I was exhausted with trying to be accepted.

Christmas came, and again my family showed how little my presence in the house and family meant. I took all the gifts that I bought over to the house the night before, as well as all the baking and treats that I had prepared. It was customary to call whoever was not living at the house in the morning and, upon their arrival, do gift opening and eat breakfast. I tried to make some level of tradition, I guess. I woke up, and no one had called me. It was about ten in the morning, so I called the house and asked why they had not called me. My mom's response was, "Well, I just thought you would get here when you wanted." I hung up the phone and cried. What a bitch. Could she be any more dismissive? If we had done that to her, there would be consequences.

I managed to get there within the hour, but I didn't know why I even made the effort. When I arrived at the house, the gifts were already opened, and everyone was downstairs waiting for breakfast; the cinnamon buns and most of the other treats I made were consumed. It was interesting how they did not have a problem taking in all that I brought, but no one thought to call me. I was disgusted with my family, if that was what I should call them. Some time passed, and my mom barked, "Are you going to open your presents?"

In my bitterness, my comment was sarcastic and harsh. "Oh, I actually get presents? Wow, how thoughtful of you all!"

I went into the living room where the tree and my gifts were. I sat by myself and opened my gifts. One sweater after another was unwrapped six people, five sweaters—not much thinking going on here. I saw a microwave there for my sister, side steps for my brother's truck, a television for my brother, and downhill skis and boots for my younger sister. I did get a gift from my younger sister; she noticed that I had arrived and ran upstairs for me to open the gift she got me. She couldn't imagine how I appreciated her thoughtfulness. She always managed to instill hope in this dysfunctional family. Again, I was disappointed in the others. I went to great lengths to get the perfect gift for each person, and I usually spent more if need be to get them what they wanted. I never gave gifts with the expectation of getting one, but their obvious disdain for me was evident by their lack of effort or consideration.

My cousins arrived in the afternoon. I had made poppycock, and I went to take the large bowl down to them. My mom scoffed. "They won't like that." How would she know, and if they did not, then so what? What was her need to shame me so blatantly?

I placed the poppycock on the table downstairs. Everyone attacked the bowl as if they had not eaten for weeks. Ten minutes passed, and there was not a kernel left. I took the empty bowl upstairs, almost to prove a point my mom. She made her anger known. I did not last the day and left early; there was only so much I could handle of their transparent attitude toward me.

I focused my attention on getting my apartment packed up and moved things into storage, as my jobs were coming to a close, and my attention was put into finding a job in the city.

THE FINAL ASSAULT

*I*t was a few days after Christmas, and I was reluctantly back at the house. I woke to a ruckus upstairs. I went up to see what was going on. My dad had called drunk, and he needed a ride home. He was so drunk that he did not know where he was. I was not getting involved in this and went back to bed. I was on the cusp of sleep when I awoke again. I went upstairs, and my younger brother was on the phone, yelling, "I do not know, I do not know." I asked whom he was talking to, and it was the police. He handed me the phone. The police officer drilled me with questions. While trying to make sense of the questions, I regrouped, and it started to make sense.

The officer wanted to know where my dad was. I explained that my mom had gone to pick him up. He wanted the license plate to my mom's car, and I told him I did not know; I barely knew mine. He continued to shout questions at me. I told him again I did not know, and I wanted to know more about what was going on. There was a vehicle stolen from a bar just outside town. My dad had asked for a ride back to town from the owners, and they refused. I knew the bar had a courtesy van to shuttle people who had been drinking, but there had been a long-time rift between the owners and my dad.

I told the officer I did not know the answers he needed. My brother was extremely anxious, as if he knew what was coming.

I told the police office that I would call him if I found out more, and I hung up. I tried to calm my brother down and get him to go back to bed.

I had settled into bed myself and had starting to drift off. It seemed like minutes, but I knew it was more. I woke to screams and things smashing in the kitchen above me. I ran up the stairs, two by two.

As I reached the top of the stairs, my brother was shaking and pointing but not saying a word. I poked my head around the corner to see my father with a hunting rifle, a .306 with a scope, pointing towards the kitchen window directed at the police car. The police car sitting on the street under the street light with two officers in it, I am sure they are waiting for my mother's car to pull in not realizing it was already parked behind the other cars not visible from the street. I grabbed my brother by the arm, as well as my younger sister, who had made her way into the hallway. I pushed them into the stairwell and told them to go downstairs into my bedroom closet under the stairs and hide. The two went without a word. My head reeled with information. The rifle and ammunition were in my younger brother's room. I cannot imagine the terror he must have felt, seeing his father take the gun and bullets. Perhaps the final assault was to follow.

I turned my attention to the kitchen and yelled at him, "Are you frigging kidding me?" I heard the words as they came from my mouth. His attention was broken, and it turned to me. Was I going to be his victim instead? He turned from me and headed toward the front door with the gun. As he entered the front living room, I saw my mom clobber him across the head and back with a broom. He stopped, turned, and then put the gun down on the kitchen table. Then he pushed past me, went into his bedroom, and passed out.

My mind was still trying to put all the pieces together. Everything happened so fast, and nothing was registering. I turned to look out the window. The police car started up and pulled away without coming into the house, divine intervention or had they just given up. They would never know that their lives could have ended that night.

I looked at my mom in disbelief and turned to make sure my two younger siblings were okay. Our mother was not concerned what effect this had on the family. My brother went to his room and hid the ammunition. He moved out and to another city shortly after that.

I knew this man I called my father was beyond help.

There would be no further discussion about what happened, as usual. I could no longer push down the emotions of what was happening in the house. I was ready to crack. I knew leaving and never returning was my vow to myself, if I wanted to live. Would his next assault be what killed everyone? Would everyone finally know the terror that happened in the walls of our house? I was not going to stick around to be a part of what would happen next.

It was now approaching the New Year. I needed to get everything out of my apartment. I put my furniture in storage in preparation of leaving. I had several calls for jobs, and with each call I felt my happiness starting to return. My days were numbered, and soon I would be away from all the obvious disdain from these people that I called my family. I celebrate New Year's Eve with my friends and left shortly after the New Years countdown was completed. My friends were very disappointed that I was leaving.

There was a huge snowstorm, and the highways were closed. *Are you kidding me!* I called the office, and they were working New Year's Day; they rescheduled the interview for the following day.

THE CATALYST FOR CHANGE

*D*espite the road conditions, the trip was safe and very enjoyable. The traffic was light, and the winter wonderland glistened with the fresh coat of snow—a sign of new beginnings, perhaps. I knew that this was the beginning of the healing for me, and yet I was unsure of what that would look like. Still, I knew that my life needed to be different.

I located the office, and as I walked in for the interview, I was a little intimidated. There were maps all over the walls, and the office was computerized. As I scanned the room, it was like I had been in the space before, but I knew that I had not, at least not physically. It was the beginning of computer age; no more accounting in ledgers. They hired me on the spot. That seemed to happen to me a lot. I had no place to live and barely a week's worth of clothes. I accepted the offer. I would work three-quarter time, and the pay would just cover my costs. The office was small, fourteen people at most, and they were in their twenties.

I did manage to contact one of my old schoolmates from the commercial baking program, and she offered her spare bedroom for a month while I located a place.

My week began. The company did international import and export, and I would do cost accounting of the shipments and other general accounting tasks. The job came easy, and the group was lots of fun; we melded quickly. I kept hearing how things would change once the manager got back from overseas. I thought, *No one could be that be that bad.* I thought I had seen the worst of the worst.

I was quick to learn all the machines: telex, mimeograph, the mainframe computer system, and the contract-processing computer. Then the door opened, and the manager walked in. I could feel the energy of the office shift: it was a mix of fear and dread. I had never experienced that kind of shift before outside of my family. He came into the accounting office, a twenty-foot by twenty-foot room with a desk, two large computers on tables, and a file drawer; this could be an office for two. He introduced himself and then wandered away. The office did change; it was sad that good people were so repressed by this man. The men were treated different—that was quick to see. I continued working my part-time hours but was quickly called into the manager's office and told that I need to work longer hours, because it was bothering the others when I left early. I knew he was lying. I told him that I want more pay if I worked longer hours. He told me, "Women do not need to make a lot of money; they have boyfriends and husbands." I thought to myself, *so that is how it will be, is it?* I went back to my account manager and told her about the discussion, I said that if I was to work more hours, I wouldn't do it without more pay. She said she would see what she could do.

My hours changed but my pay did not, I wrote an e-mail to the manager so that I had a record of it. He replied again with the whole "women do not need money" thing. I wasn't truly sure why, but I knew that I needed to print the response.

Weeks passed. I began to see some familiar energy with my new boss and my dad. The verbal abuse started in the office. There were five receptionists in one week—they would not put up with what was happening and left. The sixth receptionist arrived, and I shook my head. How long would she last? I heard her tell the boss, "I am here to make you look good." Oh no, I'm not sure I was going to be able to handle this one. As she walked out of his office, she rolled her eyes. She saw that I noticed, and we both snickered. The other staff started talking union, and I explained to them the union would not touch an office of fourteen employees. There were other ways to deal with people like him.

I was trying to save money so that I could find a place of my own. I loved the time with my friend and her family, a husband and two great kids. I bought groceries and looked after the kids as a way of paying them back for letting me stay with them.

It was the weekend, and I started my search for a place to live. I was driving around the city and became overwhelmed with its size and the amount of traffic. I needed to pull off the main road and regroup. I intuitively heard to take the next turn off. I turned to the right and parked. As I did, I saw a "for rent" sign, and I chuckled. Was this a little more divine guidance? I knocked on the door and apologized for just showing up. The young couple was not concerned and was happy to show me the basement apartment. It was still under construction; the kitchen was small, but the other rooms were large. I asked the price. I got my bearings and knew it was a good walk from downtown, but it was on the bus route. I told them I was interested. The wife said she would need references, and I said that was not a problem. She asked where I was moving from, and I told her. She looked surprised and asked me if I know her friend. I chuckled and told her that they were next-door neighbors to my mom and dad. We both laughed, and she said, "No worries—if you know her, we do not have to check any other references." The apartment would be ready by the first of the next month. I gave them a deposit and all my local information.

I told my friend that night that I had located a place. I knew this was all meant to be.

THE INNOCENCE OF A CHILD

———❦———

Something in my life finally felt right. My friend wanted me to go out with her and her husband, and I told once I got settled. I would be happy to babysit the girls when they went out.

She asked me to bathe the girls and put them to bed. I had no worries and thought it would be fun. The girls and I played and had a good time. I put the youngest to bed and ran the tub for the four-year-old. I was sitting at the edge of the tub, and we were playing with all the toys that now enveloped her small body. I was getting ready to rinse her off from all the bubbles, and she said, "Auntie, you didn't wash my pee-pee." Every cell of my body went into shock. I couldn't touch her. I did everything in my power to make excuses to her. I was overwhelmed with emotion and started crying uncontrollably. I could feel her stroking my hair and saying, "It is okay, Auntie. I will wash it." I tried to gather myself as my friends returned home. My girlfriend came into the bathroom and saw what was going on. I couldn't speak and got up and go to my room. I could hear the young girl explain to her mom the best that she could; she felt bad that she made me cry. That broke my heart. It was not her; all my past had hit me like a brick wall. The innocence of a child had broken me that day.

Some time passed, and then my friend entered my room, and we talk. She knew nothing about what I had been through growing up. I explained that the simple, innocent request had broken all the walls of protection that I had built. My friend comforted me but did not know what else she could do for me. I told her that her being there was enough. She was the first person I told; I knew deep within me that this would be the beginning to the end.

Finding My Center

———— ◦○○◦ ————

Missing the connection of my old friends I call them. As I embraced the energy of the friendship, my friend's husband got on the phone and asked, "Where are you?" I told him I was at home. "Yeah, where the hell is home?" I was shocked with his anger toward me. I asked what all this was about, and he told me he went to see me up north, and I had moved. I found it interesting; if he had called, he would have known that I had moved. I was always there for people. I was someone that people counted on to be there; that was who I was. I tried to figure out if there was more, but he was expressing only anger. The conversation ended shortly after.

I went into my room and tired to process the conversation. I realized that this was about our mutual friend. Did he not know that there was someone else in the picture, and that was why I left without telling anyone? I did not think I needed to, but apparently the guy I thought had I was in relationship with had other plans.

I was barely in my room ten minutes, and my girlfriend knocked on my door to tell me there was a call for me. Who could it be? I took the call, and it was my ex. How did he get my number? I was shocked that my friend had done this. I questioned my ex as to what he wanted. He said he was concerned about why I'd left. Was he kidding me? I asked him about his roommate, and he quickly got quiet. It was interesting how he wanted it his way and felt no remorse for betraying me. I told him that I was moving over the weekend, so he should not use this number. He began to question me more. His only concern was that I was moving in with a man. I was done with the conversation because he did not apologize for anything, and neither was he making any effort to talk about what he wanted, other than he did not want me moving in with anyone. Why was it that men did not feel they had to apologize when they hurt someone? Was there no accountability that men felt for their actions, or were they raised to believe that their needs supersede the needs of women at any cost? My frustration with that lack of compassion would set up me up for years of betrayal and disappointment.

CREATING A SAFE PLACE

The weekend came, and I went to get my furniture from storage. I was so excited to move into my new place. I got the phone set up so that it was there when I get back. I had the chance to see some friends and give them my new contact information.

It was a quick trip, and I spent the remaining time unpacking and setting up the basement apartment. I couldn't find my alarm clock and resorted to calling my girlfriend to ask if she would call me in the morning, as a wake-up call. I headed to bed exhausted.

I jolted out of bed thinking I had slept in and did not get my wake-up call. I ran from the bedroom and jumped in the shower. As I raced to get ready, I remembered there was a clock on the stove. It was half an hour before I needed to leave for work. I chuckled and let myself settle into the free time that was available. I was disappointed my friend had not called, but my attention switched to getting to work on time. I would walk to work for the first time, hoping I had timed out the walk correctly. As I walked, it was as if the sounds took me into a meditative state. I breathed in the morning air and came into a place of peace. My day would start and end with walking and breathing and I found a new sense of appreciation for my space as each day passed.

I called my friend later that day and asked why she had not called. She stated that she had called, and some man had answered. I confirmed the phone number with her. She also told me that my ex had called her, and she had given him my new number. I was disappointed with this but knew that I did not want to put her in the middle.

Organizing and making this place my home was what would consume the next week. As I claimed my personal space, I realized how angry I was, at least internally. I tried not to let people see my hurt or anger. I knew that I had to get some help, but where did one go? It was not a question one asked the local shopkeeper.

My phone didn't ring for days, and for me that was usual. I called one of my friends, and she said that she had been trying to get hold of me, but some man kept answering. I called the phone company, thinking that perhaps they hooked up the phone to the upstairs suite, and I told them I could make calls but couldn't receive them. They told me that I had the wrong number. I chuckled, thinking that everyone that called the number would have gotten the mystery man. I wondered how many calls I had missed.

I called the number that I had been given originally by the phone company and got a man. I say hi, told him my name, and then asked if there were any messages for me. He was surprised at the question, and I explained the mistake and apologized for the error. "Should anyone call for me, just give them my number." We had a chuckle over the mistake, and he told me that he got an inquisitive call from a male, wanting to know who he was. I knew that that was my ex and told him so. I thought to myself, *now he knows how I felt when I called him and got his new girlfriend.* The only difference was that this man was a stranger. I thanked the stranger for his time and apologized again.

I tried to create some sense of balance in my life. I did sports, went to the gym, and went dancing. I realized that I had to deal with all this emotion inside me. Being physical was the way I burned off the emotion, or at least some of it; I also kept mentally busy. I knew that I needed to talk about all the years of abuse. I could hear my dad's voice: "If you tell, I will kill you!" He had already come close, so who was to say he would not finish it?

Setting Boundaries

———⌘———

ach time I walked into my office, it triggered all the emotions from the past. My emotional storage room was full; there was no more room to hide any more emotion, and the abusive actions of the office manager was pushing me to my breaking point. I made a powerful choice not to be a victim of this office drama and started setting boundaries.

I was sitting in the accounting office. We were located on the eighteenth floor and faced the river valley. My computer desk was right beside the window. I felt something outside the window and turned my head. I was eye to eye with the most incredible looking pigeon; its colors were vibrant. I knew this pigeon was out of place that far up. Then I heard a voice intuitively, and the voice was familiar to me. It was my Grandfather's voice, I heard, "You are going to be okay, and everything will work out." I had this huge sense of peace come over me. I continued to stare eye to eye with this pigeon until someone walked into the office, and I turned to answer a question. When I turned back to the window, the pigeon was gone. My head was trying to process this information and the emotions. I chuckled and thought, *Yup, I have finally snapped. I am talking to pigeons.* The day would continue, and then a powerful wave of remembrance hit me: my grandfather raised pigeons with his brother.

I would continue to get information and guidance; it was getting stronger, and it was like having a regular conversation because I could hear the answers to questions. I remembered this was what it was like as a young child when I spoke to God. My life would take a huge turn in so many ways. The guidance brought a sense of trust of the good that would come. As the days passed, there would be bits and pieces of the conversation with my other grandpa, who had come when I had fallen from the roof. He had showed me different times and things that would come to me in the future. I was living that future now.

The stress was getting to me; this was not a fun place to work. I saw the others folding under the abuse. I didn't feel well one day and went home; I had incredible pain in my abdomen. I spent the rest of the day in bed. That did not go over well with the boss. He approached me the next morning and asked how I was feeling, I told him it was better; I just went home and slept with a heating pad. I knew he was not asking out of compassion but rather judgment. His next comment shocked me. "Well, perhaps we should get some of those in the office so you women don't have to go home." You could have picked my jaw off the floor. Was he kidding me?

I was still not well the rest of the week, and so I went to the doctor's office; I saw his replacement because he was on holidays. The new doctor suggested that I get an ultrasound. I told him to look in my file and count the pink result forms in it. He did, and there were thirteen. I then asked him to look at the dates on the result sheets; they spanned the last twelve months. I asked if he thought if one more would make the pain go away. He said no. I asked him if he would remove my right ovary. He was willing to schedule the surgery but wanted my surgeon to do it. I agreed.

Weeks passed, and I was called for the surgery. I sat in the hospital bed, and my gynecologist appeared in the room with a female doctor. He snapped, "So what, you're scheduling your own surgeries now?"

I was quick to reply, "No, a real doctor scheduled the surgery." The female doctor was standing there with a shocked look as the confrontation continued. I tell him this was my choice to have the ovary removed; it was obviously not working, and I would not continue to live with the pain. I went on to tell him, "When you have me open, you can scrape my left ovary; it has a small cyst. Also, remove the obstruction in my colon, if it's not too much trouble."

Was this about my health, or him? He turned and headed for the door with his final assault: "What the hell do you know?" The other doctor remains shell shocked at my bedside. She looked at me, and I shrugged my shoulders. I asked her if she was going to be in the surgery, and she nodded. I told her, "Please check for the two other things that I mentioned." She nodded again and left the room. I couldn't imagine what she was thinking.

The orderly arrived to take me to surgery, and I asked God to watch over me and guide the doctor into integrity.

The surgery was completed, and I was back in my room. The gynecologist appeared in the room and explained that my omentum had wrapped itself around my right ovary and strangled it. There was a small cyst on my left ovary, which they'd scraped, and then they removed the obstruction in my colon. He turned without an apology for being so rude and left the room. I was more than upset. I had suffered for over two years with this, and that was how he handled it?

As he left the hospital room, I blurted, "I am sorry. What don't I know?" He left without further comment.

I knew that not everyone had this ability to sense what was wrong in their body, or perhaps people had just forgotten. I did not understand why doctors did not want to listen to their patients. Why was it so hard for the medical industry to be in partnership with their patients? Was it fear? Were they so insecure that someone might know something that they did not? With complication after complication, I became well versed on the functions of the body, much to my doctors' dismay. I became the body mechanic, if you will, knowing what to watch for, noting signs of distress in the body, and then rebalancing it. That was not so complicated, was it? All I knew was I was fighting to survive and they did not want to listen. That in itself was a theme in my life. No one had ever listened when I was in pain. No one ever stepped up to help when I asked. I resolved to no longer ask for help, and it saved me a lot of disappointment.

As I lay in the hospital bed, one of my coworkers appears. He was a gentle soul, and his name was Glen. I was a little surprised that he had come. He came with flowers and a card. We chatted for a while, and I knew that he had something more to ask but was embarrassed to do so. I prompted him, and he confessed that he has been sent by the manager to find out how long it would be before I returned to the office. Now, how should I answer this? I came back with a question that he could take back to our boss. I asked him how long he would want off if they had to remove one of his man parts. I could saw the red come to the face of my coworker, and I knew he would never be able to say that. I didn't truly expect him to, and we both had a little chuckle. I told him I would check with the doctor—if we could have a civil conversation.

I returned to the office a few days after. However, I was moving slow and was not ready for any crap from my boss. The

office issues started soon after my return, and I had had enough.
I started to gather information: memos that he sent out that
were discriminatory, e-mails, and of course the harassment at
the hospital. Some accounting issues had stood out, and when
I questioned him, he told me to overlook them; I noted these
instances. We had Dictaphones in the office for the salesmen,
I used one to record the rants that happened more often. One
of our summer couriers got a promotion to coordinator of
transportation, and he was responsible for organizing the ship-
to-shore transportation of domestic property. His hesitation for
doing his job came from his lack of training. I did my best to assist
him even though it was not my job.

Things started to get explosive in the office. What happened
in this office was that everyone was fully aware that a small area
and open desk concept did not allow for privacy. We had clients
at the reception area, and the manager stormed out toward my
desk and the desk of the young transportation coordinator. I
knew what was coming would be nothing good, and I slipped
the Dictaphone to the top of my desk and hit record. In the next
second, the manager grabbed one of the old-style, eight-line
phones, threw it at the young man, and screamed, "When I tell
you to phone someone, phone them!" The young man ran and
ducked under a desk, and a crash followed as the phone hit his
desk. The clients that were sitting at reception were frozen in
fear; their eyes were large saucers as they their bodies pressed into
their chairs.

I filled in the missing information onto the recorder as the
events occurred. Hoping to break his trancelike energy, I said,
"There are clients here to see you." Without a blink, the manager
turned and invites the clients into his office. My body responded
at every possible level—this was my father all over again. As the

manager's office door closed, one could feel everyone exhale. We regrouped, trying to regain some level of safety.

I was done. It was now the beginning of June, and I had been subject to enough abuse in this office and in life. I gave my two weeks' notice. The others were sad to see me go, but I told them I had a parting gift for them, but they would not be able get it until after I left. No one knew what I was up to. I gathered all my information and put it in a courier package with a cover letter, and I had the receptionist send it to the head office.

I had no job, but I knew it was important to be out of this environment. I had the weekend to sort things out, regroup, and figure out what this was supposed to look like. My intuitive guidance was strong during this time. I went into complete trust of this guidance. It did not mean that things came to me on my time, but more so on divine timing. I learned to listen and act accordingly.

I noticed that the old emotions were starting to come up. I would have horrible nightmares, and my past would fill my dreams. I would struggle to keep my life in balance. I became very aware that I needed help. Where could I go? If I told, would my dad find me and kill me? He had threatened so many times over the years. These questions spun through my head day after day.

It was the weekend, and I went out dancing. This was something I did often, because when I danced, I felt free. Something happened that night that triggered me. An extremely drunk man felt he had the right to grab me, and every cell of my body filled with fear and anger, remembering the hundreds of times that my drunken father had grabbed me and took from me. I was shaking from my core as I broke free from his grip to go home. I knew if I did not go that I would have taken all of the anger from the years of abuse and directed it at this person.

I knew that I would probably kill him as the rage poured out of me. I spun with emotion, and my need to binge eat hit me. I stopped at the corner store on the way home and grabbed bags of junk food before heading home. I started stuffing the food into me. It was not long before I felt this rush of self-hatred for letting this get to me. I purged the food out of me, sat on the floor of the bathroom, and cried.

I managed to make it back to the bedroom and saw the message machine flashing. I hit play. It was my dad's voice: "Just calling because we haven't heard from you in a long time." What the hell was that about? I had never received a call from him! The message made my skin crawl. My emotions were raw. Was this a sign that he would come for me? I hit erase and slid into the bed shaking as the emotion and fear left my body. If I never saw my father again, it would be too soon.

It was Sunday. As I entered the bathroom, I looked into the mirror as if I could see into my own soul. The words that came were of self-hatred for all of the anger that was in me. I heard the words as they left my lips: "I hate you. I hate how angry you are."

I went for a long walk and processed last evening's events. I got home, and there was something in my mailbox, a community booklet with different advertising. I was sitting on the couch with a cup of tea as I went through the booklet. There were some classified ads, and as I read the ads I came across an advertisement that was for sexual abuse recovery for men. I started to rant over this ad. "*Men* are the abusers! Are you kidding men, a recovery group for men?" I called the number and asked if it a mistake in the ad. The lady on the other end gently told me that men also suffered abuse. It was as if I had been hit by a brick wall. That was so out of my reality. She realized how upset I was and told me there was a group for women coming up soon; it would be fifty dollars. My heart sank. I did not have fifty dollars—I had thirty after my bills were paid, and that was for groceries. She took my information and assured me that she would call me upon confirmation of the class for women.

Taking Charge of My Life

onday came, and I went to pick up my check from the import-export company. Then I went to the bank. I walked down the street to a placement agency that the import-export company used. I filled out all their forms and did all their testing. I was told that no one had ever done as well as I had, and no one had ever finished it. I chuckled at the fact that they had said to quit if I could not answer a question. I had to stop there and to go no further. I did have questions I did not know the answer to, however I knew the answer too many of the questions after. I guessed at the questions I did not know and moved on. I did not live in a world where I let things stop me. Pushing through was what I did. I never settled for what people thought I should do. I spoke to the coordinator and told her that I did not want any job that resembled the ones she sent her receptionists out on. She promised that she would not.

The office assistant was excited to have me on the roster. I shared with her that I was going out to submit some resumes, and they should call me if they found any jobs. I never left my destiny to anyone, at least not in the physical world.

It was as if I was being pushed down the street. I was at the corner and was drawn to look down the block. There was an old gray building. I could see the sign on the building: it was the newspaper. I heard my intuitive voice say there was a job there.

I walked in and asked where the HR department was, I was directed upstairs and eagerly went as if I had been there before. As I reached the second floor, I came across an open desk concept, except for a few offices that lined the outside wall. A woman greeted me, and I asked if they were looking for anyone in accounting. She pointed at a piece of paper on the wall and said those were all the openings they had. I looked; one was for the warehouse and another for a driver. I asked, "Are you sure there is nothing in accounting?" She shared with me that I could apply for one of the jobs posted, and they would at least look at my resume, the circular file drawer, and no thanks. I had a feeling; I wasn't sure what, but I stood there for a few minutes. The woman that I had been talking to started bouncing in her chair; I think she was a little strange. She waved me toward her and said, "You're not going to believe this, but this is a request from the accounting office—it is exactly what you are looking for."

I told her that was great and that I would take it. She tried to explain that was not how it worked. I chuckled to myself. She took my resume and told me to have a seat until her supervisor was off the phone.

I was approached by the supervisor, who said, "Well, this never happens!"

I thought to myself, *really? It happens to me all the time!*

She interviewed me for an hour and a half, and then she went out and made a call. She came back and asked me if I would be willing to have an interview with the office manager and the supervisor of accounting. I said yes!

The next meeting would be in the accounting office; the department supervisor, office manager, and purchasing supervisor were in the interview. They interviewed me for what seems like hours; they wanted to check my references, and then they would call me. I left knowing the job would be mine—something inside me just knew.

I was barely in the door of my apartment when I got the call. It was the HR department offering me a job. I tried to stay calm as she shared all my references checked out. She told me what the offer would be. Before I could register it, I heard myself ask, "Per month?" The HR coordinator laughed and said, "Oh no, that would semi-monthly." I asked if that the best she could do. I heard the concern in her voice that I would not take to offer, and she told me that I would be up for a review in three months, which would come with a pay raise if it was positive.

I accepted the offer knowing I had nearly tripled my pay from the import-export company. My hire was the talk of the office. Apparently the hiring process for the company usually took two to three weeks. I chuckled. I believed if I listened to my guidance, things like this happened.

I felt like I could breathe again. Everything in my life had calmed down. I had a good place to live, I had a good job, and my body was healing.

I started my new job, and things seem to fall into place. The office I was in was not on the main site. I did circulation accounting. The job itself was easy. I was intrigued by how the group of people engaged in group dynamics to get me into their social group. I was quick to assess whether I could trust someone energetically—so when people came in with warnings about whom to stay away from, it was usually them I had to watch. This situation was not any different. Never one to jump into the office drama, I simply took my space and watched the agenda of others surface.

FACING MY EMOTIONAL PAST

y past was becoming my present, and all the emotions came at me whether I was asleep or awake.

The first week at the new job ended, and I was getting dinner ready. My phone rang: it was the lady from the sexual abuse recovery group, checking to see if I wanted to sign up for the group. My heart raced and I became dizzy. Could I do this? Could I actually talk about what had happened to me? I heard myself say yes. My mind was a bit of a blur after that. The group would start in one week, on Wednesday nights. I got all the information, and as I hung up the phone, I knew my world was about to change. I was aware of the emotions flooding my body. I did everything I could to stay in balance within my physical body as the emotions surfaced.

As the week started, my emotions were raw and at the surface. I tried my best to separate my old emotions from what was going on daily at work. There was a situation at work where money was missing from the deposit bag that came from a retail location. I questioned the missing money and brought it to my supervisor's attention. I was waiting for a call back from the other location regarding the missing money. They explained that they balanced and did not know how the money could have gone missing; it was in a locked bag when it left the other office and was delivered to the office downstairs, and then to my desk. The supervisor from the other department was quick to send out an e-mail to top management that the money was missing, and the only person who would have access was me. Was he kidding? I showed the e-mail to my supervisor and stated that I was going to send a response. She wanted me to hold off until we heard from the department who had sent the money. I got that call, and the girl on the other end told me she thought she was over, so she pulled the hundred dollars and stuck it in a file in their office.

The problem was solved, but the manager from downstairs office wanted to make a point and certainly did not want to have mud on his face. He insisted that I have someone supervise me while I opened the bag. His department confessed that it messed up, but he would not hear it and insisted on pointing his finger at me. I was not sure what his problem was. My manager finally addressed the issue with him and told him to back off. The man reluctantly did so. Who was this person, and what was his need to trash me? This would trigger money issues with me again. I would later find out he was mad that I got the job without the position being posted, because the people in his department didn't have the opportunity to apply for the job. I wondered why he did not address his concerns with the management team but would rather choose to attack me.

Wednesday came, and my emotions burned from the inside out. Even though the office energy was settling, the internal emotion of dealing with the abuse heightened. I got through the day and set out early to get to the first group meeting; it was in a church basement. I was greeted at the door, and no one asked if it was the sexual abuse group; they skirted around why we were all there. I thought to myself, *Wow, we have managed to get there, and still no one can say the words. This should be interesting.*

The group gathered, and we introduced ourselves by first names only. The group ranged in age; the youngest was sixteen and the oldest was sixty-two. I felt the pain of these people as they spoke. The oldest woman struggled to say the words. I wondered what it would be like to hold that painful secret for so long. I could not even imagine; I would have probably killed myself before then.

It was my turn, and the words come out. I felt the fear of my father's threat shake through my body, but I continued. I kept telling myself that if I kept quiet, the attackers would win. They would not win—I would not let them. They would no longer have control of me, I vowed. I would not keep the secret, and I would not allow them to win. As I disclosed my truth, I realized that no one could shame or control me with the secret any longer. Yes, I was sexually abused. Yes, I was no longer going to be a victim by allowing my abusers to control the truth. If I told the secret, it was no longer a secret, and I had nothing to protect. That day I moved from being a victim to a survivor.

There were a total of eight women and the counselor. I learned the power behind abuse in this group. I saw how people had hurt themselves, believing they did something wrong and deserved to be punished. I also learned that abuse was not something that only happened to poor people, like I believed. There were people that came from a lot of money in the group; the abusers were doctors, priests, lawyers, and judges. My mind struggled with this knowledge. I had told myself the story that this only happened to poor people. I had believed so strongly that lack of money and education created abuse. My world would again have to shift into that new understanding. Whom could I trust? I would look at people differently knowing this, and I did not like how that changed me. Any hope that I had was sucked out of my body and spirit. In my child mind, I vowed to have money so that abuse did not exist in my future. That belief was shattered. How was I to guarantee that abuse did not happen to me again? If money was not the answer, then what was? When a belief one had was the foundation from which one built their world, and then that belief was false, one's foundation shattered. How did people rebuild their lives after that? I would learn about how many of my beliefs were false in the days and weeks that would come. I had told myself things to justify the actions of my abusers—things that would allow me to stay in the family, to make it normal and allow me to survive.

We make a pact that night that we would not take our lives as we dealt with the abuse. That request made me realize how fragile the group was. In my mind, if I killed myself, then they won. It was hard to believe that people had managed to get out of the abusive situation and would now want to kill themselves. My brain was on overload—and this was only the first evening. I would return home that night with the realization that my world would change drastically.

I would learn that people in the group thought they might have been abused. How could they not *know* they were abused? My brain was in for a rude awakening that was for sure. Being in a room with eight abuse survivors was going to be a huge learning experience for me. Perhaps some lessons were ones that I did not want to learn. I had recorded everything—times, dates, place of the abuse—in my mind. Nothing was forgotten. Not remembering was way outside my reality. I would learn how powerful the mind was and what lengths our bodies went to protect us from feeling things that we endured. The thought that people did not know if they were abused reeled in my head.

All of my fears of telling would come to the surface, and I would not sleep much that night, trying to convince myself that my father would not appear from the dark and kill me, as he had repeatedly threatened.

Did my sister remember? I made it my mission to fill in the blanks. I wrote a letter to my older sister, telling her that I was in a sexual abuse survivors group, and it had come up that some people did not know or remember; they just had feelings. I get a letter back. She was happy that I was in counseling and confirmed that she did remember the abuse. She told me that she had always been jealous of me, because of how I handled things and how I succeeded in life. Her perception of the effects of the abuse on me surprised me. The abuse made me angry, and the anger was what fueled me to pursue change. She thought that this had no negative effects on me, but she was so far from the truth. Abuse survivors chose to act out sexually or become abstinent; I chose abstinence. My relationships were, for the most part, non-sexual or at least very limited in sex. I would have strong emotional relationships, but sex was secondary.

Our letters continued. It was the most that my sister and I had ever shared, and the only time we ever talked about the abuse. One thing I did realize was that we were on the opposite ends of the spectrum as to what we told ourselves about the abuse. One thing was that sex was not love. For me, giving myself to someone sexually was sacred; it was like giving them a part of my soul and that would not be given to just anyone. My sister admitted that she manipulated our dad around money. She was always in a lack of energy around money. She would continually play the victim with money. If they wanted her home for Christmas, they would have to pay for her gas or transportation. She would swoop in and gather presents but never give them. If they wanted her to get married, they would have to pay. This was a huge sore spot with me. I said, "That makes you a prostitute—you are just paid later!"

Her response was, "He owed me!"

I thought to myself, *and what does he owe the rest of us?* Her selling herself disturbed me. I did not want his money—there was not enough money in the world to replace what he had taken from me.

My sister was eager to have a baby. I asked her if she was going to let our dad near her kids, and she said yes. Every muscle in my body tightened, and I was sick to my stomach. I shared what he asked me when I was thirteen: "When are you going to make me a grandfather?" I asked her, "Do you think he will abuse his grandchildren?" Her response sickened me. Her husband and she talked about it, and if they saw any signs, they would not let him near them again. I couldn't hold in my anger. I screamed at her, "If you see signs, you are a day too late! Are you kidding me?" Would handing over her kids ensure her payment plan? What would be the payout for handing over her firstborn? What would it get her financially? The rage in me magnified as she spoke; if I could have reached through the phone, I would've smacked her.

The letters and phone calls stirred up a lot of things between my sister and me, but as I continued with the group and dealt with what triggered in me, I saw within the group that my expression of responsibility and accountability triggered them. Some were mothers who allowed their children to be abused, and others accepted money to ease their abuse. It would prove to be a healing experience, but also one that triggered morals and ethics within the group. What exactly was the payout that would make the pain go away? How much money or material stuff healed the wounds of abuse? Death would be the only assurance that it would never happen again, at least in my mind.

I barely got to work on time. I was completely distant from my coworkers, and they are aware of it. With four accountants working in a twenty-by-twenty room, our desks faced two by two; there was not much privacy to process what I had been through the night before. My emotions were raw and at the surface. *Back away, and no one will get hurt,* was the thought that races through my head. I managed to get through the week, and again it was Wednesday.

The group gathered, and I listened quietly to all the perspectives of the other group members. I saw the dynamics of their families and how people managed to hide the abuse. The stories unfolded over the eight weeks, and it was as if I was rolling down a hill and couldn't stop. The flood gates for remembering wave after wave came at me. When I thought I had remembered everything, more memories came rushing in to replace the ones that had been acknowledged. Would it ever end? I was shocked at things that came back to me: the words, emotions, and pictures, but most of all the abandonment that I felt from my mother flood my body. I felt the need to purge all of this out of me. I acknowledge in that moment my need to purge came from it was never about the food it was about the emotions that I had stuffed over the years. If only getting the emotions out of me were so easy.

The weeks would unfold, and the energy among the group would change as one person would respond to what the others said. Victims demanding accountability from their mothers for not protecting them was a huge issue, and I agreed; in my eyes my mother was as much of an abuser as my father was. The cycle of abuse repeated if a mother allowed abuse of her children; she needed to be accountable. There was no question in my mind on this one. Pushing each other's emotional buttons created fear in the group. There were a few expressing physical aggression, and I found myself sitting in my car a few blocks away to see who would be at the meeting. I did manage to force myself to go into the meeting. I strongly voiced my concern and let the two know that I was not here to take any more shit from anyone, and if I had to protect others or myself, I would. My words were taken in, and the energy settled quickly. The others knew I was not kidding around. The meeting would end without incident that night.

That night I ask my guidance why my mother never protected me. The answer astounded me when I heard the words: "Because I knew you would survive; the others would not." In some way I knew this to be true. If she stepped out of denial, it would cripple my siblings. They would not be strong enough to deal with the truth. I knew the answer in my head.

I did not sleep much after each meeting; my mind processed all of the memories each time I closed my eyes. I was in and out of sleep that night, and I slept past my alarm. I was half an hour late for work, and my boss was furious with me. She came out and yelled at me about having to work late to make up my time. I said fine. If only she knew what I had endured the night before. I think not one of these people could go through what I went through and keep it together. All I heard from them was whining and bitching about things that were meaningless in the scope of things. The energy in the office was tense. I kept to myself, only speaking when I had to, and that was not often. I worked through my lunch and stayed late, just to prove a point. As I was packing up for the day, I wanted to go into my boss's office and explain. I was shaking. It was one thing to sit in a group of abuse survivors, but I had never let anyone I knew professionally learn about what I had gone through, and I certainly had not told anyone that I was going to a group. After all, I had mastered the craft of illusion. I asked my boss if I could talk to her, and I explained to her what I had been through and that I was going to group Wednesday nights—not out party, as the others had indicated. She sat at her desk speechless, and then her eyes filled with tears. She expressed how sorry she was and how bad she had felt for the day's events.

The next day I was sitting at my desk, early this time. The energy between my boss and me had shifted, and her support was noticed. The others were expecting the energy of the day before and were disappointed, feeling that I should be dealt more sternly. One of the girls brought in lilacs for each of the desks. I thought to myself that I had not noticed the smell of lilacs for years. I loved lilacs. Within minutes, my head begins to pound, and I feel nauseous. In the next minute, I was running to the bathroom, I was barely in before I threw up violently. Everything was spinning. I felt myself passing out, and then a memory came back to me. It was the one where my father was sexually molesting me in my bed at the age of seven. As his adult body crushed me, the smell of lilacs and the sights, sounds, and image of the room as I floated out of my body during the assault came rushing back to me. Every cell in my body shook as the memory returned. I was now on the floor of the bathroom crying uncontrollably. I had pushed this memory down into a place that was deep and dark, hoping never to retrieve it. What else had I forgotten? What seemed like seconds ended up being much longer. My boss was now at the door. I tried to gather myself so that I could get back to work. She looked at me, but I couldn't tell her what had just happened. I went to my desk and asked everyone to take the flowers from their desks, because I was allergic to them. All were aware that something had happened, but they were unsure of what, so they did so without question. The rest of the day was quiet for me.

Emotions would rage through me, and I had to stay present and not deflect them onto others. This was not a simple task. My spiritual connection with guidance would become stronger during this time. I would have my conversations with God. These conversations were auditory, as if there was someone in the room with me. I never questioned this and trusted the guidance. Even the guidance could not take the pain from me. If only it could be that easy.

Group would continue. I was now getting to the anger from the abuse. I was angry that no one had stopped it, that no one had protected me. I heard my child voice demanding answers to the pain. Why had no one stopped this? I thought of how many people knew, and how many times the police were at our house, with nothing ever done. This was done *to* me—I did not ask for this. I was the one who had to deal with the pain and consequences of what was done to me. It did not affect the abusers that were for sure; they continued merrily along, as if they had done nothing wrong. Was that their truth? What had they told themselves in order to cause this pain and suffering to another person? When did their belief system get shattered? When was what they did become acceptable behavior?

I would struggle with my eating disorder, and the need to purge the emotions out got greater as I experienced memories that I had shoved deep. I had to come up with some way of distracting myself from binging and purging. I would start crocheting, just so that my hands were busy. For months on end I would make baby blankets, stockpiling them. The pile became symbolic of my false sense of control over the binging.

Maintaining Balance

━━━◦◦◦━━━

While trying to maintain some sense of balance and control, I put my energy into my career. The small group that I worked with headed out to the mall for lunch. We were sitting in the food court. The mall was having a sidewalk sale, so there were tables stacked with merchandise in the hallways. I heard a young girl who was obviously intrigued with all the items on the tables, and she kept saying, "Mommy, look. Look, Mommy!" The young mother was having nothing to do with the displays or the needs of her daughter. The mother stopped and reprimanded her daughter, telling her that if she did not stop, she would be taken to the bathroom. The little girl pulled back; it was obvious that she knew what that statement meant. The mother headed down the side hallway to the bathroom. The young girl was screaming, "No, Mommy, not the bathroom! I promise I will be good."

The energy and attention of what was happening ripped through the people in the food court. I saw the terror on the face of the young girl. I stood up as I said to my coworkers, "If I am not out of the bathroom in ten minutes, call the police." They tell me to sit down, but I did not listen to them. I made my way down the hallway and pushed the bathroom door open. I saw the daughter crouched, awaiting the smack of her mother's hand. I knew this was not her first bathroom beating. I heard my voice echo in the bathroom. "If you so much as touch that child, I will beat you ten times worse." The mother froze mid-motion. The bathroom stalls were filled with women, and no one was making a sound. I looked the mother in the eye and informed her that if she wanted to beat on someone, to come over and beat on me—and I would be happy to return the experience to her. I pleaded that she gets help. I then addressed the little girl and told her that her mom would never hit her again. I made the mother look her daughter in the eye and promise. I then told the little girl, "If your mommy ever hits you, you need to dial 911." I asked her if she understood, and she nodded. I stated to the mother that if she was not out of this bathroom in the next five minutes, I would follow her out of the mall, take down her license plate number, and call the police myself. The young mother nodded, and I left the bathroom.

I returned to the table and watched for her to exit from the bathroom. As she exited she was looking for me. She left the mall in full stride, looking over her shoulder in fear of being followed. As I sat at the table, one of the women that held out in the bathroom stall, doing nothing, told her friend what she had just witnessed. The women that had remained at the table looked at me and gave me a smile, knowing I was the women who stood up for the young girl. We returned to work, and nothing more was said about what happened.

A few days later, there was a job posted for the main office; it was more of what I wanted in a job because I could use more of my accounting skills. I got the new job. Lots would change: I would be working downtown, the office was an open cubical concept, and there were eighteen in the advertising accounting group and another eight in the credit department. More energy and more drama would present itself. I realized something about myself quickly: I did not let people into my life. They were quick to want all the information on me. The family question came up, and I was quick to respond I was an orphan; the conversation ended just as quick. I was trained for five people's jobs in order to provide backup for holidays. I did so willingly, but I was quick to learn that five people times five weeks of holidays each, plus doing my own job, would amount to a lot of work. I had no time for the office politics. I was still dealing with my abuse and truthfully did not care about what was going on in this office or in any of their lives. I knew that was maybe harsh, but for the first time in my life it was going to be me first in line and if that was selfish, then so be it.

We had a dress code and a clean desk policy. The dress code was something that I had never worried about in any job; I had always dressed professionally. However, I realized that as I dealt with my past, my body weight shifted. I had some work to do in knowing how to dress my new body. I would purchase some suits and dresses and would soon become aware of how dressing up gave me a sense of pride. My body image started to shift, and I liked my body for the first time in my life.

STAMP OF APPROVAL

The sexual abuse survivor group would end. Was eight weeks enough to deal with my sixteen years of abuse? Some of the group members mentioned that they were going to a psychologist for counseling. Did I need to go, or was I going to be all right? Was there more that I needed to finish? What did being finished look like, anyhow? I was on a mission to contact someone who might be able to help. I called one office. I had a good feeling about this one, knowing that he would be the one that would help. I was speaking to his receptionist, and she told me he had a four-month waiting list. Every cell in my body screamed. I felt the panic and was quick to ask that if he had a cancelation, would she call me. I was sure I could get out early if I needed to. She agreed, and it was as if I knew that she would call me shortly.

Three days passed and my office phone rang. It was her! My heart raced as she told me that there was an opening in two hours, and she asked if I wanted it. In panic I said yes, and then I realized I would have to tell my new boss. I went to her office, and she was not there. My heart raced as my mind tried to figure this out. I heard the words, "Just tell her you have a doctor's appointment." Calmness came over me. That was not a lie, not really! She came back, and I went in to tell her that I had just gotten a call from my doctor, and he needed to see me right away. She expressed concern, but I assured her I would be fine. Inside, I hoped I would be. *What have I just gotten myself into?* I wondered.

I left and headed home to get my vehicle. I was still not familiar with the city, and I circled around for some time. I heard my guidance again: "Turn here; go up about half a block on your right." I followed the instructions given, and I was soon in front of the house converted into the counselor's office.

I went in, and the receptionist was very friendly and chatty. She asked me a lot of questions, almost to the point of making me uncomfortable. I was not used to sharing who I was with people. "Where did you work?" I felt my wall for protection go up. I meekly said I worked at the newspaper. She perked up and told me she knew someone who worked there. I acknowledged it was my supervisor from circulation accounting. I felt my body become rigid at the fear of opening this line of conversation. She said, "You will have to tell her I said hello." I thought to myself that would not happen—no one was going to know I was going to a counselor. She was quick to tell me she couldn't believe that I got in so quickly, because this never happened. I knew that things like this happened to me a lot. I smiled as I went into saw the therapist.

He was young about five feet seven. I instantly like his energy as I took a seat. He looked at me and asked, "Why are you here?"

The words astounded me, and I could feel the fear pulse through my body. As I regrouped myself, I could hear the words as they left my mouth. "I was sexually abused by my father and older brother." I had never told a man that. I instantly acknowledged the fear that he would not believe me.

He looked at me and said, "Great. Now we can get to work." He explained that he recorded the sessions, and that I would have five sessions with him, one session per month. I would have to work on what came up in the session, and then I was done—he would not see me past that. Was five sessions enough? I was happy and focused, and we got straight to it; deal with it and get out. I knew we would work well together.

The session began, and he asked me questions. My past unraveled, and with each topic he would ask, "So how did you feel about that?" Feel that was an unexplored topic of conversation. No one had ever asked how I felt about everything that I had gone through. My feelings were buried so deep that we would need a pick and shovel to get to them. Having feelings were not allowed, according to my parents; I was to suck it up. Was I going to be able to open this door and still live?

The session would go for ninety minutes, and I realized something about this man. I knew he could see what had happened to me. He brought up things that I did not verbalize. I was intrigued. I had never met anyone who could do what I could do. I knew that he was the right person to work with. Again I had been guided to someone who could help.

SESSION ONE: SELF-ACCEPTANCE

We got through the feelings and what had been placed on me. I had all the visuals of what happened to me, but I was detached emotionally; it was like watching a horror show with no sound. It was like becoming a witness without any attachment to the experience. I became aware of a sense of denial, as if the experience had no effect on me emotionally. I did not want to give my abusers the power of knowing the damage they were instilling in me. I was overwhelmed with the experience and had no control over myself; the only way to gain control was to separate from the emotions. Emotions were not allowed in the family: "Shut up and take it" was the rule. Mother said that there were things she had "chosen" to forget. *How did one "choose" to forget?* I wondered. Where was that button that one pushed? The memories continued to pound on my emotional door daily. Was healing going to come through connecting the emotions to the pictures, in order to validate the experience that I knew had happened? Was it the denial of the emotions that kept closure from occurring? Where did I find people who were safe to express emotions with?

As I reflected on emotions and my past, no one had talked about what they felt. I knew because I could feel their emotions yet saw them redirect people to believing something different. When I called people out on the truth of their emotions, they would be shocked. I think it was because they did not have a safe place to express what they were going through.

I explored my fear of men. I did not trust them to tell the truth, and certainly not to be integral in their emotions. I looked at how this belief had damaged the relationships that I had with men; I almost went into the relationships with an expectation of disappointment. I saw how my mother's denial around emotion resulted in an acceptance of physical abuse as a trade-off for the relationship. I wondered where she had learned this. The suffering as a penance of the relationship—was this bearing the cross from her religion, or somewhere else? Had I learned this emotional detachment from her? I needed to bring balance into having an experience and feeling it fully.

In truth I was afraid of sex—yes, afraid! I again needed to separate the abuse from the physical act of sexual intimacy, and I remembered the connection that I had with my last relationship. I knew that was sexual intimacy, but I saw how my inability to communicate how I was feeling created the separation and confusion between us. I also saw how having this relationship was a huge part of my healing. If only I could go back in time with my newfound knowledge, to reclaim that relationship and do it better. My heart sank in that knowing that I failed that relationship because of my past.

I explored how angry I was about having to keep the secret of abuse. Secrets hurt, and no one could tell me differently. I held a lot of guilt around not being able to stop the abuse; I was angry with those who could do something but did nothing. When one did not have the power to change the situation, that was one thing, but when one did have the power and did nothing, that was another. I saw how when I was put in a place of choice in situations, where I had the power to make change, I took it even if it put me in a place of compromise. I was fully aware of how, by stepping up and taking a stand, I made others uncomfortable; perhaps it was their acknowledgment that they were not in their power.

I saw how my life had become this intense experience of dealing with abuse and trying to reclaim some sort of balance. I needed a safe place to relax. I longed for that peaceful place, as if the desire was a place outside of myself. I realized that it would come from within.

I left with my homework instructions and a sense of safety. The month went by quickly. I focused on my homework and on getting closer to what being healed from my past would look like. I wanted to get through all the crap and get on with it; I no longer wanted this to be the focus of my life. I wanted the good stuff that others had, all that seemed to come naturally to others. I did not want to fear men or relationships. I did not want to protect the secret anymore. I did not want the pain that was in me to hurt me or anyone else.

Second Session:
The Revenge Vow

Session two came, and I was nervous about what it would bring, but at the same time it was like running a race and being focused on the end. That pulled me through the nervousness.

I had awareness that I had melded myself into others' lives, tried to figure out how to be accepted into their world, and placed my needs second. I saw the resentment that I had when others were not concerned with my needs, and it was a huge sore spot because this replicated my family dynamic. If I did not feed the relationships or friendships, they died. I learned to step back from my relationships. I saw how others expected me to be the one that fixed things when they broke or destroyed them. I was the one that needed to call; I was the one who needed to travel to see them; I needed to plan the evening out, and they were just in for the ride. I was that person who made sure that my friends got presents for their birthday. I celebrated their successes while I got nothing in return. Things became very clear as to my belief of having to earn my position in their world.

I realized how people were killing me emotionally and physically dominating me in order to control my emotions. As I started to sense emotions of others around me more, I realized that I did what I could to make them happy, safe, or whatever it was that would shift them into a calmer state, so that I did not have to feel their hurt. I did not want to feel my emotions, and I certainly did not want to feel others'. I became witness to others' expectation of me, and I did not like it. I started to step back and let them have their emotions without my interference, and they were anything but pleased. I saw how my rapport with others was not reciprocated.

As the session continued, we moved into my need to understand the sexual promiscuity of my father and brother. What in their consciousness believed that having sex with a child was appropriate? I watched their actions toward me. I was confused with their choices. I saw myself go into my head to analyze what was happening. I realized when I was in my head I separated from my emotions, which I had believed created safety. My separation from emotions took me away from feeling the truth of vulnerability. I did not want to be weak—that was my mother.

When placed in emotional connection with men, I found the easiest way to deal with them at their level. I challenged them to see who they were at all levels. I challenged them in order to prove that I was in control. I used bravado to shock them and put them in their place, in an attempt to keep them from loving me. Perhaps that was the little, seven-year-old self who vowed that she did not want anyone to ever love her again, because of her mother's definition that the abuse was how my father expressed love. I knew that I would never let anyone get close enough to induce that kind of pain on me again, in the name of love.

The shame I held was from the judgment for not being able to stop the abuse. I realized at the adult level that this was unrealistic. To think that a child could stop the abuse was senseless. The child, at a self-preservation level, took on that responsibility when the adults failed to do their job. I would have to release that responsibility and leave it with the adult, the way it should have been.

The pattern of abuse needed to stop before it continued into the next phase of my life. I promised myself that I would not carry it any further. I knew that if I did not heal this, I would self-destruct. I knew that my family needed to heal so that the abuse did not continue. I knew that they would have to admit there was a problem. Was it possible to bring them into consciousness after all the years of denial?

The clearing of the rage, sadness, and death energies needed to be a priority in order for me to move forward. The abuse of the body was instigated by the intellect's need for control, and that was the recipe for death. The transfer of wanting to balance the scale and all to pay for their acts could take me into a place of death of myself, or of the man who dared to take me on. My body came to experience love, and the intellect was what held the revenge, to have the scales of justice in balance. I focused on releasing the vow of revenge so that I could let in pure, sacred love, whatever that looked like. All I knew was that it felt right. I saw how this had affected me throughout the years, and I was exhausted with all that it had created in my body and life.

THIRD SESSION:
LOVE AND ACCEPTANCE

I had been ridiculed by my family, as if I was the dumping ground for their anger, rage, and hatred. Their actions filled me with all the emotions that they did not want, as if to see how much it would take before I was dead emotionally or physically.

I lost the body safety, and I would go within to hide. My body weight would buffer me from the pain and separation that was created through their actions. I had believed that the feminine energy was not strong enough to make the needed change, so I moved into the masculine energy in order to survive. The physical action of protection would dominate who I had become. I believed that I deserve this type of treatment as a feminine person, so with that I shifted into another experience, of the masculine.

My ability to sense when someone was lying kept me safe, and the balance that I needed to achieve this was a very fine line. When people's actions did not support what they said, that was a huge issue for me. If one wanted to see walls built fast, one had only to lie to me. As I started to reclaim my life emotionally, I realized that rather than take the time to understand someone, it was human nature to judge from fear. To rip someone from their life energy through shame and guilt was anti-love. To reflect their own shame onto others created distance, giving the abusers a sense of power and stripping one's right to stand in the powerful self. This truth became very clear within my relationships in this lifetime.

To have a belief that abuse was normal, and to have to repeat this experience triggered the law of creation. Shifting this experience to one where love was normal could only be achieved if one changed the old belief. I had several beliefs that would have to be reviewed, to move into my powerful self. I would have to work on the separation of sex and love. As I practiced this experience, I found that others were in the same situation. As I stood with an open heart in love and acceptance, others took it as sexual attraction. When I set the boundary with them, there was resentment and anger for not wanting them sexually. For those relationships that I wanted as intimate love, I would have to create the separation from a sexual experience to a sensual, gentle, loving, and nurturing experience in order to welcome it in fully and leave the sexual aggression behind.

I recalled the old relationship that I let in so deeply. I saw how my fear of sexual escalation held me back for so long, and then after letting it in, the intensity scared both of us, and we retreated from the overwhelming charge from the experience. This would be a huge shift for me, to realize and to allow the gradual progression of future relationships to develop so as not to create the need to run emotionally or physically. I also acknowledged our timing of readiness to explore the relationship was out of synch, and because of that the encounters that took place created resentment between us. The expectation that the other was ready to heal the old situation would result in someone getting one's fingers slapped, because the other was not ready to go there. The continued battle to explore what could have been was never completed. So with that awareness, I would take into consideration the failed attempts as lost opportunities. Perhaps the healing would take place, and forgiveness would come through knowing we were growing and healing our pasts without being able to communicate this with each other. I was in complete gratitude for the relationships that helped me to discover who I was and how I needed to heal, even though some of them ended in hurt and misunderstanding.

My sessions would end that day. The counselor stated that I had enough information to move forward, and he called me out on being there for a stamp on my forehead that read "Healed." He entrusted me with his verbal stamp and sent me on my way into the world, armed with the truth. As my grandfather had stated, I was not the abuse; it was what happened to me.

I ventured out into the world, but trust was a lesson that would take years to heal.

RECLAIMING MY WORTH

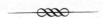

had decided to move from the basement apartment into my own place. I was excited and feeling safe as I created a new home. I come to the realization that I did not feel worthy of having things, let alone my own home. As I wallpapered and painted the master bedroom, I slept in the spare room. I woke from a deep sleep, sensing my grandmother's energy. I figured I must have been dreaming about her. I turned to see the time, and the clock had stopped. I would have only been sleeping for an hour, if the time was correct. I realized the power must have been out. I get out of bed to check the wall clock in the living room. As I did, I could see into the kitchen and all the digital clocks. I turned to the television, and the clock setting on the VCR was fine; no other clocks were flashing.

It took me a moment to figure everything out. I sensed my grandmother, and I heard her voice quietly saying that she was doing fine. I ran to the closet where I kept my photo albums. I flipped through them and found my grandmother's obituary. It was exactly seven years to the day of her funeral, and the time on the clock was the time of her passing. My mind went back to the spiritual reading I had done with my college friend. I had asked to speak to my grandmother, but she was too weak to come through. I had requested that she come to me to let me know, when she was strong enough. She fulfilled the request that night. Perhaps she could see what I was doing and came through to acknowledge what I had worked through. I was at peace as I headed back to bed. I reset my clock, and it woke me on time the next morning.

The women from the sexual abuse survivor group who had chosen to continue independently were losing their focus. I could feel that the group was good, at least for a while; I started to see people just wanting somewhere to belong. They were not doing their work to make changes in their lives to support healing. I got to the point of leaving the group and ending my relationship with them. They saw the work that I had done, and they fear it but were also intrigued. The drama of the group continued, and I resolved that I didn't want to be a victim anymore. I wanted to become a survivor.

My Third Death Experience

was still having trouble with my body. I was in good shape, and my six-pack abs returned due to my exercise program. My addiction was working out instead of alcohol, sex, or drugs. I could feel that my body was not right. Something was happening inside me. Unsure of what, I energetically scanned my body.

My body was failing me again. One thing I did notice about myself was that when I was sick, I pushed people away. I did not know what it was like to have someone to support me when I was vulnerable; I would struggle with that for years. It was easier to deal with things on my own. There was no conflict that way, and no risk of disappointment when people were not able to give me what I need.

I went back to the doctor and was booked to have an exploratory surgery, to look inside my abdomen. It was a laparoscopy, and there were small incisions made, one for a tube with a gas, and another one for a scope. I was on the operating table, and everyone was kind and explaining things to me. The only person who had attitude was the gynecologist; he hated the fact I knew when things were wrong with my body, and he was almost defiant toward me. I did not know much about ego, but I could definitely say he had one. He was on a mission to prove me wrong. I was unsure of his purpose, and at the time I did not know I could request another doctor.

It was time for the anesthesiologist to administer the gas that would put me unconscious. I started to count down and then I slipped away.

The next thing I knew, I was going through a tunnel, and then there was light. As I went through the light, I appeared in a room with a round table. A voice told that I have crossed over and was with the counsel. I sat at the round table with seven of the masters, and I reviewed my life of thirty-two years. They showed me a scroll with a list of things that I said that I would do in this lifetime, and then another scroll of what I had done. The second scroll was three times the original list. With that, I was asked if there was anything that I would have done differently. I thought to myself that I did what I needed to do to survive. I realized that my life was just that, survival. I truly did not live life—I survived it. The only regrets that I had were not being married and not having a child; that was about it. Obviously I wished my family had been able to heal, but that was not due to me not trying. What would that have looked like if others wanted what I did and were willing to do the work needed?

The questions from the counsel were more in relationship to who I was in the experience. They showed me my life, and truly my life passed before my eyes. They continued to show me all the times that I wanted to surrender to what was happening to me, but I would continue to face what life had presented and chose to be happy. The pain and anger rested inside of me, though I could see it. There were times that I lashed out with it, but I quickly realized that I was acting out my anger. I had cast it upon people who had not caused me the pain. I was quick to fix it when I realized what I had done. The list was not only the physical things I had accomplished, but also things at the spiritual and emotional levels. As I witnessed the images of my life, I realized how the abuse kept me from relationships and experiencing joy. The resentment that I held in my body from the experiences had done things to me. The counsel told me that everything in life was a choice. I could have had the relationships; the men were there in my life, but the fear that I held was greater than the desire to be loved. I held onto the memory of what my mother expressed when I asked her, "Why did daddy do this to me?" I thought of all the men that came into my life to show me a different way, and I was unable to move past the pain. It saddened my heart. I knew that I felt broken and that no one would want me; the truth of the experience was made known to me. Again my thoughts ran through the experiences, and I was shown what could have been if I had allowed the experiences in. There was no judgment in what they showed me, but rather awareness. I was incredibly humbled by the images as I saw inside the hearts of the ones who came to love me. I realized that by not letting them in, I hurt them, too.

I became witness to my family and all the abuse. I was told that I came to teach my mother how to be happy and how to experience the human body. My older siblings were healing past life issues, and as for my younger siblings, I had been their mother in another time. I died early, and they held abandonment issues that we needed to clear. As for my father, he had numerous lifetimes of abuse, including this one, and I was to teach him accountability.

That was when they told me there was one outstanding item on my to-do list. I had one outstanding spiritual contract that remained unfinished. I was unaware of what a spiritual contract was and requested that they explain. They stated, "Agreements with other souls are made before we enter a life, to resolve any outstanding teaching for our souls to evolve." They told me that if we were able to see situations from both sides, we gained tolerance and acceptance. The counsel went on to tell me that the unfortunate outcome was that the human aspect had moved into greed and control rather than love, compassion, and forgiveness. I did not like the word "forgiveness." I asked how one forgave another when so much violence had occurred. They explained that within the lesson was another lesson, one for the abused and one for the abuser. To learn and understand that the actions are what we are accountable for, we had a choice in each experience of who we chose to be. The words comforted me and brought me into a spiritual peace. I got it: even though I was abused, I tried to comfort and heal those around me. I did not act out on my anger but learned how to deal with it. In the moment of abuse, the abuser had a choice of who they chose to be, and some did choose to be in control and to harm others.

I was shown the many lifetimes that my father's soul and mine had been in together. The images were horrible, making what happened in this life almost bearable. As I was shown the experiences from the past, I realized that many of the wounds that I had on my physical body now replicated the wounds from past lifetimes. I asked why this had happened. They enlightened me that when an experience was unfinished, one carries it forward into another experience, as if to reactivate the memory so that healing could take place.

My soul had come to heal the pattern of being neglected and being left to die. To learn to be nurtured by others and to heal the body from trauma was to be my focus. The healing from trauma part I had down, but nurtured by others ... not so much. *Perhaps that is yet to come,* I thought to myself. I did become aware that my self-preservation was fight, hiding within my mind to take me from the experience around me. Making my body strong was to offset the emotional weakness I felt.

They gave me a choice. Did I want to stay on the other side, or come back into the physical world?

The outstanding contract was one of accountability, and it was with one of my abusers. I was given a choice I could stay or go back into the physical body. If I chose to stay in spirit, then I would have to take this person into another lifetime. If I went back, I would have the opportunity to finish the spiritual contract. My instant thought was, "Send me back." I was not going to take this abuser into another lifetime; he had terrorized me in this life, and I would be damned if he was going to ruin another one.

If I chose to return, my life as I knew it would never be the same. I would not come back and be normal. What I had been shown and told would put me into an understanding of life purpose, accountability, and responsibility. To squander this gift of the experience would truly be a waste. I would come back focused on that purpose.

I asked that if I went back and finished this contract of accountability, did I get to come back. They laughed and said, "No you can stay, and if you stay, you will move to Calgary, connect with a group of people who will help you grow spiritually, and help people heal emotionally through the physical body."

What? I was an accountant. What did all this mean? They wanted me to touch people? My inadequacies and fears came to the surface. They promised that everything would be there to support me, because this was not a punishment but rather a gift. Despite the fear, one thing I did know was that there was no way my abuser was welcome in another lifetime.

With that choice made, I shot back into my body. The only way I could describe it was like being in a train wreck, with every cell of the physical being blasted with energy.

As I entered my body, the physical body jerked from the operating table upon impact. I was in a seated position on the operating table when I come back into consciousness. Three nurses to the left of the table were consoling the doctor; there was another female, and she was pushing a tray away from the table to my left. The anesthesiologist was pushing a tray to the right of the table. I yelled, "Why did you bring me back? I did not want to come back!" I immediately got everyone's attention. They all looked at me but were frozen in disbelief. It was as if they there were light bulbs over their heads that flipped on and they realized that I was alive. In their acknowledgment, I felt my body slam back onto the operating table.

There was a flurry of activity around me. I felt something being placed on my face and panicked; I thought I was being suffocated. I tried to push the object away without success. I then saw the man at the head of the table. I was in survival mode and took a swing at him, trying to protect myself. I saw him go flying backward, and he knocked over the tray of instruments that he had been pushing away earlier. Then I heard a male voice in my right ear say, "It was just oxygen!" I knew it was gas and that they were trying to put me under, but truthfully I thought they were going to kill me again. Gently they placed the mask on my face, and I took a couple of breaths and was under.

I woke in the recovery room with the nurses buzzing around me as I floated in and out of consciousness. The older nurse seemed to be in charge of looking after me. "Well, now, have you been causing trouble!" she said. I was a little confused, because as the memory of what had happened temporarily slipped away from me. When I awoke again, I was in my room in the surgery department. I drifted off to sleep. When I woke a third time, it felt like I had slept for days. I became aware that I was in the four-patient room all by myself.

I felt someone walk into the room, and as I turned I saw a very handsome doctor. He stopped at the door and asked if he could talk with me. I was intrigued and said yes. He was not my doctor, but he was definitely cute, and as he came toward the bed, he was talking. I gasped and said, "Are you the one I hit?"

He chuckled and said, "You remember that?"

"Yes," I replied. "That and a whole lot more."

He asked if I would tell him what I remembered, and I agreed, but he would have to tell me what happened in the operating room first. He agreed.

He explained the exploratory surgery as if I was unaware of the reason I was in the operating room. He stated that the laparoscopy was a procedure used to scope the abdominal by going in through the bellybutton. "We filled the cavity up with gas to inflate the abdominal wall. Once inflated, we inserted a small scope to check things out. It sounds simple, but unfortunately, due to your overdeveloped abdominal muscles your stomach was not inflating, so we administered a second dose of gas. That would be the fatal mistake. The gas went up and stopped your heart and lungs. We tried to revive you, but to no avail. You were dead for twenty-five minutes before returning to your body." His voice showed signs that he was scared by the experience yet intrigued.

Then it was my turn. He asked, "Did you see a bright light?"

Truly, it was what happened on the other side of the light that was important. I spoke about this as if this was a normal experience, but I knew I had experienced something that most people had not—at least anyone that lived to tell about it. I also acknowledged that it was important I remembered.

I began to tell him the experience of leaving my body and crossing over, going to the counsel, and sitting at a round table reviewing my life. I shared about the counsel showing me the scroll and my to-do list that I said that I would do in this lifetime. The doctor sat motionless as I went through the events; he asked questions in order to bring a sense of understanding to the situation. I was unsure I could comprehend everything at the time. I knew how this would take someone out of what they had been taught religiously. "Spiritual contracts, masters, and the counsel—what is all that?" the doctor questioned. That was definitely not in my understanding, either, but I heard myself explain this to him as if it was a routine experience.

I expressed the magnitude of my awareness of all that happened to me and around me. He sat there and took in all the information. He seemed taken aback from all he had taken in. He thanked me and left. I would not see him again.

With the impact of being told that I had not finished what I came for and needed to go back, I knew my life would change. I had worked hard to overcome my past, and now I was about to be thrown back into the fire. Things became very complicated and very clear in the same moment, as my mind raced through the events of that day and those of my life. Did the years of abuse have a purpose? Was it all a part of a bigger picture? Apparently so!

All of the information flooded my mind as I lay in my hospital bed. While still trying to make sense of everything that was beyond my reality, I went into a state of spiritual awakening. If I was not finished, what else I had agreed to do? In addition, with who had I made the agreement? Questions reeled through my mind. I felt alone and connected at the same time.

That was what one would call a pivotal moment in life. That was where my life ended and my spiritual journey began.

I was released from the hospital but was not sure if I was ready to go back to work. I needed time to process all of this. I went to speak to my boss. She was shocked as I told her what I had gone through, or at least parts of it: the surgery, dying on the table, and my need to have the time to process all of this. She assured me that whatever time I needed, I could take it.

It was as if I did not belong in my own skin. Everything had changed, and I knew nothing would ever be the same. How could someone witness everything I did and be the same? Perhaps that was the point: I was not supposed to be the same.

THE NEW EXPERIENCE

J would go to the mountains to recover, at least for a few days. Being in the mountains reminded me of the time I spent with my grandparents. I loved the peace the mountains gave me, and I really needed peace right then. I loaded up my car and headed off. I realized that the quietness of my vehicle allowed for the processing to begin. I had heard guidance since I'd died at age eight. I did not put all this together, but it was all making sense now. Were the voices I heard that of the counsel group? Had I been getting direction from them all this time? Was this part of the God consciousness? Everything I thought I understood about life was shattered. Was everything I had been told in this life a lie? I liked this spirituality thing over religion that was for sure. I saw that there were lies within religion in order to control and govern people in society.

I knew what it was that I had not finished; that was obvious. I had just left my family. I knew that I could not make them change, nor did I want to; they had created their experience and seemed to be happy with what they created. It was not my job to make them change. At least, that was what I had thought. Now I was armed with the truth, and there was in fact an outstanding contract: I would have to finish this experience with my family.

When I moved away, I created a life without family. Living life as an orphan worked for me. By knowing that I could not change the past, I also knew that I was socially responsible for making sure that I took what I knew to be true and helped others in times of need. I would volunteer for the Big Sisters Organization, United Way, and many others. I participated in many community events, working with the newspaper. I had created a life without abuse, and I liked it; I did not live in fear anymore. Safety was something I searched for my whole life, and I had found it—or perhaps better put, I created it. I knew that we as humans had the choice as to what we created in our existence. That was the most empowering thing that I acknowledged through this experience.

The impact of seeing that I had not finished what I came for and needed to go back haunted me. I had worked hard to overcome my past, and now I was about to be thrown back into the fire. If I had to complete this spiritual contract of accountability, I would have to go back to what I had just left. Things became very complicated and very clear in the same exact moment as my mind raced through the events of that day and those of my life.

Was my safety an illusion? Was all the energy of abuse sitting behind a closed door? Was returning to complete this going to be the death of me? I had worked on healing myself and creating the life I wanted. Why now?

I knew that I would have to do this accountability thing, and that scared me; my entire little girl fears came up. But my fear of having to face the council again and not doing the work was greater. All of the information flooded my mind, and my emotions flooded my body. I was scared of what I needed to do to finish the spiritual contract, I was unsure of how this experience would change it my life—and the healing from my whole death experience would need some energy.

FAMILY MEMORIES

As I got closer to the mountains, I could feel my safety triggering from my childhood and flooding my body. My grandparents lived here. They had both passed at the time, but the energy of being there was what I needed to heal. Upon my arrival, I went to their gravesite, and as I sat my body surged with the emotion of how much I miss them. I wondered if they know how much the time I had spent with them meant. They were not perfect, but I loved them for what they gave me emotionally. My grandfather would call me Big Eyes and always watched over us when we visited. My grandmother always made me laugh; she was the Catholic grandma, but she was also the one who would take me to the Legion when I was very young. I remembered her saying, "Don't worry, you're tall; they will never know." She would listen to eight track tapes of a comedian who swore a lot. I also had one aunt and three uncles who lived there. I watched the dynamics between my mother and her siblings over the years: they treated her the way my mother and siblings treated me. This confused me, but I remained aware of it for years to come.

I checked into the hotel. The clerk was questioning me, but I was tired and just wanted to get to my room. She asked if I was from there, and I told her no, but my grandparents used to live here. She asked their names and recognized the family name. She continued to drill me with questions. I did not want to continue the conversation; I just wanted the key. The clerk finally got the message. With key in hand, I headed upstairs to my room, tossed my things on one bed, laid across the other, and fell fast asleep from exhaustion.

It seemed like minutes, and then a knock on the door scared me awake. I was confused as I got the door; it was my uncle. I was mad. No one knew I was there. The hotel clerk had called him, and I was furious with her. I let him in, and he was drilling me with questions: why did I not phone them, and why was I staying at the hotel? I was still trying to get everything straight in my head, and I told him I needed quiet time and rest after my surgery. He tried to make small talk, but I just wanted to be alone. He invited me to the house and wanted me to make time for them while I was there. I agreed but knew that I would avoid them; I was there only for myself. I needed to sort out all that had happened to me over the past week. The questions were too much for me. I knew he meant well, but I needed to work through everything for myself, not be flooded with more questions. I had not seen them for years. I told him that I needed to rest, and he left. I reluctantly agreed that I would call him the next day. I saw how easily I was guilted into fulfilling others' needs before my own.

I slept deeply that night, and late into the morning. I went to my grandparents' gravesite and talked to them again. My tears flowed, and again I felt safe. I held them in my heart; losing them was hard on me. When they passed, we did not talk about feelings—that was also buried deep within me. I was restless and decided to go into the mountain village to walk around. I remember my aunt worked in an office in the village. I walked into the office to see if she wanted to go to lunch. I always liked her because she was easy to talk with. She had not taken her lunch that day, which she said she always did. I left for a few hours and then come back for lunch with her. It took all my willpower to be seated in the restaurant in the middle of the room. I would rather be in the corner and in a booth. I felt too exposed, but sat there reluctantly.

We were barely seated when she asked how I was. I shared about the operation and dying, and she was surprised and comforted me. She asked what I had been up to. She stated, "Every time I ask your mom, she just says you are off doing your own thing. What's going on?" She knew my mom was lying to her and wanted the truth. I took a breath; how did I answer this? I had never told any family members what had happened to me. I started crying as I explained that I no longer saw any of the family. I went on to tell her the truth about the abuse. She was not surprised and said she had known something was not right.

I was crying so much that I couldn't eat. She was supportive and insisted that I come and stay with them. I was unsure, but I did stay with them the following night. She told my uncle about what I had shared with her. I was unsure of what he would think, but he, too, was supportive. They went over the times that we were at their house and my aunt recalled a time my sister and I were coloring. As we laid on the floor, our dad barked, "Dishes." And boy, how we jumped up, put away our play stuff, and went to the sink without protest. My uncle recalled saying to his wife, "Wow, they listen well." My aunt's response was, "Yes—too well!" They recalled other times that they felt uncomfortable with his present in their home, and how my dad would make my cousins sit on his knee.

I was getting overwhelmed by this information and did not want to talk about it anymore. It was one more thing I had to process. Anything more was too much.

I would spend time with much younger cousins. My young male cousin asked me, "Are you old enough to be my mom?" I chuckled and realized I was; in fact, I was old enough to be both his and his older sister's mom. One more thing to process, I had vowed never to have kids while my father was still breathing. Had I cheated myself from that experience? Out of all the processing, I knew I would have to press criminal charges to complete the spiritual contract of accountability. Perhaps after that, I would be healed enough to have babies.

I was ready to head home, and I thanked my aunt and uncle for their support. I did not want to pull them into this; that was not the purpose of going there. I knew that all things happened for a reason, more so now than ever before.

As I returned home, I knew that there was something different, and I knew it was from within, not from without.

ACCOUNTABILITY CONTRACT

———— ∞∞∞ ————

I returned to work while still recovering from the surgery, and now armed with the knowledge that I had to face my family abuse head-on. I knew that the charges would have to be filed in the area where the abuse took place. The city I lived in had an independent police department, and the RCMP governed the area where the abuse took place. I found the police department phone number from a suburb of the city in which I lived now; they were a part of the RCMP. I pulled the phone out into the living room and rested it on the love seat. I started to dial the number, got about four numbers dialed, and hung up. This would continue for a week. I finally managed to complete all the numbers, but I continued to hang up again and again. I did this about four times that sitting. I dialed again, and the phone had not rung, but all of the sudden there was someone at the end of the line. I panicked. I couldn't get the words out, and the person at the other end asked if I was all right. I stated yes and then said, "I have a question and hope that you can help me. What is the process to report sexual abuse?" I explained to her that it did not happen here; rather, it was in the north. I could tell she was trying to make sure I did not hang up with her. She was doing her best to keep me on the phone while I said to her I could call back another time. She insisted I stay on the line until she could locate a police officer to handle this. I could feel my need to run from this experience. It was February 6, and there was the most incredible storm I had ever seen. She asked if I could come in to speak with someone. I explained there was a storm, so perhaps tomorrow. She insisted that I do it that night. I assured her that I would. As I hung up, I realized there was no turning back from this. I sat with the phone in my lap and talked myself into going. It took me about forty-five minute before I got out to the car, and another thirty minutes to get to the police department in the storm. As I drove in the storm, I was the only one on the road. The roads were drifting as the wind blew; it was almost eerie in the silence of the night. Perhaps it was symbolic of the journey I had been on, because I did it alone.

I got to the police detachment and was greeted by a cranky male officer, who said, "What are you here for?" I stated I was to speak to someone to make a report. Before I got any further into the conversation, a female officer appeared and told me her name. Without another word, she came out and escorted me to a back office. The male officer stood there confused, but truthfully I did not care.

I sat in the room, and a female officer came in and introduced herself as Constable Diana. She told me she was sorry that I had to wait, but she had ended her shift and was just leaving when they told her that I was coming in. I felt bad that I had kept her. She asked me to explain why I was there. I started to tell her what I had been through. She frantically wrote notes. It was as if the words were purging out of me, and I couldn't stop them. I asked her, "Do you not usually record the session? I've been watching too much television, I guess."

What seemed like minutes turned into hours I could see that she was getting tired from writing, and I asked her if she wanted me to write for a while. She was grateful for the offer and took me up on it. She excused herself for a few minutes and brought back a glass of water for both of us. I was also getting tired, and it was as if I hit a wall, emotionally and physically. I did not have to hold this in me any longer; this was different from telling in group, but I could not explain the difference. It was as if there was finally space within me to breathe.

The meeting ended, and they said they would send everything to the northern detachment. I was told not to inform my siblings about the investigation because they would also be a part of it.

I headed out into the night; the snow had stopped, and there was calmness in the air. I stood there a few minutes and just breathed, my breath fogging in the cold air. The peace of the outside was the peace that I felt inside. It was as if I had become one with the world around me. I drove home slowly, only because I did not want this feeling to leave me. I entered my house and knew what I had done was right. I would sleep deeper than I had ever done before.

I went to work the next day, and even that was calm. The office drama had no effect on me that day. Was this what people called the calm before the storm? I would embrace every minute of it in hopes that the feeling would never leave me.

REBUILDING MY WORLD

tried to focus on myself. I was able to work out again, and getting back to the gym gave me a sense of connection with my body. I did notice that when I was physical, I felt more grounded. My body was getting lean and healthy. As I achieved a lean body, my coworkers were quick to criticize the change that I was able to attain. I wondered why being healthy was such a threat to those around me. Was it their lack of accomplishment or focus that set them into sabotage?

Why was it that women couldn't support one another in their successes? Had the battle for success become so tainted? My body no longer needed the protection of the excess weight. I finally felt safe, at least from my past. My coworkers, not so much! I never understood jealously. I watched as they went into overdrive to sabotage my weight loss.

I was at home and got a call: it was from my younger brother. He was angry and was yelling at me. "How could you do this?" I asked him what he was talking about, and he tells me the police had just left his house after questioning them about dad. My younger sister was living with my brother and his wife at the time. He went on in his accusations as to how I destroyed the family name. I was shocked at what I heard him say and reminded him that I had the same name. He was completely oblivious as to the effects the abuse had on me. As far as he was concerned, it was not what our dad had done, but that fact that I told—that was the destruction of the family name. His concern about what people thought was interesting; he was more concerned with people knowing the truth than he that his father was a sex offender. I asked to talk to my sister, and he told me she did not want to talk to me. I hung up and did not call again.

It would be months before I got another call, this time from my sister-in-law. She told me that my brother was not comfortable with me coming to their house. I barked at her, "So is he comfortable having a child molester come to his house? Don't worry I won't be a part of the family. After all, I never was." She wanted me to come see their son and be a part of his life. I explained to her that I was not going to sneak around and play this bullshit game. If I couldn't walk in the front door, I certainly was not going in the back door. I hung up and that would be the last that I would speak to them.

THE NEXT STEP

$\overline{}\text{\textbf{\textcolor{black}{∞}}}\overline{}$

I did not want to be in this life anymore. I remembered when I was on the other side, and the counsel said that I would move south and meet a group of people who would help me grow spiritually. I wondered what that would feel like. Would these people be able to sense energy the way I did? Did they get messages from spirit? I wanted to fit in—I did not want to be around people who didn't get it!

I returned from my workout, and there was a meeting in the boardroom. Everyone was there except me. I was at my desk when the meeting ended. I questioned the boss about the meeting. Was I the only one who was not invited to the meeting? She was sheepish when I asked her.

The meeting was to notify everyone that there was a special project starting up in one of the southern papers. The project needed people who wanted to transfer. There had been a recent takeover of the newspaper, and they were centralizing the accounting groups across Canada. Once the project was complete, they would be laying off the divisions. I asked her why I was not invited to the meeting, and her response was that I had been through so much that year. "I didn't think it would be something you would be interested in." Shouldn't that be something I decide? I expressed my interested and wanted to know what I had to do to apply. She was disappointed that I was interested. She told me that the resumes were to be submitted by noon the following day. I told her I would have it to her in the morning.

I gave her my resume the next day, and she repeated her concerns. I did not want to be in this city anymore. Why was this so confusing for her? It would be weeks before the interview. I did not make it this round, but they want to re-interview me for phase two of the project, which pacified me.

Back at the office, I was disappointed that I did not get the job. I settled back into the daily routine. The others commented how stupid I would be to go to the project. "Just wait for the severance package and then move," they said. In the meeting, they were told that they would get a number of weeks' pay per year that they work with the company. The others were calculating their future payout, and many of them spent it prematurely. I knew intuitively that it would not turn out the way they thought. I watched as they led themselves into a false sense of security. I thought back to my former male friend's comment: "You always do what you say." I remember my response well. "If you do not follow through, it is only lip service." I had flashes of all the promises made but never fulfilled from my childhood. I never understood why people would say something and never follow through. My trust issues surface when this happened.

THE WHEELS OF JUSTICE
MOVE SLOW

*T*hings snapped back to reality when I get a call from the investigating officer. The questions would go back and forth for eight months. The next call would be from the crown prosecutor. He called me at work with an offer of fifty thousand dollars to shut my mouth and make this go away. I was furious and asked him if he truly thought this was about money. "If you do, you need to find another job! This has nothing to do with money!" I told him. My dad would plead guilty, and he would go to jail. I slammed the phone down and left the office to go for a walk, trying to wrap my head around all that was happening. Was this justice—men protecting men? I wondered how lawyers slept at night.

My high school reunion was that year, and I had planned to attend; it would be the first time I was in my hometown in some time, and my emotions were high. I arrived at the Friday night registration. My classmates were excited that I was there. I asked why they were surprised, because I had registered months ago. They shared what my older brother had been telling them: if I showed up in town, he would kill me. Once an abuser always an abuser, I wondered if he realized what people thought of him when he said this kind of stuff. When I pressed charges with my dad, I also named my brother, but the court system looked at it as experimentation, and the crown would not pursue it. So when someone forced himself on me and threatened me repeatedly, was that experimentation? Was he experimenting on how to become an abuser? Perhaps if the courts looked at this for what it was, it would stop future abuse from happening. Laws were written by men and for men, I concluded. He did not like feeling powerless, and that would get under his skin. He would continue to make threats and get in my face any chance he could. *I am not your victim anymore, so go ahead and push me, see where that gets you,* I thought to myself.

As the stress increased with the court case, my body was taking it on, and I was struggling to keep things in balance. I would work out more, hoping that'd help. I would try to maintain a normal life: working, sports, and dating. The man I was dating at the time knew nothing about what was going on. I couldn't bring him into this part of my life. He knew something was happening but never questioned me. I realized the duality that I had lived: the truth of what had happened, and the world I created to survive.

Weeks would turn into months before I would hear more. The investigating officer would call with updates. It was late October, and he explained to me that he wanted to bring charges against my mom. I stated my issue was with my dad; if they wanted to press charges against her, they would have to call me as a witness—it would not be me instigating the charges. In my mind, she was a guilty as he was, but I figured her fear of God's judgment was enough to cause her stress. I would never understand how a woman could lay with a man who had done this to her children. What did she need to tell herself so that she could live? Just pretend that this was all right, so that her world would not shatter?

The police did not bring up the subject of charges with her again.

About a week later, I received a letter from my mom. She told me what a horrible daughter I was, and she regretted having me. I was nothing but an angry, miserable person. How could I do this to her husband, who was the most loving and supportive man?

Excuse me, most loving and supportive man? Had she forgotten the beatings she'd received over the years? I realized that my mother was mentally and emotionally sick, if she could honestly believe what she had written. Her rants fill a two-page letter, and it was appalling. The words cut through me like a knife. I realized that day how incredibly messed up she was. In my option, she needed therapy, and a lot of it. Would she ever be strong enough to heal? I wondered, but in truth I knew the answer.

The investigating officer called me. It was now Halloween, and in between the kids trick-or-treating, we managed to have a good call. I shared with him about the letter, and he wanted a copy of it for the file.

It would be a month before I heard from anyone on the preliminary court case. We were almost ten months from the date I had made the original police report, and I would be going to preliminary. I had to go to north to meet with the crown prosecutor. I got to the room, and he was a chubby man and was wheezing as if he was a hundred years old, but he was only in his late thirties or early forties. His comments were inappropriate, and he made my skin crawl. He asked if he could smoke in the room, and I told him no because I was asthmatic. He was angry with my response, got up, and walked out of the room. He was gone for about fifteen minutes and returned smelling of smoke. He flipped through the pages of the case and then proclaimed, "Well, at least there are no animals involved in this case!"

I was shocked, to say the least. I asked him, "Do you think that was remotely funny? If you do, you're a sick bastard."

I realized that having to deal with these types of cases may taint you, but who says shit like that? The fact that I had to deal with him disgusted me; he was just one more man that had no boundaries.

I was staying with my former boss and friend while I was there. She had invited some of the guys that used to stay at the hotel at which we worked. I had not dated these guys but knew that they had my back. A few came and gave me hugs, and others commented that now they understood why I did not date them. It was good to be supported, but at the same time if felt awkward to have my secret out. I never really knew how people would handle the truth. Not everyone was happy about the disclosure. It was interesting how some people would rather believe the lie than the truth. They didn't want to believe my dad could do this to his daughters. Well, he did, so get over it. My dad was the good old guy, buying drinks at the bar for my friends. They did not see the violent man I had to witness. I wondered why they did not question the fact that I never wanted to be around him.

As I walked into the courthouse, my sister was there, and she was angry. She was registering as a witness, and I was standing across the foyer from her. Her then husband was agitated and was complaining he was hungry. "How long is this going to take?" I heard him ask. My older sister would be called to testify as a hostile witness, which meant she does not want to be there to tell the truth, or at least not willingly. Was all this threatening her financial security? I couldn't imagine her not wanting to tell the truth. That would never be something I would be able to wrap my head around. Why would she not want this finished? Did she get the same fifty-thousand-dollar offer and take it?

I was escorted into the witness room and sat there with my friend and the victims advocate. I knew this was the right thing to do, and it would bring closure, if there was such a thing. As I sat there, the door opened; it was the investigating officer. I had never met him face to face. He walked up to introduce himself, but he went to my friend. I corrected him and stated that I was the one he was expecting. Perhaps he was looking for someone a little less confident. I did not look like most people going through this; I had healed and was emotionally in a good place. I took that as a compliment. All those years of work on me had paid off.

I was called to the witness stand first. My body was shaking, but I tried to hold my composure. As I was sworn in, I couldn't believe how nervous I was. I was there to tell the truth, and I was still nervous. Perhaps too many television shows placed false expectations in my head. The crown prosecutor was the first to approach, and told me how I needed to answer questions, and to ask him if I did not understand the question. Just by looking at him, I felt the disdain for him I had when he was making the insensitive remarks in the first interview.

As the questions came, I was able to give dates, events, and places. I had all the details of the abuse as they flashed through my head. Some of his questions were twisted; if I said to him, "If you mean ..." and redefined the question, he got hostile with me. I thought to myself that he was suppose to be defending the victim here, and then I saw that something else was going on. There were simple questions like "Where did you sleep in the house?" as well as ages to events and when things stopped or changed. My answers came quick and to the point; my recall was matter-of-fact. The questions came faster and with a little more attitude.

It was now the defense lawyer's turn, and he was actually a former neighbor from when we lived on the farm. I knew things about him that I was sure he wished I did not. I answered his questions, and he spouted on about how my dad was a pillar of the community. Pillar of the community, really? Was this what a pillar of the community looked like? I thought, *Run, because this town was about to crumble.* I heard him say how my dad would give the shirt off his back. I could no longer hold my tongue and said, "Well, perhaps if he had stopped at his shirt, we would not be in this court room today!" There was a snicker in the courtroom, and the defense lawyer was pissed off. Truthfully, I did not care. I thought we were here to tell the truth, but so far they were not even close. He was shooting questions at me, and when I answered in the affirmative, I used the word "correct." He'd blurt out "Correct?"

"Yes, correct!" I responded.

As he questioned me, he stood between his client and me. I acknowledged the defense lawyer's obvious move to protect his client. I turned and look at the crown prosecutor to give my answers and would not look at the defense lawyer, who got frustrated and moved to the crown's side of the courtroom. My tactic worked; he was no longer in front of my dad. I quickly looked at my dad and made eye contact with him. The man who once scared me was not looking so tough now. The lawyer realized what I had done, and he quickly moved back to his side of the courtroom to protect his client. I made eye contact with the lawyer and gave him a little smile. If they thought they were going to bully me, they were in for an experience like none before.

He asked, "When did the abuse stop?"

I stated, "At the age of fifteen—at least, the sexual aspect." He asked why, and I said, "Because we moved to a house that had doors. I blocked my abusers out with the door when I went to bed."

That confused him. He asked, "You did not have doors in the other house?" I said no. He had to wrap his head around this, and he realized then that the abuse could not have gone unnoticed if it was not behind closed doors.

The questioning continued for some time, and then he asked me if I had ever had a baby. My body collapsed, and I grasped the sides of the witness box to catch myself. I was unsure of what just happened. The judge asked if I need a break, but I declined. He asked again, and I told him no.

The questions kept coming. I was asked, "Why take this action now?" I told the court that the family needed to heal. I did not want the abuse to continue in this family. I was not going after money, despite what my family had told people in town. I did not want my nieces or nephews to be abused—end of story. I could not live with myself knowing that I did not do what I could to protect them. I may never see any of them, but at the end of the day, they may ask why I was not a part of the family, and someone maybe would be brave enough to tell them that I went to court to protect them from being abused. I knew their parents would not be strong enough to do what they needed: give them a voice and keep them from abuse. I would not hold any guilt should the abuse continue.

The questions ended, and then I was allowed to sit down. I sat with the investigating officer. I tried to work through my reaction to the question of having a baby. What had I forgotten that triggered that response? Nothing would come to me, but I knew that I would need to get the answer to the question.

It was then my sister's turn. She stood in the witness box and was sworn in. At the first question she was asked, I could see her become rigid. The crown prosecutor asked, "Did your father sexually abuse you?" Her anger was obvious, but she replied yes. That was all that we really needed from her. She crossed her arms crossed as she stood there, reluctant to say anything else.

The crown continued to ask questions, and with each question she looked at our dad. He lowered his head, and she would reply. If he turned his head side to side, she would not answer the question, stating she did not remember. I noticed that he was coaching her from his seat and pointed it out to the investigating officer. He stood up and made it known to the judge. The judge acknowledged it and handled the situation. With her answers to questions, it became obvious that she had shut down and was not sure what to do or say any longer. She was asked where she slept in the house, and she couldn't answer the question. The obvious shock of the prosecutor was noted. He knew he would not get anything more from her, and he released her from questioning. She returned to sit with her family.

My disappointment in my sister was beyond words. I knew that our relationship would end that day. She showed me her true self. If she could not give herself a voice, how would she ever be able to be a voice for her future children? After all, that was what this was about, right?

Our abuse happened, and nothing in this courtroom would alter the fact. No amount of denial would change it. It was, however, a catalyst for change—time for the truth, and perhaps healing could end a cycle of abuse. One couldn't heal what one could not admit. The lies were hurting me, and I needed to tell the truth. I knew that keeping the lies inside of me was killing my body. My body was getting sick, breaking down, and becoming numb. I did not want to live my life that way anymore. That was what this was about for me. Forced to have an adult experience the little girl within needed to heal. The strength on the outside was what people saw, but I was shattered on the inside: abandoned by my family, spending years trying to find a safe place to exist. One would hope that within a family, there would be some sort of support, but I guessed that when there was dysfunction, it was easier to stay in denial. The support I did have somewhat came from cousins and a few aunts and uncles, and strangers that I now called my family.

Preliminary proceedings would end, and it would be almost eight months before I heard anything more.

MORE FAMILY DRAMA

One of my aunts passed away that year. I would travel south to her funeral and knew that the rest of the family would be there. I was not sure who knew about the pending court case, and I was cautious about going. I greeted my cousins and tried to console them. I said my good-byes and said a prayer for my aunt. I had a different belief about death because I had experienced at least some of what went on behind the veil. I thought of the secrets within the family; we did not talk about the obvious. What would it take to heal the pain? It was such a waste of time. I went back out to the foyer, where I joined thirty people who had gathered, mostly family. I was there with my aunt and uncle, and my cousins from up north; they knew about the court case and brought me comfort. I walked by my oldest brother, and he was making snide comments about my aunt who had passed. I shook my head in disbelief at his incredible lack of compassion. *If you have such negative things to say, why are you here?* I joined my cousins again, and as we chatted, my oldest brother came up to me and got in my face.

He was still trying to intimidate me, and he pointed to the viewing room of the chapel. "That is where you belong, in there!"

"Are you going to put me there?" We were nose to nose in conflict. "Go ahead, big man, and perhaps I will get you a father-son cell. How does that sound? I am not scared of you anymore, and if you think you are going to push me around, you are sadly mistaken."

My Aunt Lil realized what was going on and stepped in. He was furious and stormed out of the funeral home. As he left, the force he used almost took the door off its support.

The funeral service was simple but nice. I did what I could to support my cousins, and I tried not to let what was happening in my own family distract from their time.

We headed out to the farm of my uncle's sister. I remembered the summers spent there; those were good memories. I had good visits with Auntie Ethel. The children seemed to be drawn to me, and they came and went as they needed things: food, clothes, and hugs. They were unaware of what was going on; they only knew that their grandma had gone to heaven. I thought of their innocence and thought back to what was happening to me at their ages. My heart saddened as I realized what the abuse has taken from me. My Aunt Ethel told me she was surprised that I had not gotten married and had children; she said I would be a natural. She was unaware of the abuse, or at least we did not talk about it.

I left the next day. My uncle from the coast caught a ride to the airport in the next city. We had always had a good relationship, and I knew that losing his sister was hard for him. We talked about things, and he shared with me a way I had never experienced with him before. I was happy to be there for him. I always wished he were my dad. It was late when I dropped him off at the airport and continued home.

MORE MEMORIES COME

———— ⌘ ————

I had more time to process, and the healing would continue. I processed a lot in my sleep. It was a Saturday morning, and I got up exhausted. I stood in the shower, and the memory of my father taking my younger siblings into the car flew into my awareness. That day was the day I felt as if I had been broken, and I realized I could not protect my siblings. It all hit me like a wave. I heard myself start to wail from my soul; the pain of emotion that left my body was indescribable. I was having an out-of-body experience. I could not stop the process, and neither did I want to. It was as if I could feel the grief leave my body. All that emotion that I had tucked away behind the wall of toughness poured out of me uncontrollably. I was unsure how much time had lapsed, but I was brought back into a conscious state with ice-cold water from the shower hitting my body.

My relationship with food shifted that day. That was the day that I stopped binge eating. It was as if that memory was what I had been stuffing, trying to purge from my body the whole time. That memory was buried so deep, and now that I had cleared all the other stuff, that sat on top of it as if I had pulled the root of a bad weed. I would start to build a healthy relationship with food. It was now my source of survival and not a punishment to my body. I would feed and train my body, taking pride and feeling connected at a different level now. I would dress it and feel good about how it looked; no more negative images. I remembered the first time after that day that I had sex, and I actually enjoyed it. I realized that my body really was mine for the first time, and it was an incredibly powerful experience.

The year continued to unfold, and living the truth presented its own challenges. I realized that most people did not hold themselves responsible for what they created or allowed in their lives. They played the blame game of why their life was less than what they wanted. I knew that it took work to stay accountable. My weight was my Achilles heel when I fell from my spiritual truth.

It would be a year of passing of friends and more family—an emotional roller coaster on top of everything else that was going on.

COURT CONTINUES

I hoped for some time to breathe and relax before anything else happened. It was late one night when someone came to my door. It was a process server with a notice to appear. I would not sleep much that night. I would have to disclose what was going on to my boss; I had worked with them for nine years, and no one that I worked with had any idea about what I had gone through except my first boss, and even then, she only know about the abuse—she did not know I had pressed charges. The stress of having to tell my boss was almost debilitating. She was shocked but told me she would make the time off happen. I could feel my body deflate in the support.

As the time came closer, I returned to my desk, and smack in the center of my desk was a photocopy of the company's absent policy. According to this, I would not be given the time off without using my holiday hours. I was furious, first because she had left this in the middle of my desk for whoever to see, and second because I was days from leaving and had to deal with this. I walked into her office, closed the door behind me, and expressed how pissed off I was with what she'd done. She was taken aback with how angry I was, and she sat there and listened. I explained if she was not prepared to deal with this, I would.

I went home that night and wrote a letter. I addressed it to her, her boss, and his boss. I did not care how far up the chain I had to rattle—I would get that time off. I walk into her office, letter in hand. I closed the door again and hand her the letter with a few choice words added. I stated I wanted this dealt with by end of day. I turned to leave, and I could see heads peering over cubicles to see what was happening. The office manager asked me to close the door on the way out. I could feel the tension in the office; people were walking past my cubicle to see if I would fill them in. I demanded that they stayed out of it. They conjured up a story to satisfy their own needs and thought I had quit.

I would later see my boss leave her office, go into the accounting manager's office, and close the door. The tongues would start wagging even more. In turn, he would leave his office with letter in hand and headed upstairs to the HR department. The office became abuzz with speculation. It would be moments, and then he headed back to his office, then to my office manager's office, the door closed again. Soon my boss called me on the phone to come see her. As I entered her office and closed the door, she sheepishly said, "You take whatever time you need. Just let me know when you will be back."

I thought to myself, *now, was that so hard?*

As the court date got closer, I was retaining the stress in my back, and I could barely walk upright. I went to my doctor and asked for a note for some stress leave, and he asked why I needed the time off. I explained I was pressing criminal charges against someone who had sexually abused me. He was shocked and said to me that if it was causing so much stress why not just stop the process? I was furious with him. I asked him, "Would you tell your daughter that, if she was abuse?" I saw the shock of the statement, and he knew he would not. I found it interesting how things changed when people had to take the situation home; their truth changed. I asked for something for the pain; I would deal with the rest on my own, like I had in the past. The pain medication was strong and gave me relief, but I hated taking drugs. Perhaps it was a childhood trigger from the addiction issue with my dad, and all the drugs from my surgeries.

There was a huge storm the day I flew north for the court case. The theme of storms at each major point of my journey became obvious that day.

I greeted a friend at the airport, and then my exhaustion hits me. I settled in and tried to get some sleep—something that I had been lacking for months. We headed to the courthouse the next morning. As we entered the parking lot, I saw my dad, brother, and mother were sitting in their vehicle. I headed in, nervous after my brother's confrontation. I expected the worst from him, and he usually delivered. I went to register as a witness, and the clerk stated, "We do not need you!"

I thought to myself, *I was the only non-hostile witness. What is going on?* I went over to my friend in confusion and told her that I was not needed. "What does that mean?" She walked over with me, and I asked what had happened.

The clerk informed us that my dad had pleaded guilty to the charges. "Did you not get a call to tell you that they did not need you?"

All I could think was that they had called the office, but someone had intercepted the call. I was sick to my stomach. I heard myself snidely respond, "Obviously not! So what happens now?" I was told I could go sit in the witness room, and she would have someone come see me.

I was barely settled when the door swung open, and the investigating officer came in looking as confused as I felt. He asked, "Did you drive up in the storm?" I stated I had flown, and he explained he had just driven up from the city, and the roads were so bad he almost did not make it. I explained what the clerk had said to me, and he was even more confused. He left the room to figure out what was happening. When he re-entered, he informed us that my dad was in court right now, and he asked whether I wanted to go in.

Now with my friend, the victims advocate, and the officer, we headed into the courtroom. We sat at the back of the room, and the judge was addressing my dad. "Do you understand what you are pleading guilty to?" My father nodded his head yes. The judge responded, "You are pleading guilty to serious sexual assault against your daughters!" There was a scream in the room—it was my mom, and I thought in that moment that her veil of denial had been ripped from her. I sat there in disbelief. Did she seriously just get it? My attention turned back to the judge; he was addressing the two lawyers in the courtroom. "Just to let you both know that I make the rules in this courtroom not you two. You have pleaded guilty, and you will go to jail for this!" My father's reality was obviously shaken with what was happening, and he realized that he no longer had any power here. My mind reeled to make sense of what was going on. What deal had the lawyers made for the guilty plea?

In that moment the investigating officer out of uniform jumped up from the seat beside me. He addressed the court identifying himself as a friend of the court, and asked if he could escort the defendant to jail. He was granted permission to do so. The judge remarked that if the family wanted to go see him before he was taken to jail they may proceed to the holding room. I was still confused as to everything that had just happened. The victims advocate was talking to me as if to distract me while the courtroom cleared. I could feel the negativity coming from the front of the courtroom where my brother and mother were sitting. As I turned, they were coming up the aisle. My older brother pointed at me and used has hand to make a gun gesture, like he was going to shoot me. The advocate was shocked at what she saw him do, however I expected nothing less from him. He was his father's son.

We returned to the witness room and tried to put everything together. Everything happened so fast that I was numb from the experience. Two years of my life were wrapped up in less than fifteen minutes. The officer returned to join us and informed me that the lawyers cut a deal: if he pled guilty, they would let him walk. I was shocked. This was how victims of sexual assault were treated? That was justice? The officer said, "If you were looking for justice in the justice system, you were looking in the wrong place!"

I was furious with the crown prosecutor. In my anger, I said, "I guess I should have killed him when I had the chance." I realized that if the judge had not had any integrity, my dad would have walked out of the court room a free man. I asked, "Now what?" The investigating officer explained that the sentencing would happen in a week or so.

Time to Heal Fully

─────⊗⊗⊗─────

I would return to my life, put the pieces in place, and move forward. What other choice did I have? I was not sure what I thought I would feel upon completion, but I knew what I did feel was nothing like what I had hoped. I would spend some time with my uncle from the coast to put things together. We were fishing, and I asked him what had happened in the family when they grew up. The energy shifted quickly, and he told me that he would not discuss that with me. I thought to myself that this was why the cycle continued: because no one wanted to talk about it. I could see the effects of whatever hidden secrets that away at our family. I reminded my uncle of the time I hid in his trailer, in the hopes that he would take me away from what I had been experiencing. I could see in his eyes the hurt that he felt when he realized what that was about for me. That was not my intention, but it put things in prospective for him. There was really no amount of secrets that could change that. Nothing more was spoken about the court case. I saw how much he and I were alike, we went inward to process things.

The sentencing would take place, and I knew nothing about the outcome, only that he would go to jail; I was not sure where or for how long.

The court process left me feeling used. The system was not there for the victim that was for sure. Closure was not a word that could be used to describe this process. Later, my cousin informed me that the sentencing would amount to six years. Six years, for sixteen years of sexual abuse toward multiple victims? It hardly seemed fair, but if that was justice, so be it. I guessed the real justice would take place when he passed over, and I found solace with that.

I had now dealt with the outstanding spiritual contract of accountability that I had been sent back to do. Was moving the next step? Was that when all the past was suppose to melt away, and the good stuff would appear? I would now focus on the rest of what I was shown when I had died on the operating table.

Doors of Opportunity Open

⸺

The centralization project was at its next step. I held hopes of transferring and getting on with the next part of my life. That next chapter needed to happen, and I wanted out of this city. I needed to turn the page, because there was nothing left here for me any longer.

I would have to reorganize the past to move onto the future. So what did I know for sure? I knew that I would never be a part of my birth family, at least not the immediate family. I knew that I could not change the past but would have to deal with the impact of the experience. I knew that dying three times and going to the other side made me different, and I could not change that. I knew that I had abilities that people did not understand. I knew that I could communicate with the other side, and that took people into fear. I knew that people did not have to suffer from this; their bodies could heal. I knew that I could not change anybody except myself. I knew that I would not be a victim to my experience. I knew that I could only be powerless if I gave my power away. I knew that my life was only as limited as I believed it to be. I knew that if I did not like what was happening to me I was the only one that could make the decision to make things different. More importantly I knew that I was in the driver's seat, if I wanted this experience to be different that I needed to make a different choice.

My first focus was my body. With all the surgeries and stress, it had become sick and out of balance. I would start working out to lose the weight that I had gained. My skin was yellow from all the drugs administered during surgeries, and my doctor stated he could not do anything to fix it.

ALTERNATIVE WELLNESS

I sought a way to heal my body and get all the drugs and toxins out of my body. Eight surgeries in nine years, plus poison and drugs pumped through me, was too much for my body to be able to clear. My internal body was fighting to rebalance, and it became exhausting for my physical body. Upon talking to a coworker, she mentioned reflexology. I ask her what it was and how it worked. She explained that the practitioner rubbed one's feet and the body detoxified. I thought to myself, *Right, you rub my feet, and I will heal. Sure!*

A few days passed, and my mind went back to the conversation about reflexology. I heard my guidance to pursue this way of healing. I grabbed the phone book and flipped it open to look up reflexology. I was not even sure how this would be listed, other than the obvious. I found one person listed, and she lived within ten minute of where I lived. I took that as a definite sign, and there was little room for making excuses. I made the call and was unsure of what to ask her. I booked a session and headed out to my appointment a few days later.

I had my introduction to the practice of reflexology, a holistic technique to detoxify the body. This would be a huge opening to my spiritual growth. An older woman greeted me; she was tall and lean and held a presence that intrigued me. She explained, "The feet are the road map to the body. There are twenty-one points that link to the internal organs. By triggering the points on the feet, it will detoxify the body and bring it back into balance."

I laid there as a skeptic but allowed the process to prove itself to me. As she triggered the points, the pain was obvious. I was sure she was from the school of "No pain, no gain." I cringed as she continued, but I committed to the experience. I reassured myself this was nothing compared to what I had been through already. She explained to me which organs were out of balance, which were most of them. With what I had studied about the body, it all made sense. The session ended, and I wondered if I was going to be able to walk home, or would I be crawling? She stated that I would need to get three sessions a week for three weeks.

It would only take me two sessions to see the process work for my body. I was unsure of the whole concept at the time; all I knew was that it was working. The color of my skin would return to normal, the whites of my eyes would go from cloudy to clear, and I could feel the sluggishness of my body disappear. I would go back to my doctor, and his first comment was, "What are you doing?" The difference was substantial; by then I had completed two weeks of treatments, and I explained to him I was doing reflexology. He said he did not want to know, but I should keep doing it. His response surprised me. Why would a doctor not want to know about something that was healing and could make a person well? My naiveté of the conflict that sat between holistic therapists and the medical community was obvious.

As my body healed, at all levels people began to take notice. The weight melted away and my health returned. However, I could sense something was missing. I realized that with all that had happened over the past years, I had not let anyone get close to me, and perhaps not wanting anyone in this mess I called my life. I had not been touched in a very, very long time. I would be working out at the gym, and the massage therapist there would come and chat, trying to drum up business. I had never had a massage and was not sure how that would be for me. He would continue to solicit his services. It would be three months, and I was starting to soften to the idea. I had another conversation with him, and I knew that given what I had been through, having someone touch me may not be a good thing.

PHYSICAL TOUCH FOR HEALING

I knew in the past that being intimate would send me reeling in flashbacks of my abuse. I informed the massage therapist I would try it, but if I did not like it, he must stop. He agreed without knowing my history. The massage was booked, and I could almost feel my body twist with the potential outcome. The appointment arrived, and I was nearly panicking but showed up. The massage started, and my body and mind were flashing and twitching with all of my past. I heard my guidance: "Just breathe." I was confused by the message, but I felt myself taking deep breaths and releasing. It was as if the breath took away the memories from my body. I was wrapped up in what my body was doing. I would get through the session. I felt like I had run a marathon and lost forty pounds all at the same time. I would continue with massage as a tool to unravel the past from my body. I had dealt with the abuse with head therapy. What was this? This took healing to a whole new level for me. If my conscious mind had let go of the memories, why did the process of touching the body release so much? The flashbacks came each time he put his hands on me, but I did not tell him what I was experiencing. I trusted my intuition. I listened to the guidance to take me to the other side of this experience.

Each time I had a massage, the flashbacks were lessened. I felt my body dance within the freedom as the memories left my cells.

All this intrigued me, and I sought out what this was truly about. My belief was that memories were stored in the brain, so why did physical touch release past trauma? I sought to understand, and with that process, self-discovery would begin.

I would hold this gift of healing and honor it for what it was. The human body had intrigued me since the day that I had fallen off the roof and left my body. I had read many books, but nothing had told me about the concepts of reflexology or how emotions were stored in the body. I would make it my mission to find the answers to how the body operated at this level.

DIVINE TIMING

⸺✦⸺

$\mathscr{I}$ became aware that the universe had a plan, and we needed to listen and follow, not demand it in our time. The universe saw the whole picture, and we were merely a fraction of the experience; every one of the players needed to be in place before divine timing took place. Patience was a virtue, just as it was stated.

My daily life was in need of change. I recalled the message about moving, given to me when I went to the council. I wanted everything to happen now; I was ready.

A few days later there was an announcement that my workplace was recruiting people for the next stage of the centralization project. I applied again. This time the interview went well, and I was excited. It was down to the day of selection, and I received a call from the manager in the project. She told me that they wanted me, but my boss would not allow me to transfer. I was shocked at the disclosure. I asked her to give me twenty minutes and then call my boss.

I headed to my managers office and closed the door. I could see the blood drain from her face. I asked her why she was blocking me. I explained what the project manager had told me, and I was less than pleased. She was taken aback that I knew what she has done. She explained, "You have been through so much over the past year. Perhaps you should wait until the project is more stable."

I said I wanted to go onto the project now, and she needed to stop blocking me from this. I knew she was not about to do battle with me. I forced her hand, and she folded.

The phone rang a bit later, and it was the project manager. I returned to my desk, and within minutes I got a call from what would be my new boss. She asked what I had done to change things, and I told her that I wanted this move, and more important, I needed it.

Word would spread through the office like wildfire. On and on the questions came as their fears and limitations surfaced. As the centralization project was executed, the people in the divisions would be packaged out. For many this was the only job they knew, and the idea of someone choosing to leave was beyond their grasp. People were spending their severance pay before they saw it. They were planning to pay off mortgages, planning holidays, and buying things. I knew intuitively that none of them would see a financial package. As my transfer finalized, people in the office were less than excited to celebrate with me. I went through the office farewell and held in my excitement for ending this part of the journey; there was more resentment than celebration here. I relished in the knowing what would truly come as the project moved forward. I knew the project would not last more than one or two years. When the project ended, those of us that took the opportunity would be packaged out, leaving those in the divisions less than impressed. I got what I wanted. They moved me and set me up in an apartment until my home sold.

Out on Good Behavior

———— ∞∞∞ ————

*M*y joy was short lived. I received a call from a friend who lived up north. After a quick hello, she said, "Guess who I saw today?" My mind reeled as to whom she could have seen. She blurted out, "I saw your dad!"

My whole body froze.

She was having lunch, and my dad and brother had walked into the restaurant. I was close to being physically sick. My feelings of safety disappear, and panic replaced it. I thought to myself, *is he going to show up and kill me, like he has threatened over the years?* I thanked her for telling me, but I need to get off the phone to regroup my emotions.

I was barely off the phone when it rang again. Every muscle in my body tightened, and I hesitated answering. I told myself I had come too far in this to retreat. I picked up the phone, and it was my cousin. I knew why she was calling. I heard it in her voice: she had seen him, too. She was shocked that I knew. She worked in the motor vehicle registration office, and my dad needed to renew his driver's license. She told me how she tried to avoid him. She left the floor and went into the back, just to get away. She told me she saw that he had an ankle bracelet, used for tracking him. I was grateful that my friends and extended family had my back; that brought me solace. My body rushed with emotion as I excused myself from the call.

I headed to the bathroom, threw up with another rush of emotions, curled up on my bed, and sobbed myself to sleep. Sixteen months for sixteen years of abuse—so this was what justice looked like. I wondered how long it would be before he chose his next victim.

The Spiritual Journey Begins

———∞∞∞———

The move south was complete, and I started to create my new life, the theme of my life in this city had moved me from victim to survivor, but I wanted more. I wanted all the good stuff that seemed to come to others effortlessly. I wanted to thrive and experience living joyfully. I wanted to create a state of peace, leaving all this healing work behind.

The next year and a half would have lots to offer. I got involved with sports, and I would meet more people in thirty days than I did in nine years up north. I realized that with everything I had been through, I had not been living; previously I was so focused on healing. The people were different here, in a good way. I loved this experience.

At work, I would learn the computer system for the new accounting package. There was something about computers and my brain; they seemed to process information the same. When most people feared technology, I celebrated it. There would be a corporate takeover, and the new owners would scrap the centralization project. Those of us who took on the project would receive packages, and the people in the divisions would keep their jobs, just as I had gotten intuitively. The project team would be let go in stages, and as the team shrank, so did the enthusiasm. The final stages would be to hand back the workload to the divisions. My former coworkers got the news that they would keep their jobs and not get a package. Perhaps their disappointment was fueled by how poorly they had treated me.

I would focus on the next step. My home had not sold, and truthfully, there was no way that I would move back. I started to plan my next move. I found out what companies purchased the accounting package that I had trained on, and I was told they were mostly oil and gas companies. I would send out six resumes targeting the companies on the list. I had five interviews in four days, and by the end of the following week, I would receive four job offers. My house would sell, and I would get my severance package from the newspaper. I accepted one of the offers.

I knew intuitively that I was not supposed to be in this industry, but I negotiated with my guidance that I would only work for a year or so until I could make the money I needed to take holistic classes; I was told that I was meant to do that. The remembrance of my time spent on the other side came flooding back, and there were specific things I needed to do to step into helping others.

One year would turn into five. I would purchase a house and a new vehicle, and I started to travel. There was always a need for more money; I worked hard, and the industry had a great rewarded program, but I struggled spiritually with my choice to stay.

LET THE TRAINING BEGIN

⸻❀⸻

*R*eflexology was the first holistic training I did, and with my certification in hand, I started working with clients. When I worked on my clients, I would pick up on their emotions. This was not new to me; I did this as a child, though perhaps everything else I had gone through had distracted me somewhat. I began talking to my clients about what I found. As the years passed, I would become aware that anyone holding anger struck it in their liver, rage in their pancreas, and old trauma in their colon. Sexual trauma was held in the reproductive organs. As I triggered the twenty-one points representing the internal organ systems, the pattern of emotions stuck within the organ would prove to be similar in all the clients. The health conditions of the people would support the negative emotion, shifting the body into dis-ease.

I knew the physiology of the organ system, and it made sense that the people were holding those specific emotions in those organs. To give an example, people holding onto their emotional crap would have trouble with their large intestine; their physical crap would create constipation issues or other colon-related illnesses. Other clients were unable to digest their emotions, and these people would have digestive problems. Each client brought a new experience and more information.

I would reflect back to my own surgeries and allergies. Everything became very clear. I was excited to share this information with my clients and help them to understand their bodies. Most people were surprised when I would make the connection with their emotions to their physically body. What came out of that was, "Deal with your emotions, and your body will heal. I again reflected on my fifty-two allergies that I had in my mid-twenties. As I worked through my abuse and the emotions that went with it, my allergies all but disappeared, going from fifty-two severe reactions to three sensitivities. With that came the remembrance of my allergist's reaction. He asked what I did, and as I went to tell him, he held his hand up to me and said, "I do not want to know—you would put me out of business." The picture was very clear to me: the health care system was a business; it was not a method of healing in my mind. God forbid people should get well.

I sought out another massage therapist. I could feel my body getting out of balance with all the changes in my life: work, school, working with clients, sports, and renovating my house. I would find someone, and as we were chatting during the massage, he mentioned he went to a meditation group. Meditation interested me. He asked me if I wanted to go to the next group; it did not take much for me to agree. I asked him where the meditation group was held, and he gave me the directions. I chuckled because it was only minutes from my house. Again, I knew that meditation was supposed to be a part of the experience.

The meditation group was interesting. I realized that the dreams that I had over the years would be images that came back to me through meditation. It was as if I traveled in my sleep to this time, people, places, and experiences that were familiar. My dreams were full color, had audio, and were very detailed. The more I meditated, the more vivid my dreams became, as if I had unleashed a pathway to knowing. I would see what was to come in my life, and also for others.

One dream stood out. I was on a group trip. Upon arriving at our destination, we put our luggage into our rooms, and then we went across the stone sidewalk to an area that had cinder block walls. As we entered the area, there was an herb garden in the front of the L-shaped building. Over the building was a sign written in a foreign language. I walked out of this area and down the stone sidewalk, and I turned right. I felt an energy pulling me down the pathway in my dream, and as I turned to the left, there was a courtyard with statues. The statues were beautifully colored and were majestic. I had never seen statues like these. I was unsure at the time what they represented, but I embraced their beauty just the same. My attention then went out onto the walkway and to the left. I felt a pull to go into the next entryway to the right. It was the most peaceful area, a meditation garden. I felt safe and blessed to be in that space. What I saw was so out of my knowing. I was unsure of what this dream meant at the time, but I added it to my list of dreams of flying over towns and cities, dipping in and out of experiences that would later come to be.

I would live a dual life once again: my corporate one and a spiritual one. I did not let people know that I was intuitive, and I would continue to take classes and tap into the part of me that knew things as a child. I would realize that this self-discovery—or should I say reawakening—would be what I was told about when I had died on the operating table. Now I lived in the south and had joined a group that would help me grow spiritually. I knew that I was not supposed to be doing the office work however I still held fear about stepping into doing healing work. I needed to know more, or at least I thought so.

Time would pass, and I become visible in the company. I ran the corporate campaign for United Way for several years, and I was very active in the social club. I initiated changes in processes within the department, for efficiency. I stood out; I was not trying to, but it happened. As I worked with people, I did not realize that the messages I got for them was healing, and it was not about doing physical treatment on them.

I was happiest when I was busy. I loved the life that I had created. I was truly happy for the first time in my life. All aspects of my being were nurtured physically, emotionally, mentally, and spiritually. I was full.

I noticed how people struggled when they saw that I was in a good place, and because they had not found that place of joy, they would try to take me from that place of contentment. I watched as their fears surfaced, and they went into sabotage rather than trying to find their balance. I found that when people were balanced at all four levels of being, they did not need to feed into fear, drama, or a lack of energy. I chose to be happy, and that in itself was hard for people to handle. They did not know how to work from that place of self-joy. I thought the most important part of balance came from knowing who one wanted to be in a situation. I knew that was something the counsel told me: it was a choice.

Most people knew struggle, fear, and a lack; they did not know how to move from that and experience joy. Unfortunately, when they saw someone that attained the proper state of being, and they felt they could not achieve it, they went into aggression. Perhaps that was what happened in my family. When I came to the realization that I was not the abuse, and I was allowed to be happy, my family lashed out, trying to take that happiness from me.

My joy was short lived. I had spent five years in oil and gas, with mostly women. I did my job well and did not want to get caught up in the office drama. I kept myself busy working out at lunch; it gave me the personal time I craved. I would find myself trying to defuse the drama when it came to me, trying to open up people's perspectives rather than feeding the drama. I realized quickly that people would rather create drama than deal with the truth of a situation, again not taking responsibility for their actions. With that, I became a target. I recalled the message that I got when I left my body and chatted with my grandfather: "This is just an experience; we are here to learn and grow and heal situations from other lifetime experiences and not to get stuck in the experience." I wished more people got the memo.

I could never figure out why women couldn't work with one another without getting malicious. If only people could support and encourage one another to be their best. Was that too much to ask?

Now the drama came from my supervisor. She cornered me in my office and blurted out that I was overdressing for my status in the company. Was she kidding? So what did someone of my status wear? I biked to work, so I had several of my outfits hanging behind my door. In my anger at her obvious attempt to attack me, I flung the door from the wall and went through the outfits, listing the prices I paid. I bought quality clothes that were usually on sale; nothing I had was extremely expensive. I was furious with her but was not going to let this women bully me. Perhaps she should focus on how she dressed for her status in the company instead. I returned the door to its open position and headed down the hall to the manager's office. As I stood in front of her, I asked was there anything wrong with what I was wearing. She told me, "No, you always dress well." I asked if I was overdressed for my status in this company. Again she told me no—she wished more people dressed the way I did. HR had just sent out an e-mail days earlier regarding dress code, it and restated that it was business attire.

My manager realized how upset I was and asked what had happened. I told her about the conversation. She was shocked and asked who said that to me. I pointed down the hall to where the supervisor was standing; she realized what I had done and was heading into the office. I asked the manager to deal with this, because if it happened again, I would take it to the HR department as harassment. I walked out of the office. Nothing more was said, but I would be continually set up to fail. The team lead and supervisor would start creating situations and then point fingers in my direction. Let the sabotage begin. Fortunately, I was detail orientated and would prove their accusations to be false. I had worked on a project, and the team lead got up to present the project to the manager, the supervisor, and the other members of the group. She was claiming the work as hers. I was shocked that she would even think of doing this. She continued to take credit. When there was a question, she tried to deflect it to me, but I told her no, I was interested in how she came up with that result. She stood there with her mouth open—she had dug a hole, and I wanted to see how she was going to get out of it. She gave me a stern look as if to demand I answer the question. When I did not budge, she then confessed to the group that I had done all the work. This did not go over well. The manager asked me to present the project, and I did so without further incident. I would always give credit where it was due. I was disappointed with the group and knew I would have to watch my back. Integrity, respect, and honor—was that too much to ask for in the corporate world?

Our group was asked to mark down everything that we did, as well as the time spent on each project, for two weeks. We would then have to sit with our team lead and go through what we did. My chart was complete, and I could account for forty hours' worth of work. The team lead told me that I had to take some of the things off the list. I told her no—I did all of it, and I was not taking off any of it. She was less than impressed. I wondered what she was up to. I would never understand why an employer would sabotage a staff member who was doing her job well. Fear, insecurity, and jealousy would seem to be the driving force. Why did people need to go to that ugly place instead of trying to be their best?

As I worked in the corporate world, I would have the ability to sense when people were lying; it was as if their energy would shift. I would struggle with this. In one way it was a great tool, but at the same time, it would trigger my trust issues with people. I would give them a chance to redeem themselves, but unfortunately not very many took the opportunity.

I was getting sick of all this drama. I realized that I needed to get out of this and step into the healing work, but I was scared. I had worked corporately for fifteen years and did not know any other way. I needed my guidance now more than ever.

Opening the Door
to Spirituality

*I*t was now late December 1998, and some members of the meditation group were planning to go to India in February 1999. They asked if I wanted to go with them, and I laughed. "Right, a small-town girl was going to travel halfway around the world to India!" I heard myself dismiss the trip, and then I heard my intuitive voice: "And why can't you go?" I heard my mother's fears and limitation in that choice. I decided to look into this opportunity more.

The trip would be five thousand dollars and two and a half weeks. I had to think about this. I would have to see if I could carry forward some holidays into next year. I went into my manager's office and shared about the opportunity. She was excited for me, and I got her approval. I started to make plans. I needed to get a passport, an India travel visa, and a ticket. Everything happened fast; what would normally take eight weeks took me two weeks. My trip was booked, and I was getting excited.

The supervisor was quick to express her disapproval with me carrying holidays forward. Perhaps she was just mad that I went to the manager instead of her. There was a group of three workers with a team lead, a supervisor, and a manager. Sometimes who we were supposed to go to was blurred. All the drama over four days of holiday carried forward. I saw jealously rear its ugly head. She was relentless and stated, "Well, you'd better have all your work done before you leave."

I thought; *I have to cover the others' desks when they go on holiday, but obviously I do not get the same luxury as the others. No problem—I will do what it takes.* My trip couldn't come soon enough.

It was now February 16, 1999, and the journey began. I would travel alone and meet the others in India, because they have already left. I flew into London and had a twelve-hour layover. I did not want to sit in the airport for that time. I threw on my backpack and headed to the tube, to explore London for a day. The tube shot down the track, and I was instantly aware of the differences between England and Canada. I was standing on the train, and there was a small girl sitting with her mother. Her mother told her to get up and let me sit down. The girl was only about seven years old. I was shocked by the mother's command. I told her I was fine and had just had a long flight, so standing was needed. I chatted with the young girl. She stated I had an accent, and I chuckled at her. I told her all the things that I was going to do: see Big Ben, the Palace, Trafalgar Square, the National Art Gallery, and whatever London had to offer. She asked if I was having tea with the Queen while I was at the palace. I smiled at her innocence. Soon I arrived at Piccadilly Square, and I said my good-byes.

As I exited the tube and made my way to the street, panic hit my body. All of a sudden I realized where I was, and I had to ground myself and take a breath before I headed out.

Site-seeing filled the day. The Canadian flag was everywhere; it brought me solace and put a smile on my face. The National Art Gallery took my breath away; I did not want to leave the intense energy of the gallery. As I hit the streets again, there were statues everywhere honoring lords and lions. Before I left Canada, I saw a documentary on London and their high-tech tracking system, I saw the cameras everywhere. I was sitting just outside the palace with the crowds, and we watched the guards. Then a car from the royals appeared; it was Prince Harry. The frenzy erupted, and as he passed he opened his window and waved. I had been lucky enough over the years to see and even speak to some of the royals, and this added to the excitement of the day.

As I sat on the steps just outside the palace gates, there was a huge commotion. Police cars were everywhere and circled a car, did an arrest, and then were gone within minutes. The crown was dumbfounded by the experience.

I became aware of my body as a wave of exhaustion hit. I was unsure if it was the jet lag, the adventure-filled day, or a lack of food. I grabbed lunch at a pub, which seemed to help. As I got back to the airport, my emotions got the best of me, and I sat in tears from exhaustion. I was able to sleep for about an hour before my flight left for India. I willingly stretched out on a lounge chair and drifted off to sleep.

INDIA: I WAS HOME, I WAS HOME

———— ∞∞∞ ————

The flight to Delhi was long, and the plane was packed with travelers. I was seated with two men who were inquisitive and very blunt with their questions to me. One was from New York and the other was from Delhi. Their questions were overt, asking how much money I made, how old I was, was I married, and did I have children. I was taken aback from their questioning, I felt myself pull back and become quiet for the remainder of the flight.

The Airport was full and lined with guards. I did not feel any threat, but I quickly noticed the difference between countries. The tour guide greeted me as I exchanged some currency, and I looked forward to the hotel room and a shower. We were still awaiting a few people; my roommate would be from Chicago, and she would not arrive until later that night. After we cleaned up and felt a little more human, the small group headed to the market. We were unsure of exactly where it was; the locals tried their best to give directions with hand signals and broken English. The aroma hit us, and as we found our way to the market, our noses led us to a pizza place called Hot Breads. The smells triggered my very hungry stomach—I couldn't wait to sink my teeth into my lunch. The smells did not let our taste buds down. I mingled with the others that were there; some people from Canada and others were from Germany, the United States, and India.

We headed into the marketplace and did some site-seeing and a little shopping. The rows of vendors had jewelry, garments, and artifacts. My eye caught a young woman sitting among her handiwork; there were many detailed pieces of tapestry. As I started to look at the many pieces that she offered, she was quick to tell me the prices. The exchange rate was twenty-seven rupees to one Canadian dollar. I looked at the incredible detail to her work and couldn't believe the she was selling it for so little. It was customary to haggle, but I could not even consider offering her less then she was asking. I went through the motions of bartering with her. We come to a price that would be an insult for such work. I handed her the payment; it was five times what we had just haggled. I gave her a wink, and she smiled and bowed her head to me in gratitude. Even with what I had paid, I got a great deal and knew that each time I looked at the pieces, the memory of the experience would return. I asked her name, and it was Anju. She was draped in a beautiful green sari, and she agreed to have a picture with me and the items that I had purchased.

We left the market and headed into the busier part of Delhi. The streets reminded me of Mexico, and the diesel smell almost sickened me. It bought back childhood memories of the diesel stove we had used for heat. I spent this part of the day with my nose tucked behind a handkerchief to block the smells. The streets were filled with vehicles, carts, scooters, and buses. There was something different here, and the cars jockeyed for position: a small honk and the driver ahead would move over to let the other cars by, with a wave to notify the other driver it was safe for them to move forward. There was never any yelling or swearing. With the volumes of people, there was a sense of order and respect for right-of-way. We came to a large traffic circle with a man directing vehicles; it was as if he danced in his movement, and the drivers all moved in the flow with him and without hesitation. Even with the bustle, the courtesy of the people outweighed the need for position. People were willing to stop in the midst of all the traffic to give directions. It was almost comical. My eyes and mind were trying to take in everything. We managed to get back to hotel and spend the evening in with room service, and then we were off to bed.

My body shot from the bed as I awoke from a horrible dream. I had just dreamed that the guide for the trip had died. I knew that many of my dreams came true, and this disturbed me. I tried to fall asleep when the hotel door swung open. I felt my body jolt from the bed again. It was my roommate from Chicago. I was still upset from the dream and was less than welcoming. I said hello and then rolled over to go back to sleep. I tried to sort out what had just happened in my dream.

The morning came quickly, and I properly greeted my new roommate. We were chatting when breakfast arrived at our door. Getting used to this kind of service would be easy. We continued to chat, and she told me she had been to India before, so she already had expectations of the experience. My new roommate was inquisitive and asked me if I was all right; she could sense I was agitated. I hesitated to tell her of my dream, and I was not sure of how to say what I saw. More important, I was unsure of how she would take it. I did manage to tell her about the vision I had. She was taken aback and told me we were safe. As I heard her words, I knew that what she said was true and felt a sense of peace.

As we finished eating breakfast, we got ready to explore Delhi as a whole group. The temples and mosques were abundant. The architecture was amazing, and the stone work, which had been done hundreds of years before, took my breath away. Many structures were built for prayer and for honoring the dead. Kutabs graced the skies; the crafted stone with the conceptual design was mystical for the year in which they were built, and their beauty and energy touched me deeply. The towers reached high over the city, each level offering a greater view. We were in the middle of Delhi, inside a courtyard that sat quietly behind cinder block walls. The buildings each offered a view into the past; there was attention to detail and workmanship everywhere we looked. As I explored, I came to a wall of small chambers, big enough for someone to stand in. The roof was dome shaped, and the energy that I felt as I stood in the space was spiritual. They explained that the spaces were prayer chambers, used for chanting prayers. I returned to the chamber with this information. As I stood in the space, I started to chant, and the sound of my voice hit the top and vibrated down, around, and through my body. It brought me to tears. I couldn't explain the experience other than it touched my soul.

After a long but exciting day, we headed back to the hotel to get ready for dinner. Prior to my trip, I had taken Indian cooking lessons and was excited about tasting authentic Indian food. Indian food was vegetarian for the most part; with the influence of the outside world, there was some meat eaten, but it was rare to find. I had been eating vegetarian for a while, so the missing meat was a non-issue. We walked over to the restaurant only a few blocks away from the Bright Star Hotel. My attention pulled me in many directions, and I tried taking in all the amazing sights and sounds. Dinner was great, and we talked about the day's experiences and planned what would come tomorrow. Noise from the street greeted us as we left the restaurant; it broke the calm energy that we had enjoyed over the past few days.

As we made our way to the street, crowds of people, mostly males, were dancing and shouting, and firecrackers blasted. They carried Chandler-style lighting as they danced in the night. I asked one of men what this was about. He explained it was a wedding precession. It was the groom's family; they would dance their way to the bride and her family, who waited for them. The man asked us to come join them. We moved down the street with them, and behind the crowd was the groom with his mother and father on a wagon-style vehicle. The aunts and uncles danced around them, and their voices broke the silence of the night with screams of celebration of the union. The crowd moved into a tent, and the groom was draped with flowers. Everyone in the tent was exquisitely dressed. We watched from just outside the tent. The bride sat at the front with her family. The sights in the tent disappeared because the doorway was draped once the groom's family was inside. This unexpected event was a great way to end the day.

Our meal was a distant memory with all the excitement from the wedding, but that too would be overshadowed by the exhaustion of the day. We arrived back at the hotel and headed back to our rooms to sleep. The next day we would travel to Agra to see the Taj Mahal—more history and beauty.

I awoke with the clatter of dishes and voices from the kitchen of the hotel, as they prepared our breakfast. The excitement and nervousness of the day hit me. The two-hundred-mile trip would take us hours. We would be hampered by poorly maintained roads, carts being pulled by oxen, and people on bicycles pulling carts of sugar cane or supplies. There were trailers filled with grain wrapped in burlap stacked fifteen feet high and pulled by camels. As the carts moved down the road, the grain bounced with its weight. Trucks filled with handmade bricks moved slowly to the next village for sale. I did not see limitation here, only doing.

I tried to focus on what this place had to offer, but I become aware of my restlessness after only a few hours into the trip. There was a continual stream of tractors, scooters, and bicycles jockeying for position on the road. I couldn't even imagine what the trip home would offer; most modes of transportation did not have lights. Safety was a definite concern.

The journey took us to parts of India that most did not want to admit existed, but others looked with acceptance as they went beyond the tragedy and saw the beauty within the poverty. The shanty towns appeared along the roadside, vendors repaired poorly maintained vehicles, and people sold their products from the fields, from carts. Each vendor stood proudly by their wares, prepared to deal with all the people slowed by the traffic. They faced their situation with pride; they did not see the poverty but rather their wealth. Within their existence, community, family, and honor took precedent. They believed in karma: do good and good would come. It was not something everyone from the West could claim. They helped their neighbors, offering chairs to people who came into their shops or a place on their mats. The dignity that was in the streets was powerful. As we passed through the villages and countryside, there were hundreds if not thousands of people in what would be a four-hour journey.

THE TAJ MAHAL

⊗⊗⊗

We unfolded out the vehicles and needed to walk to stretch out. I did so quietly as I thought back to all those who we passed on the roads, and I wondered how they would feel after their travels. Mine were minor to theirs, I was sure. We got to the gates of the Taj Mahal, and the guards wanted to receive a bribe to let us in early. With some haggling, we got in. The palace was breathtaking, the courtyard stretched forever, and the white marble glistened in the sun. As we approached the building, it seemed to rise from the earth. The size of the structure was overwhelming, and its beauty was majestic. As the history of the Taj Mahal was told through an interpreter, the story unfolded as a love story. He explained how the building was built to honor the love between a man and his wife. He was devastated at what would emanate, his grief consuming him as he expressed his love for her. He built the structure to honor her. His son got angered by the amount of wealth he put into the project and had him jailed and sent to the Red Temple, which was situated just across the river from the Taj Mahal. The intention of the son's gesture was obvious. The palace was the Niagara Falls of India, and newlywed couples flocked there in hopes of a receiving the blessing of the energy for which it represented.

The honoring of love, and how that love was behind the creation of this incredible piece of art, was humbling. The white marble inlaid with finely crafted stones shimmered in the bright February sun. The pillars of the Taj Mahal were set at each corner of the structure and leaned slightly to the outside, in a way to protect the main structure should the pillars fall; the builder very conscious of his actions. The courtyard filled, and as the day continued, newlyweds came to pay their respects and ask for a blessing for their own marriages. Men who were using oxen to pull old-fashioned grass cutters stood out in all that was happening; everything here done by hand. Looking at the attention to detail was awe inspiring. There was no one walking around and expressing disdain because of the conditions here; they were in the moment. It was as if time stood still in the walls of the space; everything was simple but pure.

The feeling within me from having this experience was beyond words. As we left, I was at peace, seeing what one man would do in the name for love. This felt pure. I would hold this in my heart always. Each experience here superseded the last. By taking in the sites, energy, and history, I was deeply connected; just by walking this space, I seemed to become a part of it.

We headed to a factory where the craft of carving the gems used in the detail of the Taj Mahal still existed. Finely carved pieces of gems were shaped into flowers petals one by one and then inlaid into the marble. They used the inlay process to create amazing art. I wanted to hold this experience, and when I left I purchased a marble elephant with the inlay. The delicate workmanship was done by children, and the natural instinct to protect the young hit me deep as I remembered that this was the way of the land. I stepped into acceptance as I saw the smiles on the faces of the children. They were not feeling victimized by their experiences. At the age of seven, they were grinders, and by the age of nineteen they would advance to the position of doing the inlay. The inlay process involved gluing the petals into place, and then the sanding began. At the age of thirty-five—my age then—they would have to retire because their hands would no longer be able to continue due to the pressure put on their fingertips. Instead, they would train the next generation. Everything here had its cycle.

FILLING THE SOUL

⸺∞⸺

The impact of the day hit me, and all I wanted to do was sleep. We loaded the cars and headed back to Delhi. The drive back proved to be tragic; the roads become even more dangerous as night fell. There were several accidents, with freight trucks smashing into brick carriers, vehicles hitting cane wagons, and grain trucks toppling over from their weight. It was not a place where I would want to be behind the wheel at night. I tried to sleep in order not to become overwhelmed with the experience, but even that became impossible as the tension of what was happening around us became evident.

We arrived back to the hotel safely, but the strain of the day showed on the faces of our group. It would be a light dinner in the room and then off to bed before our trip up north to Rishikesh.

We set out at 8:00 a.m. in hopes of avoiding the midday heat. The morning was crisp, and everyone was eager to get to the Ashram. The roads twisted us out of Delhi and into the countryside, once again putting us face to face with the obvious poverty and lack of necessities. The great outdoors were people's facilities, and the walls of the homes were made from bundled twigs, which hardly protected the occupants from the scuttle of traffic outside their world. The dirtiness and smell of the city gave way to green space and the vastness of the countryside; the cleanliness was soothing to my eyes. I allowed myself a few private moments to take in the transformation that happened before me, as if we had shifted into another dimension. The roadside was speckled with farmers as they tended their fields. The patterns of the crops enhanced the beauty of the countryside: sugar cane, rice, and grain caressed the roadside. There was an obvious awareness of quietness; the people became less as we moved further from the city.

We stopped to stretch our legs, and there was a large sugar cane crop to the left, with people cutting the cane and stacking it. The people on the right side of the road collected the cane from the stacks and took it to a manual pressing machine. The cane then pressed through the device. Their efforts were obvious; the machine was old and large, and the sugar cane juice streamed down a flute into a vat. The vat was buried in the dirt on one side to help maintain the heat. The vat was at least six feet high, and women gathered sticks and dry cow dung to burn. Everyone helped in this event. The sugar was heated into a liquid state for hours, creating a thick substance to which they added a stabilizer. The thickened sugar cane was then poured into a large fry pan the size of a large, round dinner table; it was stirred to assist in the cooling process. There were four men who sat on its edge and rolled the cooled substance into balls. They would sell the sugar, which people used for cooking and added to their drinks. They were selling one kilo of gourd for 120 rupees, which was approximately 45 cents Canadian. I purchased some to taste and to take to the cooks at the ashram. The whole process took place into the middle of a field—not the most sanitary conditions that we in the West held as a standard. *Only in India,* I thought to myself.

India was a country that was self-sufficient. Recycling was a way of life, and one man's garbage would service another. Shopkeepers placed empty boxes outside their doors to have others collect the cardboard, precisely folding each piece and then strapping it to the back of their bikes. Shopkeepers tossed any food rubbish and any vegetables not sold at market that day onto the streets, to serve as food for the cows that roamed freely. The cows were then followed by people collecting the hot dung as it hit the ground. Everything was relative; it was as if the food chain was presenting itself before me. The dung was used as fuel to heat the homes or use for cooking.

India may not have the amenities of Western countries, but she had the incredible ability to live up to a standard that we could not hold a light, as far as taking from the world what she needed and using it until it had no more use.

CULTURE SHOCK

———— ⚬⚬⚬ ————

The roads became lined with the families returning home after their long day in the fields. People packed into carriages or scooters; four people rode comfortably on a motorcycle, happily sharing what they have. The bond that the people of this country had with one another was apparent. Perhaps we needed to learn a thing or two here. People from Canada could barely share a road, let alone ride four people to a vehicle. As we got close to the next town, the road was lined with trees. The image connected me to home; it was what we saw in the older neighborhoods in Canada. The differences and similarities pulled me back and forth between the two worlds of existence. The peace and comfort of my awareness brought me calmness. I was tired, but the desire not to miss anything on the trip kept me awake. The animals in this country were honored and were included into their lives: camels, oxen, and donkeys were used as laborers, and dogs rested in the sun and followed children home. I was unsure whether pigs, chickens, and sheep were a food source or a friend. The harmony of this land became apparent, and perhaps that was the reason for the high level of spiritual blessing this country received, due to that level of consciousness held by its people. Perhaps that was why so many journeyed here searching for answers.

As we reached the north, the Ganges River presented itself, and I was humbled at the view. People were resting, and I embrace the experience. The roads rolled up and down the sides of the Ganges, the most blessed waters. The presence seemed to be uneventful, but the power and the energy became apparent. We wound our way up the mountain to the highest point, only to descend down the next moment. The trees presented their own energy. The beauty couldn't be described. We entered the ashram area, but we couldn't drive up to the building. The roads were stone and narrow, and we parked and headed to what would be home for the next two weeks.

The accommodations were basic, and I could hear the cries of the Westerners. The beds were an army-style mattress resting on a wood frame. The rooms had open shelving for closets with a toilet, and the shower head came from the wall and shot into the small bathroom, with no curtain to be found. It was one step up from roughing it in the outdoors in Canada. I was happy to be out of the car, and I was excited to explore what came next. I heard the chants of monks from the next ashram, and I hoped their chants smothered the negativity that the group was releasing.

We put our luggage into our rooms—there was no sharing of rooms here—and were taken across the stone road to the healing center. Each yard was protected with cinderblocks walls, and as we entered the healing center I looked around and then froze in my tracks. I saw a garden in front of an L-shaped building and above the building was a sign written in script. I realized this was the dream I had five years prior. I turned to the people behind me and asked them to come with me; I wanted to go see the area that had the statues in my dream. They were all questioning me. We had been here five minutes, and I wanted to be a tour guide.

I couldn't hold back the urge to see if this was in fact what I had seen in my dream. I raced down the stone walk and off to the right, and then I turned left into the courtyard. The statues stood before me; the only difference was that the statues were in protective cages. I then recalled the meditation area, and I went off to find it with my small group in tow. We went out the gate to the left and then to the right. As I entered the space, I was shocked to find that it was an orchard. The others come trailing behind me, and as they did, they realized I was wrong.

I saw a man appear from a shack along the left wall in the orchard. He stood about five feet from me and asked if he could help. I was confused. I knew this was where it should be. I explained I was looking for the meditation garden. His face shifted as he looked at me inquisitively. "How do you know about the meditation garden?" I told him I had dreamed about it. His face shifted again, and his next comment brought goose bumps to my whole body. "This was where the meditation garden will be, but we have not built it yet." The silence of the group was deafening. I thanked him, and we left in silence.

The group processed what had just happened, and then the questions started. How did I know this? How could I know about something that had not been built? I did not have any answers to their questions. All I knew was that my dreams from childhood had come true throughout the years; this would be one more time. We headed back to the healing center and finished the tour of where we would do yoga, meditation, and massage daily. We settled in the common room and chatted before we went down for dinner. Our bellies were full with a freshly made Indian dinner prepared by our cook. We met with the doctors that ran the center and the training of future doctors; they would work with any of us that needed it.

HISTORY SEEPS INTO MY SOUL

The history of Rishikesh was vast. This region of India filled with ashrams has called too many people over the years, especially people seeking awakening and souls needing connection find their way here. The Ganges River and the Chandrabhaga River, along with the dry riverbed of the Ramjhula, trisect Rishikesh, which holds its own attraction. Rishikesh was where Yoga originated. Over the years, many traveled here and have made pilgrimages to this region, seeking the Yogi Masters and sages of the region for spiritual truths and healing. I could feel the energy of this place, and I was humbled with all that I felt.

Ashrams lined the hills, each holding its own spiritual backing. As we were about to settle in for the evening, we heard the chants from the ashram that rested on the hilltop. People were dancing around the fire and chanting, and we watched respectfully and then headed back to the rooms for a well-deserved rest.

Late to bed and early to rise let the experiences begin. Tea was served in the sitting room situated at the front of each bedroom. As I enjoyed the tea, the crisp morning air blew gently as the sun beamed through now open shutters. I heard the rhythm of India again, and the clip-clop of horse hooves hit the concrete walkway. I went out to see three packhorses carrying bricks up the hill to another ashram under construction. I listened to the rhythm, and it was like a blessing within the silence of the morning. As I finished the last of my tea, there was a man pushing a cart filled with fruits. He stopped at the kitchen door to sell his wares, which I suspected would be our breakfast. My awareness shifted from this state as the doors of the other bedrooms opened. We said our good mornings, and then it was off to the healing center.

Neti Cleansing
and Healing Begins

The first experience was netti; this was a cleansing process for the body. We gathered in a wash area, and there were jugs of saltwater and small teapot-looking containers. We were instructed on how to use the netti pot for cleansing our nasal passages. I inserted the spout of the netti pot into the opening of one nostril and tilted my head as I poured the saltwater into the nasal canal. I felt and tasted the saltwater as it filled my nasal cavities, and slowly the water began to drain from my open nostril. The sensation was weird. I continued draining and then blew air through the nasal passage to finish cleaning.

I was then given a large jug filled with saltwater; the salt ratio was high, and the objective of this was to clear the stomach lining and any mucus in the throat. I was instructed to drink the solution quickly, and as I did the natural instinct for the body was to purge. The saltwater came out as fast as it went in. This process continued until I finished the saltwater in the jug. There was an emotional trigger doing this for me. I flashed back to the hundreds of times that I had purged my food over the years, and the need I felt to be empty of all things in me: guilt, shame, anger, unworthiness—all those emotions of self-loathing. This realization of all the abuse

I had been through and how I owned it. The thousands of times that my abusers would imply I was asking for it. This was what this journey was about for me: to go deeper into my soul and heal. I kept my thoughts and emotions to myself and continued with the morning ritual. The next process was one that I could not complete. I was given a small rubber tubing, insert it into one of my nostrils, and feed it into my throat, then reach in my throat to grab the tubing and see-saw the tubing to clean intensely. *Gross,* was all I could think, *definitely not for me.*

Yoga was next. The group gathered, and the Yogi led the class into a place of oneness. I felt my nasal passages drain as I moved into the downward dog; the sensation brought me back into the room. I heard members of the group whining again. I could never understand that about people. It was something so simple and peaceful; why was it easier for them to complain? I went back into my place of peace, as if I could follow my breath into my body and disappear. The class would end, and I felt myself wanting to separate from the drama of certain people. It was back to my room and then to breakfast. After breakfast, we would experience massage, Indian style.

The massage was done by a therapist the same sex as the client. The woman who worked on me was tall but very thin; her size did not impede her ability to work me deep in the treatment. I released more of my past trauma as she worked me over. She also worked my stomach and all the scar tissue that remained from my ten surgeries. That might have been too much; my body would clear most of the day and night. Knowing I had been triggered to heal, I honored the processing of my body. This routine would continue for the fourteen days that we were at the ashram.

As I suspected, the fruit from the cart was part of our breakfast. The colors and tastes nurtured my senses. I promised myself that whatever came my way on this trip, I would embrace it. India was far from what I knew, and in the same breath, it was everything I knew to be true.

Taking in the Sights

After breakfast, it was time to explore the village. As I walked through the crowd, I saw within the people their connection to Rishikesh. The people seeking guidance and awakening only needed to be in the presence of the locals. The energy created was by all who had walked here over time, making it what it was. The streets were not quite big enough for one American vehicle, yet they were filled with shoppers, beggars, monkeys, and cows. Everything was in harmony. I could feel the energy here; it was familiar, and I felt safer here than any place I had ever been.

Shopping took up some of the afternoon, and after that it was back for a nap and then lunch with the group.

PRAYERS AND MEDITATION

———◈———

Mediation areas with statues honoring the gods and goddesses surrounded me. Early evening came, and the shops shut down. People were going to Aarti, which was prayer. Each day ended with prayer. The open-air prayer center was on the banks of the Ganges River. A marble chariot with four horses pulling it graced the archway, and marble steps led us to the seating area, also made of marble. As we entered the space, a man welcomed us and stated to us, "Please come and pray to whomever you choose; it raises the consciousness of the earth." The words brought me to tears. Why did the rest of the world believe otherwise? Religion had become so tainted. If you were born unto a Catholic family, would you not be Catholic? If you were born to a Buddhist family, were you not Buddhist? It was just one more level in which we had chosen to experience our existence. More important, if you prayed to your God, and I prayed to mine, was the world a better place? Were your god and my god at war? I think not. Perhaps it was my death experiences that put this perspective before me. I will not debate my truth against yours, because each of us has chosen a path of learning, and I will not judge your experience, just as I hope that you will not judge mine. There was a saying, "Live and let live," and it is within that message that I trust your truth will come to you.

I knew that I was in the right place, and I was already regretting having to leave India. We looked out onto the Ganges River. The sun started to set, and the monks took their place at the bottom of the seating area. Our group's presence in Rishikesh had been noticed. There were large, gold pedestal candleholders with teardrop-shaped wax circling the many layers of the trays; these would be lit at the beginning of the ceremony. While seated I noticed that Maharishi was within arm's reach; he was a master there. I watched graciously as the honoring of Shiva was done by burning the bud-like wax on the tiered candle holder. The singing of prayers began, and there were offerings done to the Ganges River by selecting people from the group of worshipers. As the holder was passed to different people, they moved the holder in a circular fashion; the energy it created was amazing. My focus was broken as the holder was passed to me, and I mimicked the motion, unsure of what it all meant. I was blessed that I had been chosen.

The prayers started; they were in Punjab, but their vibration hit me deeply. All I could hear from my inner self was, "I am home, and I am home!" There was a surge of remembrance that shot through me, bringing me to tears. I see a vision that I have walked this land in another time. I couldn't hold my emotions in me. I sat beside the girl from Chicago, and she comforted me as I released my connection to this place without having to explain. I had never felt this kind of connection with anything before, and it took me by surprise.

The day ended with another amazing meal, and then it was off to bed, only to rise early again and begin our morning ritual of netti, yoga, meditation, and then massage. They informed us there would be a private meditation with Maharishi in the gardens after our morning rituals.

Maharishi spoke about the proper techniques of meditation via breathing from the root chakra up to the third eye. He stated that the process was not easy; it would take about six months to achieve this technique. He also talked about the technique of remaining in the state of acceptance.

Step 1: Meditation
Step 2: Non-reaction
Step 3: Introspection

Repeating this process each day allowed for the permanency we were looking for.

As the days unfolded, I was grateful that I had taken the cooking lessons, because it gave me a high level of appreciation for the foods that were prepared. At least one if not more of the things that were done in the cooking lesson appeared at each meal. The fruits here were beyond description: the supply bananas, papayas, mangos, and apples were endless. Dahl, rice, and pekoes were regulars on the meal plan. I could feel my body changing as a result of the food I was taking in. I had not felt that energetic for a long time. I was sure that the yoga and massage were also key components of the shift in the concept of body, mind, and spirit that came into my awareness. It felt good to be connected to all of me. My lifestyle prior to coming was respectable; I had dealt with my emotional past, knowing more needed to be done. I had been eating vegetarian for about two years, and I was physically active, but this took me to a new level of self-awareness.

It was now time for prayer. We made our way to Aarti and sat, again to the left of Maharishi. The candle ceremony had begun, and we were all included. The service was even more powerful than the day before, and it again brought me to tears. Being here had begun my spiritual awakening. As I saw the poverty of this place, I also saw the incredible strength and love of its people. While sitting at the shores of the Ganges River, I offered my own prayer for emotional release. I knew my spiritual journey was about to take a very large step forward. The offering to the goddess Shiva was made, and it was our group that was selected. I was the first to receive a flower to offer into the river. That simple process was overwhelming, and the honors that we received were beyond words. I looked back at the experience of when I had gone to the Catholic Church, and how poorly the minister had treated me. I would take the love and openness of India any day.

My Body Shifts

he next day I was not feeling well. There was a day trip planned, but I opted out of it to rest. I managed to get through breakfast but then retreated to my room. The doctor gave me a mix of crushed papaya seeds and grains with salt, followed by a large glass of warm water. Then I went back to bed and slept for a few hours. A blockage moved from my colon and with it a lot of emotion. I continued to clear and received a crystal healing and a soul reading.

In India they believe your path is written, and that we choose experiences to learn lessons. That being the case, I had come into learn a lot in this life. My thoughts went back to the times of my life that I had huge life choices: all those moments in time came through in the reading. Sixteen years of abuse, ten surgeries, lost pregnancies, and three death experiences—and all that was by the age of thirty-five. I acknowledged that I had stepped into the fear of what was before me and chose to heal. I knew that I could have easily fell victim to what I had gone through, but rather I made a promise to myself that I would rise above it. I could have let the words of my parents crush me and the actions of my abusers limit me. I promised myself the vision for this experience was beyond what I knew, but I trusted in all that was to come to me!

I also acknowledged that healing took work. I knew how messed up I was from what happened to me, and I knew that no one could heal me. That was my job. Perhaps having my first death experience at the age for eight had connected me to the truth of choice. I made the choice to come back into my body that day. I believed the possibility of what my grandfather had shown me. I later would believe in my ability to scan my body and know what was wrong. Then I had the courage to face doctors with what I knew to be true. I was willing to fight to survive this experience.

Facing the fear and standing up for the truth was not what most people did. As I looked back, I saw themes that manifested in my life. My needs did not matter to others, starting with my family. Being strong threatened people around me, and if I had money, people would take it. I became a witness to those lessons. I knew that my life experiences had been out of the norm and they put fear in those around me. I had died and came back, I was able to see and communicate with spirit, and I was able to sense emotions in the people around me. I also knew when people were being deceitful, and I would not hesitate to confront them with the truth. What I found most interesting was that I had chosen to be happy, and that created anger in others. All this made me stand out to the judgment of others as I claimed my independence from my past. I would not surrender myself emotionally, mentally, physically, or spiritually to the interference of those people who came in to control or manipulate me. I was in survival mode most of my life, fending off my abusers and struggling with aspects of my body: what was appropriate sexually, and my relationship with food. Then there were my trust issues. People did not want to hear what I had to share with them: my mother and the abuse, my connection to spirit, and the guidance that came with it. Doctors did not want to listen to what was wrong with my body.

In each situation I needed to move into my truth so that I could get through the experience. With all that I had been through, I knew that all of these experiences were about gathering information and perspective. It was not about judgment. I knew that I did not need people to believe what I believed. I knew that I did not expect people to change and to match my experience, because they had their lessons to learn. However, they were responsible for their fear that they felt when they went into it. I knew that despite what others chose to do to me, I had a choice of who I was going to be in the experience and after it.

It reminded me of a situation when one of my relationships ended. My ex-boyfriend said to me, "You could be a little less happy."

I heard myself say, "I was happy before I dated you, I was happy when I dated you, and I sure as heck will be happy now." He did not control my happiness. All he could do was laugh, because he knew the wholeness of what I was saying.

Perhaps knowing that all of these circumstances were lessons meant I could move into acceptance. What I would not do was lie down and take any more abuse.

India had a way of taking me deep into my experiences. No one here treated me rudely or held me in judgment because of my experience. They did not fear me when I was being my best. That was not something I could say of people that had walked the path before.

INITIATION

The next day came, and I felt amazing. As we sat down to breakfast, we were informed that a top Yogi Master would be coming to the ashram and had offered to initiate us into meditation. This was a huge honor; in Canada one would pay thousands of dollars for this experience. The day was filled with excitement. I was told I needed to make an offering, both a cash donation and food offering. I went to the market and bought nuts and fruits, and incense so that I could prepare a tray to present to the teacher and Shiva. I placed my cash donation in an envelope. As I made my offering, I took my place in the room. We were led through Yoga, and then we did the initiation into meditation. Each of us was blessed and then given a mantra, and then we did the meditation. We would do three meditations, separate from the others. I could feel something shift in me after the initiation, and again I was in tears. I couldn't explain this experience other than it touched my soul once again. This connection that I was experiencing was deep and allowed me to be whole again.

I woke again as they placed my morning tea in the sitting room. I slipped into my clothes and took my tea to the balcony. I again enjoyed the rhythm of the area: the horses carrying bricks, the clicking sound as the workers chipped away on ground as they continued to build the next ashram. There was a warm breeze. We did meditation with the Yogi Master, and this class was much different from the others. The state that I came to in this mediation was as if I melded into the room—I was the floor, the wall, the ceiling and all that was in between. Coming back from this state was almost disappointing.

After the meditation and massage, we were treated to a mud bath. The ladies were smeared with a rich, red mud from India, and then we lay on benches in the warm India sun. I could feel the minerals of the mud tingle on my skin; as the warmth hit me, the mud dried and my skin tightened. The assistant washed the mud from my skin, and I could feel my body detoxify in the experience.

The day was gentle. As night came we were joined by a new group member; she was the president of the University of Delhi. Her presence was warmly received by everyone in the group, and her energy was gentle. We chatted, and she shared that she edited books. Overall she was an excellent source of energy. She was married to an ambassador of India, who then currently held office in Chicago. *The world in which we live is vast and yet so small,* I thought to myself in that awareness.

I did reflexology on Doctor May of Germany, and she was pleased with the treatment. She was almost completely blind and worked with people with balance and structural issues. She used her other senses to heal others. This concept sank into my knowing.

HAND BLESSING

new day welcomed us, and a day trip took us to the Temple of the Divine Mother. We traveled by car; the roads wound up a mountain side. I get motion sick as we weaved back and forth, and I had to get the driver to stop so that I could ground myself. The air was crisp at the higher level, and the view was spectacular. After I was settled, we continued our journey. We arrived at a parking area close to the top. A staircase graced the access to the temple, which rested at the top of 107 steps. I made my way to the top and felt the altitude for the first time; my breathing was strained. I looked out from the temple and could see for miles. The landscape was so different from what I knew. Now in the lower Himalayan Mountains, I could see down into the valley: there were buildings tucked away into the layers of the green, vibrant mountain, and it was breathtaking.

A priest was there and would do a blessing on all of us. Then we went to receive a private blessing. I again asked for emotional healing from the priest in the group blessing. We had been in many temples since our arrival. The process was to go in to make an offering and ask for a blessing. I had reflected so much over the time I had been here, and I had come through so much. I knew already that I was blessed in so many ways; to ask for anything else seemed almost greedy. I expressed to the group leader that I did not know what to ask for. I was instructed to go meditate on it, and it would come. I sat quietly outside the temple and breathed into meditation. Then I started to see my hands come to my face, as if they were waving through me. I was confused by the image and asked quietly what this meant. Then I heard the voice: "Ask for your hands to be blessed." This confused me more, but I trusted the message and went in to ask for my blessing.

We gathered outside the temple and enjoyed the lunch that our cook had packed for us. I was unsure if it was the altitude or the clarity that I felt, but the food tasted even better.

We made our way down to the car and descended the mountain. It was early evening, and the sites were mystical. The road, however, seemed even more twisted than when we went up. I made it to the bottom without incident.

We returned to the ashram and enjoyed a lovely dinner. The girl from Chicago could not come with us that day because she could not do the stairs. After dinner, the two of us went to the common room to share our experiences of the day. As we chatted, I was doing reflexology on her feet. The night air was crisp, and temperature of the room dropped, but that did not stop us because we are deep into sharing our day. She abruptly shouted, "Stop!" I was shocked and stopped working on her, asking her what was wrong. She told me to take whatever was hot off her feet; it was burning her. I stated that there was nothing on her feet—it was just my hands. I became aware that I was sweating, and my hands were incredibly hot. Then I remembered the blessing of my hand that came to me earlier that day. I shared the story, and she proclaimed, "Be careful what ask for in India. It comes quickly." We chuckled and tried the treatment again I was able to complete it this time. My new awareness to what had happened scared me and then humbled me in the same moment.

MY INDIAN BOYFRIEND

We continued to chat, and the door to the common room swung open. Within seconds the young doctor in training ran into the room, touched my forehead, and ran out as quickly as he came in. We were confused by the experience but chuckled and continued to chat.

Moments later our group leader entered the room and shouted, "Who did that to you?"

"Did what?" I asked.

He informed me that I had something on my forehead. I went to the bathroom and realized that the young doctor had marked my forehead—a way of saying that he was interested in me. I was embarrassed and flattered, and I did not tell the group leader because I did not want the doctor to get into trouble, knowing that he should not have been in our area of the ashram. He would continue to flirt with me during the stay.

In India it was not appropriate for men to show outwardly affection. I saw men hugging men and holding hands everywhere I went, but public displays of affection were not to be expressed between man and woman, because most relationship were arranged.

I was happy to see my bed and sleep deep after the full day of happenings.

GROUP DYNAMICS

————— ∞∞∞ —————

s I laid awake, I knew that something had changed, but it was not about me. As I drank my morning tea, I was joined by one of our group members. I knew that she was not her normal self, and I asked her if she was all right. She was the sister of our group leader. She told me her father had had a heart attack, and she would be leaving the group to tend to him. I remembered the dream I had in Delhi, the first night. I knew the truth of this dream; it would be our group leader's father, not him, who died. I did not share what I saw in the dream but rather lent her my support. We accompanied her to the taxi.

As I walked to back to the ashram, I came across a jeweler, and I felt a need to go in. As I entered, I noticed the energy of the shop and then the presence of the shopkeeper. Another man was in the shop, and he made his presence know to me. I did not like his energy—it was as if he was invading my space. The shopkeeper came between the two of us, and I felt safe. I was overwhelmed with all the crystals and jewels that he had, and I was unsure of what I was looking for. I made my way to the back of the shop. The other shopper tried to get into my energy again. The shopkeeper handed me a strand of quartz crystals and told me to put it on. The other man left the shop when I did this. The shopkeeper shared that the crystals would keep negative people from interfering with me. I purchase the strand and headed back to the ashram to get to my massage on time. One of the shopkeepers I met the other day came on a motorbike and offered me a ride back. I chuckled to myself; it seemed that no matter where I went, I found a man with a motorbike. Was it fate or energy?

India had a way of letting me see into the truth of the person that stood before me. With the absence of the group leader's sister, the energy shifted. There was an older woman in the group who did not handle change well. She was acting out, and all I could do was walk away from the drama. The strain on the group was substantial; everyone felt it.

MORE ADVENTURES

———⊛⊛⊛———

We would head out on another day trip; this time we were off to Kempty Falls and Mussoiri. The trip took three hours, and again the road was windy as we made our way to the hill station. The weather got extremely hot over the summer, and so the hill stations that were in the lower Himalayans provided a cool retreat from the heat. Kempty Falls was the first stop. There were walkways at the base of the falls, and we made our way over small bridges as we took in the sites. The natural sites were lush and green, and I could feel the cool spray of the water as it hit the base of the falls. Over time the travelers had left their marks, and the dirtiness was heartbreaking. As I stood taking in the beauty, a Sheik family wanted to take a picture with me. The mother pushed her young children to stand by me. I felt their obvious fear of me. The young boy was almost in tears and was unsure of what to make of this white woman.

We made our way to Mussoiri, and this was the cleanest place since I had been in India. I took it in and wanted to be still within the space. There was an obvious difference in the people here; the influence of Nepal was evident in the people. The shops were filled with sweaters made of wool, and the shoppers in the group left their mark and money in the small village. I loved the work but was allergic to wool, so I did not indulge in shopping. All the white-skinned people who filled their streets intrigued the villagers, and I became aware for the first time of the fact that I was a minority.

My Chicago friend and I headed off to do some shopping. She wanted to find a Buddha statue for her son. We came upon a shop, and the energy within it pulled at me to go in. I found a wall of Buddha statues, and we both chuckled. I was picking up different ones to examine them, and as I was holding one, my hands heated up as if they were on fire. I told her I thought I had found the one. She held it and agreed; it was definitely giving off some kind of energy. With the impact of the altitude of the hill station and the days of shopping, the group was losing its stride, and we headed back to the cars.

ANOTHER BLESSING

⸻

As we made our way down the mountain, most of the group fell asleep. I was again sitting in the front seat to avoid getting motion sick. As the winding roads became almost smooth, I felt my body continue to sway. I tried my best to ground my energy, but to no avail. In a harried state I got the driver to stop, and as he did, I jumped from the car. The night air settled me, and I was able to get back into the car without incident. The driver barely started down the road, and I signaled him to stop again. This time I jumped from the car and ran to the driver's side of the road and into the ditch, where I began to purge. The sleeping people awoke as I wretched what little remained in my stomach. As I regrouped myself, I took my place in the car. I felt embarrassed and sat quietly. We went approximately five feet, and the driver started screaming and pointing in the direction of the ditch where I had just been. As I looked out the front window, I saw the head of a snake popping out from the ditch. It then made its way across the road. The driver continued to make a fuss about what was happening. All I was aware of was that the snake now blocked the full width of the road. As its head dipped into the right side of the ditch, its tail was coming from the left ditch. It became very clear that I was just standing in that spot, and I potentially threw up on the snake. As the snake disappeared in the night, it was all like a dream. I was unsure of the totality of what had just happened.

That night there was a huge discussion about this experience. The snake was the symbol of the Indian god Shiva; the snake was a white python. Shiva symbolized rebirth and was a very powerful sign. We were humbled by the experience as one of the group members told me the story and its importance.

Saying Good-bye

———∞∞∞———

W hen we returned to the ashram, there was news that the group leader's father was hospitalized and was not doing well. We prayed for him, but I knew that he would pass. My prayer was for his choice to be honored, and for all who loved him to be supported in the experience, whatever path his soul chose.

It was March 1. I woke with sadness in my heart, knowing that our friend's father had passed during the night. We started the day with prayer, yoga, and breakfast, and then we sent our group member to take care of his family. The remaining group members did their best to support one another. This took our focus from what we had planned, and some are making their concerns known. I was again frustrated with some of the members. I was sure that the passing of this man was not with the intent of messing up our plans. The selfishness shown by some of the individuals of the group shocked me. A man had died—did they not get it? I spent time with the few that stood in compassion. Intuitive information came to me at this point, and I shared what I was getting intuitively with the small group as we reflected on what had happened.

Morning came, and the energy had settled within the group. Aarti was beautiful for two reasons. The festival of Holi had started and would continue with colors tomorrow, and our friend's father's passing has been honored in the service. There were three prayers by Maharishi, and then our group participated in an offering of boats of flowers into the Ganges River in remembrance. As we embarked on this ceremony, the family of our friend started the cremation process in their home village.

We were told that the body of the deceased would be taken to the family home after passing. The male family members would perform the cleansing process because it was a male that passed. The shaving of the body occurred; the belief was that the body was to leave the way in which it came into the world. After the shaving, the body would then be bathed in milk and then draped in a blessed cloth that would come from the village of his family. The body was taken to the outside cremation site, and the site consisted of piles of tree branches that were selected by the eldest son. The body was then placed on a large block of marble situated outside with the sticks, to be cremated. The body would burn for three days, and the son would take a bamboo stick and tap the crown of the head to crack the skull and release the soul. The body would continue to burn, and when the cremation completed, the ashes were gathered; any bones were then placed in a blessed sack. The remains were then taken for placement into the Ganges River. What had come from the earth would be returned.

I sat in gratitude at the end of the day, exhausted with emotion and all that had taken place. This certainly was not something that one signed up for when one planned a trip, but allowing the experience to happen was a gift.

HOLI CELEBRATION

———◦◦◦———

On March 2 we started the day with cleansing, breakfast, and the celebration of Holi. In India there was a caste system, but on Holi everyone was equal. As we sat for breakfast, we were smeared with a creamlike power. There were many colors, and the cooks, doctors, and all of us that filled the small breakfast area were the color of a rainbow. We celebrated the rebirth of the land and the soul. We headed out onto the streets. We women were escorted by the student doctors into the festival. Men and children filled the streets with singing and dancing. Priests, workers, farmers, and beggars were all equal today. There were high priests that came to the village for the celebration.

I stood in the courtyard and was gently guided into an area where there was a large crowd of men standing outside large doors. I was not sure what was behind the doors, and I waited within the crowd. Then the crowd of men parted like the sea, and they guided me to the front of the crowd. The doors opened, and I was unsure of what to do. Without words, I motioned for one of the villagers to go ahead, to show me what I was to do. There was a man lounging on a chaise bench inside the room, and the student doctor went before me. He walked up and bowed, and then he touched the feet of the man lounging. The man did a blessing on the student. I suspected that he was one of the priests and held a high status for this to happen. I followed the direction of the student ahead of me, and I felt humbled that this had occurred. As I stepped out to the opposite side of the room and back into the courtyard, I was given a coconut like treat. I was unsure of what it was and hesitated, and then I was joined by others. They enjoyed the coconut square, and so I tasted it; it was incredible. I loved coconut, so the treat was most enjoyable. It was not long before I realized that the treat may have had a "special" ingredient. I felt a little buzzed. I knew now that I needed to stay close to our group. We danced and sang until we could no longer, and my friend and I returned to the ashram and were faced with a greater challenge: trying to remove the color from our clothes and skin. I chuckled at the experience. I couldn't tell you the last time I had simply played. My life had been filled with heaviness, and being childlike was almost foreign to me.

The celebrations continued, and there would be a feast in honor of Holi and then Aarti. The steps were filled to capacity as we waited for prayer to start. With the departure of members of our group, there was a shift with the people who remained; certain individuals jockeyed for control. It was interesting how the people who needed control acted out when they did not get what they wanted. For me, it was too late in the journey to get sucked into this.

We were asked to be a part of the ceremony called Hoven that evening; it would be a continuum of the passing of our friend. In the Hindu beliefs, once the soul left the physical body, the soul could be in a weakened state. The Hoven ceremony was to feed the soul. The ceremony started, and our group knelt around a small fire pit as the ceremony was performed. We were instructed to throw oil and grains into the fire, making an offering to the soul so that it was strong enough to pass over—a new twist to the phrase feeding the soul.

After Aarti the small group that had formed went to the rooftop of the ashram, where there was as sitting area. The night sky was clear and crisp; it was as if one could reach up and touch the stars. We enjoyed the group energy, and our conversation took us to a new level of bonding. We talked about the energy and the experiences of the weeks that had passed. I would look back to my death experiences and realize that this was what it was about: connecting, honoring, and loving. I tried not to think about how short my time in India would be.

INTUITION AND THE
TRAIN STATION

*I*t was early, and we had breakfast and then headed off to meet up with the other group members. We would go with the family to spread the ashes in the Ganges River. We would return to Rishikesh for the night and then head out to Chandigarh on the fourth. I picked up a few things from the market before we headed out to meet the others. I got to the train station to pick up our missing travelers. We sat in the hired car; I was with my Chicago friend and the principal of the University of India. The driver and the principal were in the front speaking Punjab or Hindi. My friend leaned over and said, "I wish I knew what they were saying." I told her that the principal wanted the driver to move the car into the shade, because by the time the train arrived, we would be extremely hot.

Both the driver and the principal turned to me and asked, "How did you know what we were saying?"

I realized what I had just done. To the best of my recollection, I did not speak Punjab or Hindi. I tried to joke with them about what had just happened, but we were all confused by it.

The train station was busy; I got out stretching my legs and watching the hundreds of travelers move to and from the train platform. As the trains came, I saw that they were in less than perfect condition and were packed with riders. Everyone on the train was just happy that they had got on. It was nothing like the experience of home, where people would demand their space and certainly would hesitate to give their seat to another. They announced the next train would hold our group member.

I went to the platform with another member of our group to wait. I noticed a monkey about twenty feet from me, and I could feel that this monkey was going to attack me. My friend made light of my concerns. "He is nowhere near you," he said. I tried to shift my focus but had strong feelings that I was in danger. Within seconds, the monkey came from behind me and ripped the bag from my hand. There was a large crash as the contents smashed onto the concrete platform. The bag was filled with small metal pots filled and sealed with blessed water from the Ganges River. The monkey fled, and I gathered the fallen contents from the platform as my friend located our wary traveler.

As I gathered myself, I saw that the monkey who attacked me. He had just stolen the lunch of another traveler waiting for the train. The monkey sat and was allowed to eat the contents of the bag, and everyone gave him space. I would later learn that the animals were honored, and they also needed to eat, so if they took food no one challenged them.

We headed to the temple for more prayers and then to the river where ashes, flowers, and a small box were placed in the fast-moving river, to be swiftly carried from our site. I watched the emotional impact on our friend as he celebrated his father's passing, and all I could think was that I would not shed any tears when my father passed.

We arrived late to the ashram and were provided tea and sandwiches, and then we retired to our rooms.

LEAVING THE ASHRAM

⊶⊷

$\mathcal{M}$orning came quickly, and I packed and had my tea. The quiet morning was interrupted by the harried energy of our friend whose father has passed. I questioned him, and he realized that there were still ashes not placed in the river. I was asked to go with him to the river. My initial response was to say no. This process was extremely personal, and I was unsure whether I wanted to be a part of that. I tried to convince his close friend to go with him, but he told me it was important that I go. Less than impressed, I agree to accompany him.

The two of us headed to the prayer center to place the remaining ashes and flowers. As I started down the stairs, one of the young girls from the orphanage presented me with a beautiful yellow lotus. The gesture of the young girl took me aback. I knelt down and accepted the flower, and I give her a hug and said, "Namaste." Both our eyes filled with tears, and she disappeared as quickly as she had appeared. My thoughts were reeling; how did she know that we would be there? When did she have time to get the flower? I was pulled back to the task at hand, and we placed the flowers and ashes into the river. I felt almost embarrassed that I had touched the ashes of his father. I only knew him slightly prior to his death. I said a prayer and wished his spirit a safe journey. The flood of emotion hit me. We returned to the ashram, where the group had finally converged with luggage in hand. We took a few final pictures and then headed off to the hired cars. As we snapped pictures, we noticed that there was a blue jay that had landed just above us; it was a symbol of safe travels. It was almost eerie yet comforting—a final message of spirit of our friend, perhaps.

We headed to Chandragar, or at least most of us. Our travel partner from Chicago would remain for a month, and the brother and sister from Vancouver would also stay for a few more days. We went to the family home of our group leader for a few days before our trip back home. Upon our arrival, the first daughter of the president of India invited us for lunch at her hotel. We were followed by security for the first daughter, and for the first time here I became aware of the potential risk.

REFLEXOLOGY SHARED

───── ∞ ─────

We arrived at the hotel and received a tour. They told us that it was a five-star hotel, but the difference of the standards between East and West were noted. As we sat for lunch, I was directly across from Jaishari. She had heard that I did reflexology and was intrigued with it. She would like a session before I left India. I was unsure of the schedule but agreed if there was time.

After a lovely Chinese lunch, vegetarian style, we were taken to Jaishari's farm, where there were beautiful gardens and animals. The next night she arrived at the house with others. It was like a mini-spa session had formed. I worked on Jaishari, and she told me that she was shocked with the heat that came from my hands. The energy was getting more powerful with each session that I did since the blessings. The lineup of people came after her, boosting what she had experienced. I was a little offended at the entitlement that the others presented to me. One was from Germany, and she was trying to roll her pant leg up but couldn't manage to roll it high enough, so she jumped up off the bed and removed her pants completely. There were men in the room, and they quickly covered their eyes and started to yell in Hindi. Again cultures clashed: India's modesty and Germany's liberation.

The night was over, and I retired to my room to break the energy and process what had happened. I heard a shriek from one of the rooms and went to see what was going on. The woman from Germany was naked in her room, and the male server entered after knocking and being told to enter. There was an immediate reprimand of the woman because it went against everything that India was about. I wondered if she had not learned anything in the weeks that she had been here.

The caste system started to show its ugly head. There were cooks, maids, and others who served the rich. I was not asked by the others; they just expected it and that set me off.

Later that night they served tea and biscuits, and people had calmed down about what had happened earlier. As we sat, there was a knock at the door. I was summoned to the door and presented with a package. I asked whom it was from, and it was from Jaishari. I thanked the messenger and returned to the living room to see what it was. Embarrassed about my earlier emotions, I opened the package: it was a fresh water pearl necklace with gold amulets. It was breathtaking. I quietly sent gratitude for the gift. No one had ever done that for me.

The next morning came and I was ready to go home after all that had happened.

THE JOURNEY BACK

⎯⎯⎯◈◈◈⎯⎯⎯

nly three of us headed to the airport. One of our friends came to the airport but was traveling on another airline. After a little airline drama now straightened out, we joined our friend in the Singapore lounge in the airport. We enjoyed mango juice and conversation, and then we went to the plane, said our good-byes, and headed out. Everything that had happened hit me all at once. I could feel the exhaustion in my body and just wanted to sleep.

The time in India came to an end, and so much had happened. I could feel the change within me and was unsure of what my life would look like upon my return. It was as if I had been given more truths, just like those that were given to me when I had died on the operation table. Would my life shift yet again?

We flew from Delhi to London, and then we were off to see relatives of my group leader for breakfast and meditation. Then we went to the market, and culture shock hit me as we wound through the streets of London. Biscuits and chips, English style, were on the must-have list. I thought I might have to ease into the change in food. I just wanted to be home. A lot had happened, and I was ready to unplug. I tolerated the demands of being with these people, but I wished I was on the plane for my final journey home.

There was tension between two of us as we landed, I was strained emotionally, jet lagged, and overtired, and I was being told how I needed to act at customs. I had flown before and did not understand what this direction was about. Then I remembered that he had placed some of his purchases in my bag, as he made room in his bag for his father's ashes and the things needed during the Canadian ceremony for his father.

As my feet touched Canadian soil, I felt different and knew that this, too, would be the beginning of much more to come. It was now time to process all that had happened. I went straight to bed and woke early for work. With that thought, I was sad that the India experience was over.

SPIRITUAL CONSCIOUSNESS

———— ⌇⌇⌇ ————

I stepped back into my world, but I had changed—how could I not? The spiritual consciousness that came from a trip to India was indescribable. It was like dying: there were not words that could truly express the awareness and truth that came from the experience.

Upon my return to work, it was obvious that those who tried to block me from going were stepping into drama. Their disdain was palpable, and it was clear the work that should have been done was barely touched. No worries; I jumped back into my job without complaining and got things done. No one asked about my trip.

I was clear as the weeks unfolded that this was the message that the counsel had when I died on the operation table: the spiritual group, working with people to help them heal the emotional body. I knew that I needed to study massage and find out more about the body.

I continued to work in the oil and gas industry and take classes. I became more tapped into my spiritual gifts and started practicing readings. The office group would start creating conflict. Some knew what I was doing, and it challenged their beliefs. I also noticed that when I created options for myself, those who wanted to control me had no power. I had decided long ago that I would not fight, so when people around me created conflict, I simply smiled and walked away from the drama and did what I knew I was supposed to do. Putting energy into their fears only fueled the drama, so I would again gently take my stand, smile, and then move through it, leaving those who wanted a fight spinning in their own stuff.

I would complete the massage course and would incorporate reflexology and massage as my side business. As time went by, between working in the office, holistic healing, and renovating my house, I was busy. I ran corporate campaigns that satisfied my volunteer needs, and I played sports on weekends. My life was full and great. For the first time I felt 100 percent safe and free.

I would continue to train in holistic therapies. As I worked with clients, I would be able to assist them with releasing the emotional posturing in their body. I became aware that I was sensing their emotions in the parts of their bodies, similarly to what I did when I did reflexology. I would ask questions about what I was getting, and they would validate that they had in fact been through the experience. Once we talked about the situation and validated their emotions, they could let go of the negative physical aspect that had manifested—anything from frozen shoulders, abuse trauma, negative posturing, digestive issues, and even fertility issues.

As I worked with clients, my intuition became stronger. It was to the point that the only thing anyone had to do was walk by me, and I could pick up information. All this created sensory overload for me. I would train in energy based healing, in order to learn how to protect and clear the information that I was getting.

The conflict between my day job and evening job would start to present itself. I could walking by my boss or coworkers and know what they were thinking and feeling. As people I worked with were whining about their experiences and knowing the truth about the situation, looking for me to support their drama,

I reserved my option to keep the peace. I would pull myself from certain groups even though I could protect myself. Protecting myself from the information was hard work; imagine having this tool at work or when you were dating. Things came in pretty clear, but I tried not to alienate myself from a world where people found it easier to lie than to tell the truth. I would have to develop strong communication tools to get to the truth without them feeling attacked.

As I stepped back into my normal world, I watched as the difference of the two cultures clashed before my eye. I was less than pleased. Perhaps it was due to all that I had seen and experienced, not only in India but collectively through the spiritual connection. With my guides and an understanding of life purpose, I struggled with the drama that sat in the corporate world. I realized that everyone acted out their unfinished family issues. Abandonment, jealously, and fear ruled the actions of those around me. I did not feed into them and stepped aside; that choice not to play within their game triggered them to lash out and sabotage my energy. I was embarrassed with what I witnessed: grown adults acting like children. Short of throwing temper tantrums, they demanded attention in their drama. When that was not met, they went for the jugular and took abusive actions. I just wished they could learn to own their stuff and not demand others to take it on. More important, they should tell the truth. If you are in the wrong, admit it, and if you are jealous, go fix it instead of bringing someone else down. It was hard work, trust me. Anyone that knew me knew where I stood. I did not pretend to be anything I was not, and more important, I knew exactly where I came from, which meant I knew my faults and the work I needed to heal it. The question would be why would they attack me and not work on themselves? I wondered what that world would look like.

TOUCH STONE

⟶ ∞ ⟵

s I settled into my life at home, I reconnected with an old boyfriend. Our paths seemed to cross after either of us shifted; it was like a touch stone to mark our journey. The connection we had was uncanny. I was always intrigued as to how we grew and then reconnected, almost like a touch stone energy, that person who you trusted with your life but did not have to be in each other's life to know they had your back. We ground each other, and for the most part we had a powerful physical connection. I watched myself: the old me was no longer there, and I was more open to grow in a relationship with him. In many ways, we were different from where we had come. We guided each other through the weak spots of who we were in the relationship. This time it was in a more playful way, which made it fun. As always, we did not last long due to his inability to tell the truth. He did not know that I was an intuitive and knew when he was lying. I was not sure if I was willing to settle for that aspect of him.

I refocused on work. I would leave the accounting group and move to the land department due to the constant conflict with people trying to take me from my place of peace. I knew in my heart that I was to do the healing work full time, and I just needed to leave. I ignored the message from my guides and moved into some fear. As I rejected the urge to leave, my body started to feel out of balance. At the time I was biking to work and eating cleanly, so I did not understand why I was feeling that way.

It was the morning of what would be me first day in the new department. I had been the accounting support for this group, so integrating into the group was easy. I would receive a call from my cousin to let me know that my paternal grandmother had passed away. I was thrown back into the family and was not sure if I wanted to be there. I told my new boss that my grandmother has passed. She was very supportive. I knew that my uncle from the coast couldn't get there for a few days, so I told her I would continue to work but would need time off. She told me I could take it right away, but I would delay my trip up north until my uncle arrived. This would be the first time I had seen anyone from my immediate family since the court case.

AWARENESS OF THE JOURNEY

———⊖⊖⊖———

As I headed up for the funeral, I became aware of the growth that I had been through on this journey, whereas others had remained stuck.

I stayed with my cousins. I arrived at the funeral, and my older brother got aggressive. I told him to bugger off and went to be with my aunts, uncles, and cousins. Shortly afterward, someone slammed into me, almost knocking me off balance. I turned and I saw a female walking away. I did not recognize the woman.

I saw my brother's ex-wife sitting in the foyer. I approached and asked why she was not coming in. She stated that my brother told her she was not allowed. I told her to come in. I assured her I would not let him bully her, but she still refused. She told me that my family treated her the way they treated me. Well, that must suck! It was interesting how everyone acknowledged that I was treated differently, but no one did anything to fix it.

As the service proceeded, I thought of what could have happened in my father's family to instill the abuse and alcoholism that ran rampant within this family. My younger sister grabbed my hand and held it tightly as the service continued. I knew that she was happy that I was there with her; that was not something I could say about the rest of the family.

As the service ended, we had lunch service at the funeral home dining room before heading out to the gravesite, which was an hour away. My ex-sister-in-law's son was a pallbearer. When he came out of the service area to sit with his mom, I sat with them and asked if I they wanted lunch. Again I was told they were not allowed. All I could think was how the abuse continued. I made up plates for them and returned to join my cousins. I was slammed into again, and it was the same woman. Did my brother need to get a girl to fight his battles?

I couldn't believe my brother's arrogance. These people were a part of this family, and they were there to pay their respects like everyone else. I stayed and chatted with them. She remembered she had brought a picture of my niece, and we went to her truck to get it. I saw the picture and knew that I would never get to know my niece. My brother would make sure of that. If she did get to know me, he knew that she would know the truth about her dad and grandfather. I thanked my sister-in-law for the picture. She left but let her son stay at the burial that was out of town.

I got back into the reception, and someone banged into me from behind for the third time as I was speaking to the funeral director and an old friend. This time I confronted her. "I am not sure if you're aware, but you are at a funeral. Could you perhaps try and act with just a little class?" I turned back to the conversation I was having. I couldn't imagine someone acting that way at a funeral. What was her goal? I would later see her sitting next to my brother. He was grooming her, to see how much he could get her to do for him. I questioned what he had told her in order for her to fight his battles. I knew that he would use his control over her later—that was what abusers do. Did my brother really think that I was going to lie down and take this harassment? I saw that if he was getting her to do this when she did not even know me, then she was just a puppet that he would use to his advantage.

My cousin came and asked me what I had said to her. I told her. She told me, "She went to my brother and made a comment, and he was going to get up and put you in your place." My aunt told him to sit down and behave. Was he serious? Would he ever understand that he was just a clone of his father? His need to be in control made him out of control.

We headed out to the gravesite in a small town in British Columbia, the place I was born. We lay my grandmother to rest, and there was a dinner at the local hotel for the family and locals. My older sister was there. I had not seen here since the court case. I did not trust her because she stood in the courtroom and lied. Her comments that she would allow an abuser to have access to her children still made my blood boil.

Rebuilding Family

would spend time with my cousin and her family. She
had an older daughter and twin girls. There was a strong
bond with the girls and me, even though I lived so far
away and had not seen them much. It was hard to explain but
comforting. One of the twins crawled up into my arms and fell
fast asleep. My cousin was shocked because the girl did not go to
anyone. I embraced this moment because it was as if she already
knew who she could trust, and I was honored.

I headed back home. Hours on the road gave me time to
think, and I was unsure whether or not that was a good thing.
My connection with the girls brought me back to my abortion at
age fourteen, and a miscarriage at twenty-four. I knew I would
have been a good mom. I chuckled as I rethought that. Perhaps
I'd have been overly protective on one level, then pushing and
encouraging on another. I would not want my children to live in
fear. I reflected on my friends that had blessed me with the gift
of their children. I would take them on weekends, and we would
hang out. I would guide them when they could not talk to their
parents. I made baby blankets for a lot of them, and perhaps my
energy made its way to them through the blankets. I was Auntie
to many of them. I would not know my own nieces and nephews
because of their parents' choices. I knew that when they were old
enough, perhaps they would find me on their own, if our paths

were meant to cross. I reflected on my time as a big sister in the Big Sisters Organization. I learned from all of them that love did not have boundaries, and for that I was blessed.

I reflected on the relationships that I had. Each allowed me to grow and get closer to being my best—which sometimes was not great as I looked back. I saw so many people angry about past relationship, and the hatred between them. I looked at relationships as tools to grow. I learnt how to communicate, to fight fair, to play, and most important to love. I sent gratitude to all that had let me learn who I was in a relationship. Without them, I would still be stuck.

As I traveled south on the highway, I literally passed my life. Each city allowed me to reflect at the growth and who I had become. Again I sent gratitude for the journey. I chuckled, thinking that perhaps I could have had the journey with a little less drama. I was bumped, bruised, and shifted down the journey of life, and I still held the smile that I told myself that no one would ever take away, no matter what! I was going to win. The only way I knew that I was winning was if I was still smiling.

I returned home and I would continue studying both in the holistic therapies and for my corporate job.

STRENGTHENING MY GIFTS

I tried to maintain balance, and my life was good. I noticed that I started to see spirit more. Sometimes spirit would come through during treatments, and other times it was while I was out doing day-to-day things. It took me into some fear. I knew I was fine with getting messages from spirit, but I was not sure I wanted to be the translator for others. I came to a place that I fought the information I was getting, and the pressure in my head when I resisted the information was debilitating. I wasn't sure that I wanted the responsibility of giving people the information, knowing that what I had to share would change their world.

When information came in, I would tell the client that I was getting some intuitive information, and I asked whether they wanted it. If they said yes, I would give it. If they said no, the pressure would subside, and I could get on with their session. I would learn over time to maneuver through this. Again, this would be something that would create conflict at work. Getting information about who these people really were made me pull back rather than deal with the constant conflict. The best way I could describe it was if I could see through the walls of my neighbor's home, and I knew their truth; it would make my world different. I would discern quickly as to whom I could let into my world. I did not want to know so much about my coworkers. The world would be an interesting place if we could all see through the veils of deceit. However, one's heart may break by always knowing the truth.

I would study energy courses that allowed me to harness this information, at least somewhat. I had been a part of a meditation group for about four years, and my clients were intrigued with how I used this to get information. I did not know how to explain to them how to use this technique for themselves. This studying took me into the field of hypnotherapy. I would attain my certification in hypnotherapy, and then later I was certificated in regression therapy and worked with clients as they sought out answers for themselves.

I would find the beliefs that blocked people from what they wanted. I truly had never made the connection before this. As I reflected on all the limiting things that I was told growing up, I was surprised I was not lying in a gutter with a needle in my arm. Perhaps if I did not have my guidance, I would have ended things years ago, but I was certainly glad that I had not.

I would continue to work study and continue with the self-discovery of who I was.

Medicine versus Holistic

———— ∞ ————

I would notice something with my body again: it was sick. I scanned it energetically, as I had in the past. I knew that I had another abscess. I went to the doctor and told him exactly where the problem was. He rolled his eyes and reminded me that he was the doctor. I told him I have no energy.

Actually, there was something wrong I could feel it, I responded.

"You are just getting old," he said.

"Is that your medical option, or just your option?" I told him I wanted blood work done, to see if there was an infection or if my iron was low. He again challenged me. I refused to leave without him ordering the tests, and he did so in a huff.

I got the results. He again said there was nothing wrong and that everything was normal. I asked him, "What was my iron level?" He told me he did not do an iron test. I come in exhausted and he does not check for my iron level. "Any chance you could test that?" He reluctantly ordered the tests.

I went back again for test results. My iron was down to two; it should be a minimum of twenty. I walked out with an iron prescription. I would continue to feel exhausted. I did energy balancing and ate well to help my body heal. Nothing seemed to make a difference. I continued to do treatments with clients and work. I ran corporate campaigns and biked to and from work. I did not understand why my body would not heal.

I was biking home one night, and my whole body began to shake. I was dizzy and collapsed on the floor as I got in the house, becoming unconscious. As woke up, I knew that I would have to get the doctor to look further into this. I knew my body, and it was now screaming at me.

PAST LIFE VISIONS

—⊗⊗⊗—

*I*t was my birthday, and a friend wanted to take me to a healer who did a meditation night. I thought that it would be an interesting night out and agreed.

The healer hosted the event in her home. We arrived and took a seat. There were a few people already there, and I introduced myself and asked how this all worked. There would be a meditation, and then we would hold the energy for a healing to take place. *Simple enough,* I thought to myself. The rest of the circle arrived, and we began. One of the people took a seat to have the first healing.

I was holding the energy, and then *bam!* I started getting a vision, with full color and audio. I couldn't pull myself from the vision, and it seemed like it went on forever. I was shown a vision that was from the past. There were two men fighting with swords. They had both fallen in love with the same woman, and the only way that the issue could be resolved was a fight to the death. I watched as the fight ensued, until one of them beheaded the other. The survivor looked to the woman and said, "You're so weren't worth it." I thought to myself that this survivor would never choose a woman over a friendship ever again. Then the vision ended, and I became conscious as I sat within the group.

What was that? I had never experienced that before—at least not while I was awake. I dreamed like that, in full detail and colors, with emotion and all-inclusive experience.

I sat quietly as I processed what had just happened. The leader asked if anyone got anything. I waited to see what everyone else got. This group had been together for six months, so I was interested in what they came up with and how my information fit in. No one said anything. I thought, *are you kidding me?* If these people have been working with this woman for six months, I expected something. The healer leaned forward, looked at me, and asked if I saw anything. I was unsure if I wanted to say anything. I told her yes but hesitated giving up the information and what it meant.

She encouraged me to share. As I did, I was apologetic; I felt as if I had seen into his soul, and I was not sure I was deserving of that gift. I told the man what I saw and what it meant, and how he came to resolve this experience in this lifetime. I was not sure how he felt about me being able to see what I did, and I tried to minimize the experience.

We went back into another meditation healing, and I received a vision for that person, too. This continued for each person: I told them what I saw and how it may create struggle within their lives now. Each person took in the information and validated the message behind the vision.

It was now my turn. As I sat, I could feel and hear spirit around me. Spirit was saying, "We know it is your birthday, we know it is your birthday." Intuitively, I told them to stop fussing; I was trying to stay focused on the healing that I was receiving. The energy continued to taunt me playfully. After the healing was done, I was about to reclaim my seat when the healer said, "Spirit would like to honor your birthday and would like to bestow the keys to the higher dimensions upon you." I was embarrassed but sent gratitude and returned to my seat.

There were a few more people to receive their healings. I was not sure how much more of this I could handle, but I settled in and received more messages for the remaining members of the group. The last person was ready to go. This vision was intense that I was literally witnessing an argument between her and the masters and God. I did not feel like I should be witnessing this. I tried to pull out of the energy, and then I was told in no uncertain terms that I would witness this. I was less than impressed. The arrogance of her soul shocked me. It was as if God presented her with all the tools possible for healing, and she stood there pissed off that she had to come and walk among these humans. I would not want to be in her meeting when she crossed over.

Spirit knew that she would not listen, as usual. I was given specific instructions that she was to sit there and listen, and if she huffed, puffed, or blinked, I was to stop the message. I told her the conditions attached to her message, and truly I did not think she blinked the whole session. I heard the anger in my voice as I gave her the message. I knew it was not my emotion or intensity, and I tried to stay grounded in it all.

I finished with the message and was feeling extremely sick to my stomach. I jumped from my seat and ran to the bathroom to throw up. I started to cry because I was overwhelmed with all that I had witnessed. All I wanted to do was get out of the space. I thank the hostess then told my friend he needed to get me out of there. The only thing I wanted to do was stuff food down my throat; stuffing emotion was what I knew. He was still reeling with everything that I was able to do and wanted to talk about it. I told him to let it go; I needed to detach from it and process it in my own time, and more questions was not what I needed. We went to eat, and I binged, and then all I wanted to do was purge. I get home and purged. Old habits were hard to break.

HEALING CRISIS

I was not sure I could handle doing that, ever again. My body went into resistance. It was one week from the meditation, and I started my period. The only problem was I that did not stop bleeding. I was two weeks into this cleansing process, and there was no end in sight of it lightening up. The energy that I pulled through had shifted me quickly, and my body went into a healing crisis. Too much of a good thing was too much of a good thing.

I headed to the doctor and told him I was hemorrhaging, He said, "Well, isn't that what you women do?" I was in shock with his attitude and lack of professionalism.

I told him to find out what was causing it; all he wanted was to do was give me pills. I took the prescription but did not fill it; I knew intuitively that was not what needed to be done. I persisted with getting him to look and see what was causing this. I was now losing blood twenty-four seven, and I was now eight weeks into it. I was emotionally drained and physically exhausted. He was still being arrogant, and I told him I want to see a gynecologist. He snidely remarked it would take eight weeks. I reminded him that I was hemorrhaging, but he gave me his "I don't give a shit" attitude. I was in the bathroom every twenty minutes completely soaked in blood. I was bleeding to death, and all he wanted was to be in control.

I entered the emergency room and explain I had been hemorrhaging, and I was on my ninth week. They told me to have a seat, I was given my hospital wristband, and I sat in the waiting room. I was in and out of the bathroom, and with each visit I was getting weaker—and I was running out of supplies. I explained to the nurse, and she tossed pads at me and told me to have a seat. I had to look twice I thought my mother was sitting there at least they had the same energy. The waiting room was full, and I sat and watched people with broken bones, headaches, and runny noses getting treatment. Apparently losing all my blood was not that important. Thirteen hours later, I was still there. I was shocked with this process. I finally got in to see a doctor. I had lost blood for thirteen hours and was not sure I had any more to give.

They did a blood test on my hemoglobin and iron levels. My hemoglobin was 63 and my iron was zero; the least hemoglobin should be was 125, and with no recordable iron in my body, oxygen couldn't get to my cells and organs, creating exhaustion. The doctor came in and said I should probably get a blood transfusion. I asked if they were going to see if they could find out why I was losing all my blood. Flippantly he said, "You are probably just starting menopause," and walked away. *Could you back up your hypothesis? If I remembered correctly when I studied science we could have a hypothesis but we needed to back it up with facts; otherwise it was just your opinion.* I guessed that was no longer valid in medicine. I was thirty-eight and knew it was not menopause. He returned ten minutes later and told me to go see my doctor, to arrange a transfusion. What? I was in a hospital! He dismissed me. I went home, stunned and exhausted by this experience.

I phoned the office and told them I would not be in to work that day. I made another appointment with my doctor and told him what I had been through. He snidely remarked, "I told you, it is going to take eight weeks to get into a gynecologist." I would be dead by then! He shrugged his shoulder and walked out the room. Health care at its finest! Perhaps what I needed was a lawyer instead.

I retreated home and tried to figure out what to do next. I started with a meditation, and I intuitively got that it was an abscess.

I finally got a call from the gynecologist's office and was booked for the following week—eight weeks to the day I had contacted my doctor. I prayed that I lived to see that appointment, and my prayers were answered. I told the doctor my history and told him I thought there was another abscess. I told him all I wanted was for him to stop the bleeding. He told me, "I don't have hospital privileges."

You could have knocked me over with a feather. I waited eight weeks for this? Why was it so hard to get people to do their jobs? Complacency at every corner—I was sick of it. "So what do I do?" I asked.

He responded, "I could give you some pills." If I had the energy I would have started beating these idiots one by one, or better yet, start cutting things off and let *them* bleed to death and see how quick the medical system kicked in.

I knew I was going see the other side of this; I just needed to get a doctor who did not have his head up his ass! Perhaps doctors should get paid by results and not just warming a chair.

I go back to the idiot doctor that sent me to the gynecologist with no hospital privileges. I confront him on his incompetency with a few choice words to follow and stormed out of the office.

Two days later, I was in a medi-center, in a treatment room. Minutes passed, and the door swung open; a female doctor entered. She stood in the doorway and shouted, "You have arthritis of the jaw."

I was shocked. Was she kidding me? I asked her if she was in the right room and told her I did not have arthritis. She stood, there as if that was all she needed to do; she had not even come into the room, and that was her diagnosis. Nice! I asked her, "Well I guess you made your fifty-five dollars! Does arthritis in the jaw cause you to hemorrhage for eight months?" She was unplugged and in no way going to do her job, either! I stormed out of the office in tears.

I phoned Health Link to try to get some direction. "The only thing you can do is find a new doctor," the woman said. I told her perhaps I should find a lawyer instead and hung up on her.

I lay in bed in tears. Why was no one listening! I heard intuitively, "Has anyone every listened to what you needed?" Everything became very clear to me. With my family no longer in the picture, I was now being abused and neglected by the health care system. Great—now here was a battle I had no energy to fight.

Clearing patterns within my soul path came to me. Here I go again, working on myself. I clear emotional patterns in my path the bleeding subsides somewhat but not completely.

I continue to show up for work and deal with what I was going through silently. There were changes within the company, and the added stress was not welcome. I pulled myself from running corporate campaigns and the social club, and I reserved what little strength that I had. My boss came to me and asked if I was all right. I told her I was very sick and could no longer do everything. She was fine with the explanation and told me to let her know if I needed anything. "Yes, I need a doctor that does not have his head up their ass. Do you know where I could find one? Spirituality be dammed for now.

I would start to get intuitive information non-stop from people. My body was fighting to stay alive, and I had to pull this energy through me. I could not find the shut-off button. I knew who was pregnant, who was cheating on their spouse, and who was cheating the company. I pulled myself from anything that needed physical effort. I sat quietly in my office and did my job. Interesting enough, this created drama; tongues were wagging, but no one came to talk to me—it was easier for them to talk behind my back. My weight spiked with the stress of bleeding, not sleeping, and the physical and emotional fight.

MEDICAL SYSTEM FAILS ME

———— ✺ ————

made another attempt with this doctor to get some help. I had an appointment but sat for over an hour in his office. With each minute that passes, the blood flowed, and I was soon out of supplies. I told the nurse that if she did not get me in immediately, she would be talking to my lawyer. She got up and went in to see the doctor; I got in immediately. I butted heads with him and demanded that he do something, and *now.* He got me to a hematologist but did not look for what was causing this; he told me that there was no infection in my blood. I explained to him I was bleeding out every day—there was no blood to check, let alone to get infection. It was wasted breath again.

Weeks passed again, and then I met with the hematologist, I told him what was happening, and he said he just gave blood—he didn't look for what was causing the loss. Was he kidding me? I arrived at the hospital, and they hooked me up to the iron infusion. As the iron entered my body, I went unconscious within minutes; it was too much for my body to handle. The nurse couldn't believe how quickly I went under and had no explanation, either. Eight hours later I went home to sleep. This cycle continued every month for four years, and no one was looking for the cause.

At work, the company went through a takeover, and the new management was less than supportive. I continued to show up for work and did what I needed to do. Truthfully, the only reason I showed up for work was because I did not want to die alone at home.

The people in the office knew that I was getting iron infusions and were speculating what I might have, but interesting enough, no one asked; it was easier for them to create drama and make up stories. I left them to their stupidity. I no longer had patience for what was happening in this office. I had someone from the management team daily trying to stir things up with me. I would not play their games, and it drove them into a tailspin.

They rewarded me for going over and above my duties, and in the next breath they were complaining that I was not a team player. They challenged me as to why I did not get involved with the United Way campaign. I told them I was sick and did not have the energy. They did not accept my explanation and snidely commented, "You do not look sick." Every day the harassment got more intense. What were they after? What was it they needed from me that they were not getting?

The final assault was the VP of the department, who challenged me about my resume. "There is no way you have done everything that you have put on your resume."

Really? I thought there were probably ten things that I had left off, but in his mind the numbers did not add up. I was now out to push buttons. "Well, perhaps we should go sit in HR and go through my resume, and then you can talk to my lawyer. How does that sound to you? I ask have you reviewed everyone's resume, or just mine. Have you looked at all my annual job reviews and all the things I have done since I have been with the company?" He walks out of the office and did not come back in. I might be dying, but I was not dead yet. Bring it!

TIME FOR RELAXATION

Christmas was coming, and I usually headed to Mexico for the holidays. I decided that I would go again. Perhaps this would be the last time I go anywhere. I booked the trip, and knowing that I did not have to be around these people for two weeks brought me joy.

I arrived in Mexico, and I was unsure if it was the fact I was not being overloaded with the office drama, or if it was the warm sun, but I felt at ease. The people on the flight stayed at the same hotel that I did, so we had already bonded. On the bus ride to the hotel a young couple from a small town across the BC border were very chatty and nervous. I told if they needed anything, they could call me. I had studied Spanish and had traveled to that part of Mexico before. It seemed to settle them. We arrived late, so we were seated at the same table for dinner, not realizing that we would have to sit with each other for the full two weeks.

The weather shifted, and we were in a downpour. Most of us were sitting in the covered lounge, and everyone was getting bored. I asked if any of them would like me to read their face. The three couples sitting at my table agreed. As I read each of their faces, I told them things about themselves that I would have no way of knowing. I saw their spouses shake their heads no as I read their partners. I knew I was right, and they would tell me I was 100 percent right. I knew things their spouses did not even know. We joked about the situation, but I knew that there would be some discussion later that night between the couples.

As the week continued, the young couple came to breakfast, and I picked up that something was wrong with the man. I asked, and he said nothing was wrong. I pushed him, knowing that he was lying. He shouted out, "She was trying to kill me in my sleep!" I was shocked and knew that this was not her personality. I inquired intuitively what this was about. I got that they had bought something that had a spirit attachment to it. I asked them if they had gone shopping, and they excitedly proclaimed yes. I explained to them what I had received from spirit and explained that the object needed to be cleared, or he may not make it through the week.

We headed to their room, and they laid the objects out onto one of the beds. I scanned the gifts and found the one that was corded by spirit: it was a totem made of bone. I started to clear the object, and as I was doing so, the girl was sitting on the opposite bed and the young man was sitting in the corner chair. I felt the energy move from the totem to the chair. Then I felt an incredible surge of energy from the young man. As I turned to look at him, his chest was pinned to his lap and his arm was extended, reaching for his cigarettes. I realized the entity had left the object and had gone to him. I immediately cleared him, and his body shot upright. He was obviously freaked out. I checked to see how he felt. He explained that it was as if was very tall man had stood behind him, pushing him downward, and there were hands pushing him, and the hands were very hot. He confirmed what I had seen. I got him settled and had both of them take a deep breath to ground their energies. Both of them did so, and then at the same time blurted out, "It does not stink." I had smelled it when I had walked, but I did not associate it with the spirit. With them both settled, I returned to the pool.

Later that night I headed back to own my room; the heat had taken its toll on my body. I barely had the energy to get back to my room. I entered the room and felt a spirit in the room. I said out loud, "I know you are here. I don't have any energy for anything more. You need to leave." I got into the shower and rinsed the day off, and then I headed to bed. I could still feel the energy, and I again stated "I know you are here." With that, my attention shifted toward the patio window; the curtains were slightly open, and the outside patio light shined through the sheer. All of a sudden the light was blocked, and there was a huge man standing there, his body dressed in warrior gear as he held a spear. I did not have the energy to move, run, or even scream; even for me, this was way outside the box. I questioned him as to what he wanted. All I heard was he was there to thank me for releasing him. I told him he was welcome, but now he had to leave. With that, his energy left and did not return.

Choosing to Leave

⸻

$\mathcal{A}$s the two weeks came to an end, I concluded that when I returned, I would quit my job. Upon arriving at the office, the department VP was in my office and asked how my holiday was. I replied it was fine, and he asked where I went. I told him Mexico. He snidely remarked, "You don't look like you were in Mexico!"

I thought, *what now, I am going to be confronted about this?* I told him again I was in Mexico. He challenged me again, and I asked him, "Where do you think I went?" He told me what he thought, and I stated, "Well, I guess if anyone asks, I will tell them your version of the story—apparently the truth is not good enough." And with that, I walked out of my office.

They offered me a package to leave the company the next day. I took it and left the drama behind. *Thanks for giving me what I wanted. I win!* There was a group that thought they had just pulled off the most amazing thing. I chuckled, knowing none of them could do the work on my desk. I knew that their smirks would soon be wiped off their faces when they realized they would now have to do all my work. The funny thing with that was that they now would learn how much work really was on my desk. Weeks later, I heard that those who went after me were struggling with the workload; some were leaving the company, and another stepped down from the supervisor role because she was not able to handle the demands of everything that came off my desk. Regrets, anyone? I believed what went around came around. "Good luck," was all I could say. Sometimes karma comes quickly. The saying "Shoot first and ask questions later" came flashing back to me as I smiled.

Part 3

---∞∞∞---

Helping

LET THE HEALING BEGIN

*left the oil and gas company on Friday. I incorporated my own company, found rental space, and started doing my healing work full-time on Monday. I was booked solid two weeks in advance. My body shifted as I started doing the healing work and stayed out of the petty drama.

I found another doctor. I went through my history, and he wanted to talk to my former doctor in Edmonton. After speaking with him, my new doctor was told he should check whatever I asked, because, "She knows things!" I chuckled, but that feeling was cut short when my new doctor said, "I will determine what needs to be checked." Pop went the balloon! I was sick of this and was almost ready to drive back north to see my old doctor. The only thing keeping me was that I would have to stop every twenty minutes due to the bleeding.

Breathe, I tell myself.

He sent me for an ultrasound, and during the examination the technologist told me my ovaries looked great. I state, "Ovaries? I only have one ovary—I had one surgically removed when I was twenty-five."

"No, you have two. I could see them."

I said, "No, unless they grow back, I only have one."

"I could see two," she insisted. Seriously, was she hearing me? She proceeded to give me an anatomy lesson. "You are supposed to have two ovaries." I explained I was aware of that, but I had had one surgically removed! Again she insisted that I had two.

I told her; "Perhaps what you are seeing on the right side is the abscess that is poisoning me! Why I need to have an ultrasound in the first place." She was not getting it. I told her to stop touching me and to go to get her supervisor. She knew that I was serious.

The supervisor came in, and I explained that she was insisting that I had two ovaries. I again explained that I had had one surgically removed. If in fact there was something on the right, perhaps it would be important to mark that so that my doctor could assess what they thought they were seeing. The supervisor was less than impressed that I had challenged his staff, made a comment to the tech, and left the room.

The results were in, and I headed to my doctor to see what has been found. He told me that everything was normal. I asked him if they marked my right ovary on the exam, and he told me no. *Are you kidding me?*

I told him what I had been through and what was said. I asked if he would do something else: check out whatever was seen on my right side. He then told me it was probably just scar tissue.

I told him I want to see a gynecologist, and perhaps I could get one that had hospital privileges. He looked shocked at my request. I filled him in on the last experience and told I was at my wits' end with the bullshit that I had been through with the medical system. Again I waited eight weeks to see a specialist. Now it had been four years of bleeding, four doctors, and a truckload of bullshit. I was done, emotionally, mentally, and physically.

I went through my history again with the specialist and continued to go to the hematologist. More exams, more drugs, and more time, I knew *my* time was running out.

Spirit Activity

I continued to work part time from home and in a location in the south part of the city. The space was filled with energy, and it seemed like every day there was spirit energy grabbing for my attention. I was doing my best to work with clients, but the spirit energy was almost stamping its feet as I worked in the space.

I was cleaning my treatment room, and I felt someone standing at the door. As I looked I saw a soul energy: it was an older man. I was no longer able to dismiss the energy; the best way to clear it was deal with it. I asked the energy what he needed, and he told me he was lost. I went into the linen supply room and sat with the energy. There were not windows in the room, so as I closed the doors, the room was completely black but I could see the old man. I asked him why he was lost, and he told me he couldn't find his wife; with that, the whole room illuminated. I turned to see who had come into the room. Both doors were closed, but I looked up to the left of where I was sitting and saw the most incredible light. As I looked, I saw a woman standing in the light. I heard intuitively that she was his wife and had been waiting for him. She explained he had experienced dementia, and since he had died, he had been confused because he did not know his wife had died before him. I showed him the light, and he saw his wife. Their souls reunited within the light, and like a switch the room was completely dark again. I sat in amazement of this experience. I had never passed anyone over before, and I was humbled by the experience and a little shaken.

In the weeks that followed, I noticed an increase of spirit activity. It was taking what little energy that I had to continue to work at this level. I decided that I would set a vortex in the linen room to pass who ever needed the help. I forgot about this and got on with working the physical beings that needed my help—the ones that were paying me. I chuckled to myself.

Weeks passed, and one of my co-workers came to the front desk. She looked like she had seen a ghost. I asked if she was all right. She told me that she was in the linen supply room, and she felt like she was being sucked into a vortex. Oops! I then realized the intention that only those wishing to pass over could find it. I questioned her if she was suicidal, and she was. I readjusted the vortex and tried to balance her from her suicidal state.

MEDICAL PROCEDURES

*I*t was now December 17, 2005, four years and three months after my bleeding issue started. I was scheduled for an ablation; it was a process where the uterus was burned, to stop the bleeding, I realized it was exactly twenty years to the day since they had found my abscessed appendix. I went home after the day surgery; there was some relief with less blood being lost. It was about three days of relief … but then something else was happening.

I was gushing infection, literally non-stop. It was not pretty. I called the doctor's office but got no response. I headed back to the hospital at three in the afternoon. I called my sister and left a message that I was going into the hospital, and I was not sure I would be coming out. As I heard my own words hit my ears, I cried knowing that this may be my final exit.

I registered and took a seat. It felt like poison was flooding my body, and I floated in and out of consciousness. The emergency room was wall to wall with people. I tried to sit motionless as to not induce any more flow than what I had been experiencing. I breathed myself into a meditative state. My body was fighting what was happening, and I again said prayers.

My body was jolted awake from what was a deafening silence. I looked around, and the waiting room was empty other than a security guard and me. He noticed that I had awoken and said, "Can I help you?"

"Yes, I am here to see a doctor." I held up my arm with the hospital wrist band on it.

They put me into a room, and doctors came and went as they rotated in and out of shift. A female doctor came in with three student doctors. They were focused on the bleeding and not the infection. She rattled off the procedure to the other doctors that she intended to do. I intuitively got she was wrong in her decision. I placed an intuitive request that she be downloaded with the most beneficial procedure to assist me. Within seconds of the request, she stopped midway through her next sentence, looked directly at me, and said, "We are not going to that. We are going to do this instead," and then she proceeded to state what that would be. I sent gratitude to her and knew that she, too, was intuitive.

They went into the uterus and filled the fibroids with a gel-like substance. The procedure was an embolization, in the hopes of sealing them so that bleeding would stop. They explained that they could only do a partial ablation, so they wanted to do this to hopefully stop the bleeding completely. I could feel the infection, but they were missing this part of what I was trying to tell them. They did the procedure, and again I could feel the poison fill my body.

The nurses told me, "Today you will go home; you need to arrange a ride." I knew from my guidance that that would be the death of me if I went home. I called my sister and asked her for a ride home. I had been in the hospital for five days now, and she had not responded to my earlier call. She told me that she was leaving for Red Deer and asked if I could find someone else to take me home. I was shocked. I heard myself say, "You know what? Don't worry about it. I will take a cab. Sorry for being an inconvenience to you." I hung up.

I got another visit from the admitting doctor. He wanted to send me home. I challenged him. "Are you sending my home because it is Christmas, or because I am well? So, if you are sending me home because it is Christmas, I will die tomorrow in my bed."

He was shocked by my statement and said, "Well, I guess you are not going home, then."

"That works for me," I said.

The doctor left, and within minutes my sister appeared. "Are you ready to leave?" I explained the doctor had changed his mind. She was mad and more concerned with the fact that she had been inconvenienced than the fact that I would be staying in the hospital. She left. I knew exactly what her expectation would be if the tables were turned.

The day ended in the hospital. I woke to the morning light hitting my face. I went to move my body, and I was completely paralyzed, all I could do was scream. Fear hit me like never before. I yelled at the lady sharing the room with me to buzz the nurses and tell them I couldn't move. The nurses run into the room, and then I heard the woman in the next bed: "I'd better not get infection from her."

I snapped, "Yeah, why not make this about you! I am fighting for my life, and you are going to make this about you!" Then everything went black.

I was unsure how long I was under or what happened after I blacked out. I awoke hours later with three doctors standing at the foot of my bed. I did not recognize them, and their energy was different. I got their attention and asked who they were. I was told they were from the infectious disease department. "That can't be good," I said to them. "So what is wrong with me?"

The head doctor said, "We do not know—we have never seen anything like this before."

I told them, "Well, whatever it is, it has been festering for four years, so good luck with that."

The lead doctor was shocked at what I told him. They huddled and talked as they left the room.

My body was flooded with antibiotics, and I returned home ten days later. The process was still not over; they still had not found the source. I couldn't seem to communicate to them that there was an abscess still in me. I would continue to take eight antibiotics three times a day for a month. I felt better finally; it was now January 29.

I wanted to work out. I headed to the gym and did a light workout. Everything felt good. I woke the next morning, and I couldn't stand up straight. My abdomen had a grapefruit lump on the right side where my ovary once was. I panicked—what was going on? I intuitively got the message, "Get to the hospital." I couldn't handle the thought of having to spend thirteen hours in the emergency room, and so I opted to go to the doctor's office. I couldn't get into see my doctor, so I went to another one, and he took one look at me and told me to get to the hospital. I was still haunted by my experience with the emergency room, and I asked if he would write me a doctor's note to get me seen immediately.

I headed to the hospital, note in hand. I entered triage in the emergency department and explained to the nurse what was going on as I handed her the note. She read the note and barked, "If you think this note is going to get you in any faster, you are mistaken." I was shocked by her response and shook my head. I was registered, got yet another wristband, and took a seat. As I sat, any little movement shot pain through my body. I tried to find a chair that was independent of the others. I found a seat near the end of the waiting room.

I quietly waited my turn; the emergency room was once again full. I tried to settle the fear that ran through me. Time seemed to fade in and out. I become aware of someone saying, "God, please don't let me die. Please, God, don't let me die!"

A Stranger's Help

he next time I became aware, there was a woman sitting across from me, and she asked me if I needed some tissue. "Why I would need tissue?" I asked.

She explained, "You are crying, and you keep asking God not to let you die." I told her no, I was not. "Sweetie, you are. You are soaked in tears." I looked down, and my chest was drenched with tears. She comforted me and stated that she was going to get me some help. She yelled at the nurse, "We need some help here!"

The crabby nurse from triage came out and signaled for the assistant to get a wheel chair. The nurse came over to me and grabbed my arm to put me in the chair, but I couldn't straighten up. Her anger was evident, and she grabbed me again. The people around me were getting angry at her, and I heard someone say to her, "Stop being a bitch." If I were not in so much pain, I would have probably laughed. I hollered at the nurse to settle down; I had to do this slowly. Now she was even more frustrated with me. I think she realized that everyone was watching her because she stopped being aggressive with me, at least physically.

I managed to get into the chair, and she pushed me in front of triage and left me there before returning to her desk. I heard her tell the other nurse, "I am sick and tired of people who come in here that don't look after themselves." She perhaps needed to rethink her career path, because she sucked at this one! If only

I had the strength to confront her. With that thought, I felt my body collapse, and everything went black.

The next thing I remembered, I was in the back of emergency with two nurses who were trying to get me into a gown and get me to take a urine sample. I had no idea how I got to the back. The younger nurse walked with me to the bathroom to give a sample. I was instructed not to lock the door. I went to the bathroom and came out with the sample jar, however it was empty. I was so disassociated that I could not put those simple instructions into action. I again realized in that moment that I may not leave the hospital this time.

The young nurse walked me to the bed, and the senior nurse joined us. With a hospital gown in hand, they gave more instructions that overwhelmed me. I was grateful for the compassion of these two, and I thanked them for being so nice to me. She was surprised with my comment, saying that she was there was to help. I told her that the nurse out at triage needed to learn to be nice. She wanted to know what happened, and she assured me that she would handle the situation. They left as I got into the gown. The next thing I remember, they were rushing me down a hallway. I could feel everyone's panic. Just like in the movies, the lights blurred as they raced down the hallway. I faded to black again and awoke in yet another area. The bed was curtained, and I heard a voice from the medical staff just outside the curtain. The next thing I heard was a woman's voice: "I have an abscess in my fallopian tube, and it is going to rupture." It was like a chant. The chant continued, and I thought to myself, *I wish she would shut up.*

No sooner had the thought come than a male nurse pulled back the curtain. He said to me, "You are definitely insistent that is what is wrong with you." I was confused by his comment and asked him what he was talking about. He informed me that I kept saying I had an abscess in my fallopian tube. I felt like I was having an out-of-body experience and knew this was an intuitive message. Now if only I could get the medical staff to help.

He headed out of the curtained area and told someone what I had been saying. The doctor scoffed at him and snapped, "Does she have a medical degree?"

I heard the male nurse defend me, and then I heard, "No, but I have a really good lawyer." The doctor reluctantly conceded to run tests.

The results came back. I had a tubular mass in my right fallopian tube. Perhaps that right ovary that the ultrasound tech had seen was the abscess. Doctors zero the intuitive girl, one more for the books.

They contacted my gynecologist to do the surgery; he was on staff that night. I continued to go in and out of conscious. I was unsure of how long I had been in the hospital thus far. All I knew was that the journey was not over yet.

They placed me in the same unit that I was in at Christmas. The nurses are shocked that I was back. They converged in my room and supported me. I was comforted by their presence and concern.

I had my surgery, and there was in fact an abscess the size of an apple. The poison was still flooding my body; I could feel it. Their missing the abscess earlier shocked everyone. The days passed, and I get lost within the all the drugs.

Betrayal of Trust

I had a visitor at the hospital. She was a business associate, and I was unsure how she even knew that I was in the hospital. She came with what I thought was support. She offered to do reflexology on me, and I agreed. She was in and out of the hospital, but I was not doing well and faded in and out of consciousness while she was there.

As I laid in the hospital bed, I was jolted into consciousness because the day nurse was yelling, "What the hell are you doing?" I snapped back and realized my business associate was at the foot of the bed. The nurse demanded she leave. I was confused as to what happened after the woman left. The nurse informed me she was asking me question, and I was talking in "that voice." I realized that the person who I thought was there to support me was actually there to take advantage instead—she was getting me to channel. Channeling is the technique to tap into spirit and bring through information. That was not a bad thing when done properly, but I was drugged on morphine and completely unconscious of what was being done, which put me in incredible danger. More important, that woman knew better. I felt so violated by what she had done. I couldn't believe she would put me at risk like that. I told the nurse I did not want her anywhere near me. Her actions could have killed me; selfish was a mild way to put it.

My Conversation with God

⊶⊷

My body was overwhelmed with the medication, and I took a turn for the worst. My veins collapsed, and the hospital staff couldn't get antibiotics into me. There was a lineup of staff that thought they were going to be the one to find a vein; I was like a human pincushion. I was instantly bruised by their numerous attempts. The doctor was notified by the concerned nurses. As a last resort I would have to get an IV in my jugular. The thought of that terrified me. With all the attempts of getting an IV in my arm, they people were more concerned with being the one to get a vein. They were oblivious that I was experiencing a lot of pain. There was one final attempt, and they got a vein; they were quick to cancel the radiology process. The group went to leave my room, and the vein blew out the IV. I yelled at them to let them know what had happened, and they rushed in and removed it. My body filled with poison and no antibiotics. As time passed, I felt my body spinning with the infection.

I called the nurse, and she was less than impressed by what had happened. She stayed with me and tried to get me settled. Then my gynecologist appeared in my room, a wheelchair in hand. He was personally taking me to radiology to get the IV inserted. He was rushing me through the hallways, and I could feel the urgency that he had; I was more than a little scared. Everyone in radiology was snippy—apparently they were ready to close the department, so they were now running late. *Hey, don't worry about it; it's probably just my life that is at risk.* I was so sick of the medical industry. I did not realize that we were only allowed to be sick on *their* schedule.

I woke up in my room with a huge bandage on my neck. I was groggy and was unsure if I was allowed out of my bed. It was only minutes before a nurse appeared. She comforted me and expressed her disbelief at what I had survived. Her compassion brought me to tears.

The nurses were great and tried to keep my spirits up. I was on morphine and felt stoned. I couldn't imagine anyone wanting to willingly put drugs in their body. As days passed, I felt toxic again. While wired up on the drugs, I couldn't sleep. I was awake the whole night and through the next day. Sleep came quickly that night however I woke at three in the morning. With the urge to go to the bathroom, I slipped out of bed and tried to get the machine unplugged from the wall. I couldn't get it unplugged, and my body started to purge. I was vomiting, urinating, and defecating all over the place. I knew that my body was shutting down, and I was close to death. I begin to vomit, and the nurses knew this sound too well and came rushing into my room. Between the vomiting, I tell a nurse I couldn't get the machine unplugged. They managed to get me into the bathroom and into the shower. I was embarrassed and scared. I knew I was dying.

As I was in the shower, I was having a conversation with God. He told me that if I did not get back in that bed and do what I did for others, I would not leave this hospital alive. I also needed to get off the morphine.

I was crying and saying, "I am sorry, I am sorry." I heard the nurse out in the bedroom say, "It's all right, dear; it happens all the time."

I heard myself say, "I am not talking to you—I am talking to God." There was silence from the other room. I finished cleaning up and made my way back to my freshly made bed. The nurses were amazing—I couldn't say that enough. I was in gratitude for this; throughout my life no had taken care of me.

HEALER, HEAL THYSELF

―――――∞∞∞―――――

got back into bed and immediately started doing an
energy balance. I went to the heart chakra, and the
energy was almost nonexistent. I cried in the realization
that I was dying. Reality hit me, and I completely understood
it now. I was truly at death's door. Like all the other times, I
had a choice here: I could surrender or do what God told me.
I would complete four cycles of healing on myself, sleeping in
between each. When the nurses came into my room to check
the morphine, I told her I wanted it taken off. I refused to take
it. She was taken aback by my request and was inquisitive. I told
her about the message I got from God. She honored my request
and moved the machine out of the room. With the drugs taken
out of the equation, I felt my body begin to heal again. I had a
sense of joy.

The next day, I got up from bed and cruised down the hallway
to the patient lounge. As I passed the nurses' station, I gave a
cheerful "Good morning."

The nurses standing there said, "You're doing your stuff again,
aren't you?"

I said yes. Then I joked, "What does it take to get some
breakfast around here?" They apologized because they had
cancelled my tray, not thinking I would be around to eat it. I

knew what they were getting at and continued to the patient lounge. They hand-delivered my breakfast to the sitting lounge.

Two days later, they released me from the hospital. It was February 14, 2005.

RE-EVALUATING LIFE

⁕

y body would heal, my energy was returning, and I would try to reclaim my life. Most of the people that called themselves my friends had disappeared. I was not able to take care of them, and so I quickly found out who my real friends were. They could not support me emotionally, and they did not believe that I was in fact sick. Truthfully, I did not know how I survived what I did. Perhaps there was more I had to do here.

With the small handful of people that remained as friends, interesting enough those whom I had attracted when I was sick would soon leave when I got well. Their comment was, "You are too powerful."

Really? I think to myself. I reflected on that and realized that in a backhanded way, it was a positive thing. *Onward and upward,* I thought. I did realize how beaten up I felt, and was exhausted with everything. The little girl within wished that she could be loved and supported unconditionally.

I started working out again. As I entered the gym, I started to panic. I got dizzy, and my skin broke in cold sweats. I took what I knew through hypnosis and talked myself through the fear. My body shook in fear of my body failing me again. When I was sick, each time I worked-out, I would hemorrhage for days after; the fear of triggering this lied within me. I breathed myself through that fear each time I went to the gym. As I continued with this, the panic disappeared, and I could focus on body. I felt the movement of my body as I strode on the machines, and I melted into the rhythm and remembered the body that was once healthy. Soon my body healed.

REBUILDING

—⊗⊗⊗—

*M*y business needed rebuilding, along with my self-esteem. I was financially struggling but stepped into what needed doing. My body was now holding eighty-five extra pounds from all the stress, poison, and trauma. I did not know how to handle this body, and people were quick to judge it. After all, I was in the wellness business! What I knew in regards to the body seemed to take so much more effort, but I persevered, and my body rebounded into protection as I struggled to rebalance it.

I resorted to the medical system for help, and again the response was that nothing was wrong. I asked to have my hormones checked knowing that with all that I had been through, they were out of balance. My request was refused with the firm response that my hormones had nothing to do with what I had experienced. I was in shock, and then I remembered the conversation with God: "Do what you know, or you would not walk out of here." I did more balancing, and I found a doctor who worked outside the medical system. She ran the hormone test and confirmed what I knew to be true. I decided to work with holistic practitioners, and my body began to heal. My iron started to rebuild as I chose natural supplements rather than synthetic ones. Each day presented a challenge as my body dumped toxins.

I would work from my home and would feel a pull to work out there, in the world that was less than supportive. I shot out an e-mail and got a lead. I worked part time in a shop and continued to work from home. I was working seven days a week with my newfound energy. I did what I had to do, to regain my financial status and my safety.

There was a holistic wellness exhibit that promoted those of us in the healing field. I was still not ready to set up a booth, but I did attend the exhibit. As I walked around, I connected with many people that I had met over the years, and it felt good to reclaim those connections. I was chatting with one of the girl that I knew through hypnosis training; she also ran the ghost tours within the city.

As we chatted about the tour, we were approached by one of the other exhibitors; she had just listened to a speaker that was doing readings for a large group. The woman, blurted out, "I don't believe that people can talk to spirit." I knew what was coming next. She looked directly at me and asked if I believed that people could communicate with spirit.

I nodded my head, and my associate chuckled because she knew what I could do. I told the non-believer, "Yes, I talk to spirit."

She was quick to respond, "Well, do I have anyone dead around me?" I looked, and she did not; I told her no. She walked back to her booth.

As I chatted with my associate, she joked with me, and we both laughed at the experience. Within seconds I was being pulled into the booth of the non-believer. I heard, "Look up." It was what I heard when spirit wanted to communicate. I looked up, and sure enough, there was spirit energy beside her. I questioned her. "Remember the question you asked?" She nodded, and I informed her there was a soul energy beside her. "Do you want me to give you the message?" She affirmed, and I started the reading. I could see him and hear him; the message unfolded, and there were questions and answers that went back and forth between them. I was merely the translator between the two. The session went on for twenty minutes. After all that was shared, I asked if she had any question. She said no, and I asked spirit if he needed to share anymore. He said no. I closed the session.

The women expressed her shock at all the information. She commented, "I believe!" Her coworker who was sharing the booth with her had left the booth during the session, and she now returned and couldn't believe the details—the description, names, and events were bang on. I forgot that people did not live in this reality; it was normal for me, so it was a huge reconnect for me about what made me different. More important, I realized that what I did could help others heal.

The business started to grow, and I pulled all of my knowledge from my business training, accounting, and marketing. I got more holistic training so that my business grew. Months passed and things started to shift. The old me started to surface, my confidence increased, and the energies that I pulled through in my treatments were even more powerful. I embraced it. I moved my business from my home, and things fell back into rhythm. As the business expanded, I again reclaimed the intuition and the strength to move forward professionally.

I was working on a friend, and I noticed that there was a huge health concern, and she needed to seek medical attention immediately. I could feel the lump in her leg I got nauseous when I touched it. I knew it was cancer as a Holistic Practioner I couldn't tell as I am not allowed to diagnose. She proclaimed, "I just bumped it." I looked at her and told her to please get it checked because I was very concerned. She did and the cancer was confirmed.

She also did healing work, so over time we did what we could, but we both know that this was her life path to go through this. We also know that she would not live through the experience.

As she went through her journey, she sent me clients that she couldn't work with due to her lack of energy. I got a call to work on a child who was in the local children's hospital. I did a distant healing. I tapped into the child's energy and scanned her; I get a vision and then heard she was being poison by the umbilical cord. I knew in my intellectual mind that she was four and did not have an umbilical cord, but then I heard, "Do not judge the information." I called back my friend, who passed the information to the mother. A day later there was a call back from the mother. She told my friend that the feeding tube that the little girl had in her stomach had been contaminated. The mother was told to say her good-byes to her daughter days earlier, but she would instead get to take her daughter home because of the insight I had.

I was sitting at the reception desk at my shop, and a man walked in and asked if I did energy work. I tell him yes, and as he talked, his voice faded away. It was like the cartoon Charlie Brown, when the adults spoke: "Woont, woont, woont," was what I heard. Then as I looked at him, I saw him shape-shift and saw him in another lifetime. It was like when I did the meditation with the healer. I saw and heard the past life that would unfold in the energy of what he was experiencing in the present time. I was shocked at what I saw, but in the same breath I realized that it was what he had come to heal.

More people came, and I saw from where in their soul path the issues came, and I worked with what I knew to help them heal. I was living what I believed to be my purpose, and it worked.

It was not long before jealously raised its ugly head. I watched people around me step into manipulation and sabotage in what I had created. I would not give energy to them, and that made them spin out of control. What was this about for them? I wondered what childhood drama they were acting out—abandonment, lack of attention—and I realized I was not here to heal everyone, only those who wanted my help. And they would need to ask for it, not demand it. There was not enough time in the day for demands, and I stayed focused and moved through it.

Past Life Training

———◦∞∞∞◦———

It was now September, and it was my forty-fifth birthday. I received an e-mail promoting past life regression training. I was already a certified hypnotherapist, but I couldn't get the advertisement out of my head. I thought to myself that the course would be a nice birthday present to myself. I knew that I already saw past lives, but integrating it into hypnosis intrigued me.

I needed to study something; perhaps I felt I had lost a few brain cells during this experience, and I wanted to reclaim that part of me. The course would be in Sedona, Arizona, in the month of November. I signed up and was excited at another outside-of-the-box experience.

I arrived in Sedona for the first time, but everything looked and felt familiar.

The course began, and the energy was interesting. As we worked with each other, taking in the course, we explored the past lifetimes we once lived. I felt like I did in the meditation with the healer, years earlier. We gave acknowledgment of how we had pulled past experiences into this one—not only the situations but also the souls. This connected me to when I died on the operating table, and the counsel told me about soul contracts. So many things came rushing back: the years of living outside the box, the teachings, all of it like mini-movies as I reviewed the past soul experiences. "I get it," I said. Everything was clear.

I worked with my family and saw how many lives my dad had been on my path. I worked through issue after issue with him. I saw how all the past had infected my life now. The week soon ended, and I had had enough of this with him. I called my dad's energy into what they called a soul meeting. I told him I was no longer participating in soul contracts with him in any other lifetime. In the image I got up to leave. In that session, his rage surfaced, and he yelled at me that I was not going anywhere. With that, he grabbed me by the back of the hair, as he did when I was a child. This was shocking to me. The other hypnotherapist was doing her best to guide me through this. I stood in my power and commanded that he left me go; he was not welcome in any other lifetime. Enough was enough. The session ended, and I was shocked at what had happened. I worked through the awareness that came from what I'd witnessed.

The training ended, and we all head out to our place of origin. I realized how powerful this training was as I processed the events of the week. It gave me a sense of closure. Everything was laid out in front of me to see all that had been carried forward into this life. I returned home and embraced the incredible sense of closure with my father, for the first time.

I settled back into my routine. I had someone doing renovations in my home while I was away, and the debris was still sitting in my yard. It was now November 27, 2008. Three days after my return from Sedona, I woke to a clatter. I thought that someone was going through the debris. I got up to check my yard to find five deer there. I went to get my camera and headed out onto the balcony. As I did so, the deer formed a procession and were walking away from the yard, across the street. I thought it was a little weird, and the sight gave me goose bumps. I heard intuitively, "Someone has died." I was creped out and shook off the feeling as I started to get ready for my day.

As I got to my office, my message light was flashing. There were several calls, and the first five were from up north. Most of the messages started with, "I am not sure if anyone has called you ..." Then they stated, "Your dad died."

As I was going through the calls, more calls were coming in. I chuckled because everyone had the same comment: "I'm not sure if anyone has called you." I told the remaining callers that I knew, and no, I would not be attending the funeral. I would let his family mourn him. I knew who he was, and I did not need to sit through a service and witness everyone pretend he was someone other than who he was. I knew he could have been an amazing man, and for that I would mourn that he did not live to his potential. I would send healing to his soul, but I was not prepared to put up with the family drama.

I thought back to the deer and realized that my dad was the fifth person, from that side of the family have passed away. Was it a coincidence? I wasn't sure, but it was interesting nevertheless.

Perhaps the family would heal now. I knew that it was not my job to walk them through this. I would keep space while they did their work, if they chose. I would receive the wrath and judgment of all the family members that were not willing to deal with the abuse. They made their judgment known. It was interesting how no one asked how I was doing with this experience; it was all about that they needed. In that awareness I surrendered their judgment and shame to God.

I became witness to the power of my healing the past-life issues with him. I knew lists of things that I chose to do in this lifetime had been done. I knew that when I met with the counsel, I would have a clean record. So now what?

I moved forward, living my truth and helping others walk their spiritual path—and more important, I took time to have fun, to love, and to be loved unconditionally.

I looked forward to continually bringing the healing energies with which I had been blessed and bring them through to assist people in their healing. I stood in my truth and honored my journey. I knew that I had survived all that I had for a reason, and I didn't have to justify it to anyone. I knew that I was here to live my purpose, and I did so with pride and honor.

What Do I Know?

- I know that I will face those who fear what I was capable of doing.
- I know that some of the greatest rewards come from struggle.
- I know that whatever you call it—God, Buddha, Ali, Krishna—there is something greater than ourselves.
- I know what I have experienced challenges, what people believe, and more important that is not my problem.
- I know that we are here to live a purpose.
- I know that most people fear their own power.
- I know that you are only limited if you believe you are.
- I know that when you step into your passion and live your truth, it fulfills your life purpose.
- I know that I was not here to live others' fears.
- I know that I had the life I did so that I could help others through their experiences.
- I know that I came back to be a healer.

I step into my purpose willingly. Anything less and I would be cheating the experience and myself. I vow that I will no longer dim my light. I am on my journey, and I will no longer live in the darkness of abuse. Join me on the path if you choose, or step aside, as my journey will only end when I say it is finished.

My wish for you is:

- That you are able to face your fears so that you achieve your greatness.
- That even though others around don't understand your journey, they accept your choices so that you get what you need to heal your path.
- Most of all, that you leave this experience with a smile on your face, knowing you have done what you came for.

I am grateful for:

- All the lessons I have learned.
- All the things that have been shown to me from the other side and that I know to be true.
- All the people who have crossed my path—and yes, even the ones that caused me pain.
- All the trust I have learned.
- All the strength to stand strong in my own truth.
- All the people who did not understand me—and those who did, knowing that it was all right.
- The guidance of the other side; without that, I would have been alone for most of my life.

The journey continues—after all, it is just an experience!